YOUNG MRS. BURTON

By the same author

MANCHESTER FOURTEEN MILES
THE FOOLISH VIRGIN

Young Mrs. Burton

Margaret Penn

Cambridge University Press
Cambridge
London New York New Rochelle
Melbourne Sydney

Published by the Press Syndicate of the University of Cambridge
The Pitt Building, Trumpington Street, Cambridge CB2 1RP
32 East 57th Street, New York, NY 10022, USA
296 Beaconsfield Parade, Middle Park, Melbourne 3206, Australia

First published by Jonathan Cape Ltd 1954
Facsimile edition published by Caliban Books 1980
This paperback edition first published by the Cambridge University Press 1981

Printed in Great Britain by
Redwood Burn Ltd
Trowbridge and Esher

British Library cataloguing in publication data

Penn, Margaret
Young Mrs. Burton.
I. Title
823'.9'1F PR6031.E49Y/ 80-41544
ISBN 0 521 28298 5

CONTENTS

To
ELIZABETH BURNARD

CHAPTER I

HOSTAGE TO FORTUNE

As a frightened girl of twenty, in the last stage of labour, attempted ineffectually to mount the steep narrow stairs of a small house in Sydenham she cried out sharply: 'Frank! It's coming again! Don't let it! Come home and stop it. Please. You *must* stop it!'

Another pain tore through her as she clung to the banister rail. When it had ebbed she abandoned the attempt to reach her room and die, as she was obviously going to die, in her bed. Gripping the rail with both hands she moved clumsily down to the sitting-room where, holding on to a table, she wondered what on earth she was going to do if her husband did not come home quickly. For months she had exulted at the thought of this momentous day and until now she had never once felt the slightest fear. For months, too, both doctor and nurse had been engaged, and mocking her from the mantelpiece was a postcard on which Frank had written their addresses and telephone numbers. He had written it some weeks ago and impressed upon her that, if by any mischance she was alone in the house when her confinement began, she must ask a neighbour to telephone for them immediately. She had only herself to blame for the fact that she was alone now. It was Saturday and Frank had left about half-past eight for his temporary job in the War Office, but Mrs. Huntley, who came each morning to do the housework, had been with her until midday. The restlessness preceding the first pains had commenced about ten o'clock, and Mrs. Huntley, to whom childbirth was no mystery, had trenchantly remarked that the time was come to fetch doctor and nurse. Hilda Burton, however, despite the evidence of her senses, could not believe that her baby was about to be born, for only the previous night Nurse Cowick had been to see her and had pronounced authoritatively that she would 'go' well over the week-end and probably into the middle of the following week. 'There's nothing to worry about,' she had said. 'You're a healthy girl and there'll be no fancy business. I'll look in on Monday night and we'll see how things are shaping then. What a pretty little house this is!' she had observed as her eyes roved round the cosy but rather ugly room.

'Oh, but it isn't,' Hilda had protested. 'It's comfortable though, and will do until we find something better. It's only a furnished house.'

Nurse Cowick had looked thoughtful, and then asked: 'How long have you taken it for if it's not a rude question?'

'Only twelve months. It's not our sort of house at all, and I shouldn't like anybody to think it was. The furniture is so ugly,' Hilda had said, with a scornful wave at the solid walnut chairs and table. 'I've put away all the ornaments and pictures. They were just silly.'

'I see. Well, until Monday then, and get to bed early. My guess is Wednesday or Thursday.'

Relying absolutely upon this professional forecast, and assuring the worried Mrs. Huntley that in any case Captain Burton would be back by one o'clock at the latest, Hilda had allowed her, had indeed compelled her, to go home at her usual hour.

The pains, each one biting deeper, made her feel confused; and it was now two o'clock and Frank was not home. Supposing he did not return for hours! This possibility was so alarming that she groped her way to the kitchen door and, scarcely knowing what she was doing, shouted for help; not from her pleasant neighbour, Mrs. Fewings, but from Frank. Nobody heard her frantic cries, for all were snugly indoors. The sky, smooth as dull grey satin, was heavy with banked-up snow and, gazing up into its heartless immensity, Hilda Burton was in despair. Somehow it reminded her of the hairless, swollen body of a drowned dog she had once discovered at the reed-fringed edge of a marsh. Was she, young and strong, with help all around her, to perish like a dog? She began to cry, and stumbling back to the warm sitting-room she made a final bid for help by standing full in the window, determined to beckon in the first passer-by, for she was too frightened to risk going out. There was no sign of life in the straight, quiet road; no movement or fire-glow in the sitting-rooms across the way, for these were only occupied on Sundays. Every house looked as neat and dead as a coffin. She had been at the window for what seemed hours when a man came into view. He was elderly; from his whole appearance, she judged, a business man, and he was walking rapidly, obviously bent on getting home before the snow began to fall. Hilda, by this time half-hysterical, flung open the window and beckoned to him. For a startled moment he stopped to stare at the apparently insane young woman in the pale blue dressing-gown, her hair in two long plaits, gesticulating and screaming: 'Fetch a neighbour, please. Anybody. I can't move. Please!' He stepped hesitantly towards the gate and then, as though pursued by devils, broke into an undignified trot in his haste to get away. Hilda sobbed with rage and terror. She knew now beyond any doubt that the child was fighting its way out of her shaking body, and it fought with demoniacal strength. She *must* get on to her bed, and, bent almost double, she managed the short distance to the first stair; and there, crying out for him, some minutes later her husband found her.

'Hilda! My poor darling! There, there. It will soon be over. Oh, curse that Boche!' In her joy at the sight of him she did not hear the shocking invective directed at the German sniper who had shot away Frank's left arm in the Battle of the Somme. Although he could not lift her bodily, he managed, in some fashion that neither of them could ever afterwards remember, to get her into bed. 'There, dearest. Be brave. I'll be back in one second with some woman or other, and in minutes with the doctor and nurse.' He ran from the room and soon returned with Mrs. Fewings, enveloped in a white cooking apron, her hands all floury, her face red and frightened. Frank pushed her towards the bed, saying peremptorily: 'Look after her. Wash your hands. I'll be back in a jiffy with the doctor. Don't stand looking at her! Help her!' He was gone, and Mrs. Fewings, more frightened even than Hilda had been, washed her hands and, still drying them, tiptoed to the bed. Hilda, waiting quite calmly now for the next mad plunge, beamed up at her. Lying safely in her bed, with the dragging weight taken from her limbs and Frank seeing to everything, she was in command of herself again. For one thing—she was not going to die. Frank would take care of that! The past bewildering hours, even the terrified stranger who had passed by on the other side, were forgotten.

'Oh, thank you, Mrs. Fewings, for coming in. I tried to make you hear from the kitchen door. I shouted and shouted.'

'You poor dear! Why ever didn't you come for me when it first started? There, try to keep quiet. It can't be long now. Press your feet against the end of the bed as hard as you can. It helps.'

Hilda pressed. She was being rent in twain and could not stifle one last scream. Then all was tranquil. The baby was born and a minute later Nurse Cowick bustled in, followed quickly by the doctor, and at once both became busy with cotton wool and lint, while Hilda lay in a blissful trance. She caught the words: 'Badly torn', but they conveyed nothing to her until Doctor Mallinson smiled down at her and said: 'There's nothing further to be afraid of, Mrs.

Burton. Just a couple of stitches. Keep quite still. You've done splendidly so far, and all by yourself, too. And you have a lovely little girl. Now, quite still, please.'

Hilda, who could not have moved had she wanted to, set her teeth. She was so grateful to everyone for helping her, so astonished at finding herself alive and whole instead of in two moribund halves, that she had momentarily forgotten what all this activity was for. Then she heard the child cry. She was a mother! She had a daughter! The fact that she and Frank had so passionately wished for a boy did not now seem to matter. . . . The baby's eyes? Were they being properly attended to? In the book about childbirth which she had studied so earnestly, and every precept in which she had forgotten while her daughter was being born, there was a grave ruling that a baby's eyes must be cleansed the instant it was delivered. 'Nurse,' she called out anxiously, 'have you washed her eyes? Please bring her here and let me look.'

Doctor Mallinson assured her that all was well, but Hilda, convinced that no other woman could properly appreciate the peril to which her child was exposed, repeated her request, and at a nod from the doctor Nurse Cowick brought the baby over.

'There. Take a good look. Now are you satisfied?'

Hilda, fascinated by the creased little monkey-face, boldly asserted her authority as a mother by lightly touching the eyelids. 'Make them open, Nurse. I want to see what colour they are.'

Nurse Cowick frowned. 'It's time you had some rest, Mrs. Burton. You've got a perfect baby. Here's Mrs. Fewings with some hot milk. Drink it and try to sleep for a bit; then, if you're a good girl, I'll let your husband come in and have a cup of tea with you. Do as I tell you,' she added rather sharply.

'All right, nurse,' Hilda answered meekly. She closed her eyes but was far too excited to sleep and, though she had drunk the milk, she was so hungry that she longed for a substantial meal, but felt that to ask for it in the circumstances would be altogether too unromantic. She heard the doctor leave, and after him Mrs. Fewings. She heard Frank knock softly, and the nurse's whisper: 'In about an hour. She's dropped off now. She's been badly frightened and she's over-excited. I can't think why she didn't send for me this morning. I'd warned her about the first symptoms.'

'I'm to blame, nurse. I'll never forgive myself. I promised to be home by one o'clock, but something detained me. She was all right when I left home this morning.'

'Now don't go fretting. She'll soon forget it. They always do, you know. I'll tell you as soon as she wakes.'

Hilda smiled to herself and glanced at the silver clock on the mantelpiece, a gift from her Aunt Helen. Its confident Edwardian tick would make short work of an hour, and meanwhile she would dream about her daughter and about her dear, dear husband, and amuse herself by laughing at all those prophets of woe who had warned her of the folly of rushing into a wartime marriage with a man more than twice her age. Her Aunt Helen had been the worst of them all with her gloomy prognostications that she would live to rue her wedding day. Over and over again she had quoted, as if she had invented it, the old saw — marry in haste and repent at leisure. She had even talked to Frank as if he had been a callow schoolboy instead of a brave officer who had proved himself in battle. Frank had been in the very thick of the bloody fighting at Festubert, and Hilda knew by heart the terrible letter in which he had described this to her. In a hailstorm of lead, with bullets splitting up the ground and filling the air with the buzz of angry bees, he had been caught in the barbed wire but had torn himself free. And this was the man whom her aunt had dared to lecture! But Frank had carried the day and her aunt had remarked, rather meanly, Hilda thought: 'Oh well, if Hilda has made up her mind to marry you, I may as well, to save face, give in, for there's nothing to be done about it.'

'There's nothing else I want to do about it,' Frank reminded her.

'All the same, I think it's a pity. How can she, at her age, know *what* she wants? She's not even thought of what marriage means. She's in love, or thinks she is, and a young girl in love is incapable of thought. When I had a serious talk to her the other day she laughed and quoted Shakespeare at me! "Let still the woman take an elder than herself; so wears she to him, so sways she level in her husband's heart." What do you think of that? It came out so pat and made me feel such a fool.'

Frank had laughingly repeated this conversation to her and they had joked about it, but neither of them realized how deeply worried Helen Shepheard was. She liked Frank, and she respected him for having unhesitatingly left his job on a great newspaper and volunteered for Kitchener's Army, but probing cautiously here and there she had heard hints and whispers that she did not like at all. Hints that indicated a darker side – a mysterious side. In the open-handed fellowship of Fleet Street, Dermot McGilray had confided, Frank was sometimes criticized harshly for his unlikable habit of slipping unobtrusively from a friendly gathering in one pub and being discovered later on moodily drinking by himself in another. 'It isn't meanness,' Dermot said loyally. 'Nobody's ever known old Frank not to stand his corner. After he's vanished we've discussed him often but we've never quite fathomed him. And when we've finally run him to earth, and started chaffing him, he's turned nasty and quarrelsome – you'd scarcely credit he was the same chap. The Street doesn't approve of solitary drinkers, and if there wasn't so much else we all like about him some of us would fight shy of him.'

'Solitary drinkers!' Helen did not like the sound of that.

'Look here, Dermot. You and I are old friends. You've known Frank longer than I have. Be honest with me. What do you think of Hilda marrying him?'

Dermot was embarrassed. 'I wish you hadn't asked me, Helen, but, since you have, I think, as you do, that it's a pity. Hilda's too young for him and far too romantic, but I agree that it's no use your trying to stop her. So why not hope for the best? When she's not being divinely silly, Hilda's not without intelligence; and when he's demobbed Frank has his job waiting safely for him — at least as safely as any job on a paper can be. And if he does drink a bit too much at times, what of it? There are worse things, and the responsibility of being married to a girl as attractive as young Hilda should steady him up. She might even reform him,' he concluded with a smile.

'She might. And as you say, there are worse things. Unfaithfulness, for instance.'

Dermot laughed. 'That, I'd stake my last shilling, is something she won't need to worry about. He's demented about her. And as, if anything, she's even more so about him, perhaps the sooner the burning question is settled the better.'

Helen sighed. 'I'd always hoped that my niece would give a few years of her youth to the Cause. Oh, I know that we've now practically got our rights, and haven't we had to fight for them! But there's plenty of hard work to be accomplished yet, and after all I've drilled into Hilda it's maddening to have her not caring whether we get the Vote or not, but thinking only of herself and rushing into marriage with the first man who, so far as I am aware, has taken her seriously. Most disappointing!'

'Poor Hilda! At any rate there's one thing to be thankful for. With Frank safely out of the fighting she's not, barring accidents, courting early widowhood. And if she must work for your Cause, I can't see that being married need interfere.'

With which dubious comfort, fortified by a not unnatural desire to shift the responsibility of her romantically inclined niece to hands more willing to accept it, Helen at length gave an ostensibly reluctant consent to the wedding.

Lying there, warm and safe, listening to the gay little clock ticking so loudly, and watching, from beneath her lashes, every movement of Nurse Cowick as she ministered to the baby, Hilda humbly thanked her Maker for being who she was and where she was. Her bed faced the wide bay window, and the pent-up snow which had seemed so menacing as she stood calling vainly for help was now glorious to behold as it whirled silently down. The little clock, for all its assertiveness, ticked with maddening slowness, and to speed away the time until Frank was allowed to come to her she gazed into the glowing heart of the fire where, in tiny pictures, she recaptured the lyrical days of her honeymoon, from which Frank had brought her to this house. He had hoped to take her for the honeymoon to Carcassonne, but the war had made that impossible. Instead they had gone to Amberley in Sussex and spent all their days upon the Downs, delighting in the fertile country below, where villages and farmsteads rode the deep green fields so sturdily. There they had had the luck to come upon a dewpond being made, and had talked with the men who were thatching it with straw as though it were the inverted roof of a cottage. While she took photographs of their operations, Frank plied them with questions and that night he wrote a factual and fascinating article about the construction of a dewpond. The article appeared a few days later in a London paper, and Hilda was so proud of her husband that she showed it to the landlady of their inn. She, too, was proud of it, for Captain Burton, she confessed, was the first 'writing gentleman' to stay at her house, and she asked his permission to pin it up in the bar.

On Amberley Mount they made the acquaintance of a

shepherd who startled them by confiding that, though he would not change his job for a kingdom, 'it was terrible quiet on the Lord's day'. To Frank and Hilda it had seemed enchantingly quiet up there all the time, but the shepherd insisted that on Sundays it was entirely different. 'Terrible still,' he repeated firmly — 'terrible still it be up here on the Lord's day.' Frank had photographed her with the shepherd and Dusty, his dog, who, his master informed them, was sagacious beyond belief, and, despite the fact that he was well past his prime and had left a hind leg in a cruel gin, nipped around when on duty as nimbly as a puppy. Frank had pondered on the shepherd's assertion about the Sabbath quiet; she, too, had wondered and then, rather shyly, said: 'I think I understand what he means, Frank. It's quiet for him because it *is* Sunday. The quiet is in himself, don't you think?'

'You're right! How like a woman to jump straight to it!' For a minute or so he was silent, then chanted:

She is wiser far above me
And wiser when she wishes;
She can knit with cunning skill
And make the daintiest dishes.
She can handle knife or pen
And deal the wound which lingers,
She can talk the talk of men
And touch with thrilling fingers.

'Do you like it?' he added.

'I think you're the cleverest man in the world to make up a poem like that on the spur of the moment.'

'I'm sorry, Hilda, but it isn't mine at all. I've taken liberties with it from Meredith. But do you like it?'

'Some of it,' she said cautiously. 'It makes me sound cruel, though, and that isn't true.'

'That's merely poetic licence, darling. Listen!' They

stood still, and from across the Channel came the dull thudding of heavy guns.

'I hope to God they're ours, Hilda.' It was a flawless, burning day, but he shivered as with cold, while she, thinking of how, but for a Boche sniper, he might still be in France, clung to him and thought of one German at least without hatred.

One especially lovely evening she romantically suggested that they should take an all-night walk, and although Frank groaned within him he hadn't the heart to refuse. Why be such a curmudgeon as to remind her that for long days and everlasting nights he had been unable even to remove his boots? If she wanted to walk all night, then walk all night he must.

'Of course, my lamb. It will be fun, though I shall feel rather an ass explaining to the people at the inn.'

'Leave that to me,' she said confidently. 'I'll ask for a thermos of tea and hard-boiled eggs and we'll have breakfast away up on the Downs just as the dawn breaks. Why, I haven't seen the dawn in summer since I was a child in Moss Ferry!'

'And what grave and important reason could you ever have had then for awaiting the dawn?'

'All sorts of reasons. Outings. Bank holiday outings to the seaside. I always used to wake up early on those mornings. I was so afraid that we should miss the train, but of course we never did. Now you go and have a drink while I tackle Mrs. Simmonds.' Mrs. Simmonds, who was tidying up the kitchen for the night, received Hilda's request with disappointing calm, merely remarking: 'I hope you enjoy it, though why anybody wants to let a warm bed stand empty for the sake of a walk in the dark, I don't know. You're not the first either. Be sure to put on something warm, for you'll find it bitter cold up there. I'll have the things ready for you in about ten minutes.'

Climbing the white, stony path up Amberley Mount they stopped to peer down into the chalk quarry which bit deeply into its flank, and Hilda counted seven small fires glowing redly against the darkness.

'Oh Frank, they look like something in another world! We've never noticed them in the daylight. Isn't this exciting? I feel as if we were being watched, as if the Mount might open and draw us inside.'

'I was thinking of the Pied Piper too. But come along, pet. That ancient piper can still put the fear of God into me. You might be drawn into that new green world and I, the maimed one, be left for ever in the old. Every time I look at you I know that honey-bees *have* lost their stings, and that horses *are* born with eagles' wings. Let's see how much we can remember.'

Thus they walked on for hours towards Chanctonbury, chanting poems and ballads, until Hilda said that the dawn could not be far away for high above them a lark began to sing. This was the sign, ancient as the world, sure as the life hereafter, that day was near. Then the miracle happened and Hilda shouted: 'It's here! It's all over us!'

'Yes, darling, yes.'

The lark was singing its heart out as the first light fell over the landscape. Everything was a cold, filmy grey until away over the Weald a steely line, bright as a needle, turned to a faint rose and the sun began to rise. Hilda poured out the tea, and, while they ate and drank and watched the swirling mists vanish from the meadows as the sun climbed higher, talked serenely of the years ahead. There was to be no winter in their life together; no chilling winds; no shrivelling frosts, but always deep summer, warm and golden. Looking back to her childhood in Moss Ferry, she recalled the unspoken affection between her foster-parents. Their life, she now knew, had been narrow and hard, very different from the life which lay before herself and Frank; but their love for one another, and for their children, amongst whom they had counted her not the least, had been so deeply rooted that, like the thorn trees upon the Downs, no storm could uproot it.

Remembering all this as she gazed into the fire and waited for Frank, she determined that so it should be with her family. They would be enclosed in a circle of love which time would only strengthen. The little clock was ticking rapidly now, for the hour was up and Frank could come in.

'I've had quite a good sleep, nurse,' Hilda lied gaily.

'All right. Your husband can see you now. I believe he's been outside the door for quite a time. You can come in, Captain Burton,' she called.

As she entered, Nurse Cowick wheeled the baby's cot alongside the bed, and then disappeared to make the tea. Hilda looked at Frank. Frank looked at Hilda, and then, too deeply moved for speech, together they looked at their daughter.

CHAPTER II

THE FIRST ALARM

To Hilda's extreme dismay the doctor commanded her to remain in bed for three whole weeks and merely smiled blandly when, after a few days, she protested that she was perfectly capable of getting about and accomplishing miracles. But despite her impatience to be up and doing the days did not pall. There was always Frank, her dear, wonderful husband to dream about; there was her lovely baby to idolize; there were marvellous plans to make for the well-being and general advancement of the Burton family; and there were the entire works of Mr. Hall Caine to read. These she found entirely fascinating and blushed for her ignorance when Frank made fun of him for daring to look like William Shakespeare; for there, he added drily, all resemblance ceased. And, of course, there were the days when her Aunt Mildred and Aunt Helen came down to see her. The first time they came they seemed to be quite embarrassed to find her so brimful of happiness and pride in her achievement as wife and mother. They duly admired the baby and listened gravely to an account of her perfections, but when Hilda, dotingly and at length, talked of the pearly finger-nails as being the eighth wonder of the world, they looked as if their thoughts were elsewhere.

'Just look at them, Aunt Helen! Aren't they like pearls or tiny flowers?'

'Yes, dear. Yes. All of her is like a flower,' Helen answered quickly. 'But tell me, have you and Frank finally decided what name to give her?'

'Not finally. I want her to be called Hermione — you know — '

'Ah! *The Winter's Tale.* But why Hermione? Perdita would be far more appropriate, for like that lost "barne" of Hermione's she's "a very pretty one". What does Frank think of your choice?'

'Not much, I'm afraid. He says it's too much of a mouthful for any girl, but I think it's rather pretty and out of the ordinary.'

'So it is, but why not something simpler? Flora, for instance? Or Mary? Mary's lovely. Of all names I think it's my favourite. Call her Mary to please me and Mildred.'

'Mary,' Hilda repeated softly. 'Mary. Yes, it is lovely. All right, Aunt Helen, we will call her Mary. I'm sure Frank will like it, too, especially when I tell him you wanted it. He says I must have been quite a trial to you in one way and another!'

'So you were. But it's good to see you safely in harbour. Let's hope little Mary won't cause as many rumpuses when she's growing up. She won't have to fight for the Vote at any rate. Why, she won't even know how long and how bitterly women of my generation fought to get her a place in the sun. And she'll never know either, please God, what war means, outside the history books. You're a very lucky girl, Hilda, to be setting out, at this moment of time, on the great journey through life.'

Clever Aunt Helen! She had been so kind since knowing about the baby that Hilda found it difficult to realize that there had once been friction between them. All through the months of pregnancy she and Mildred had come every week to see her, and they had always brought a small garment for the child's layette. She felt ashamed of herself as she remembered how hard, parsimonious even, she had once thought her Aunt Helen. Once having consented to the wedding, Helen had been quite generous. She had bought her the prettiest trousseau she could afford, and given her for a wedding-present not only a cheque, but also her own fragile green and white tea-service which Hilda had always loved, and which she now treasured with infinite care. 'It was a wedding present to your great-grandmother, Hilda, and came to me when I married. I've never forgotten how intently you looked at it the first time you saw it in use. You didn't say anything. You just gazed and gazed and kept on touching it. I decided then that you should have it when you married. Keep it safely for your daughter's wedding.'

Now that daughter was here, fast asleep in her pink be-ribboned cot; and as she closed volume six of Mr. Hall Caine, Hilda lay musing deliciously, casting ahead to the glorious day when the lovely girl would walk up the aisle on her father's arm while she, her mother, exquisitely dressed in pearly grey, stood proudly among her distinguished guests. And afterwards, when the young people had left for their honeymoon and the guests had gone, she and Frank would sit and talk of their first-born, wondering for her, fearful for her, praying that her married life would prove as full and happy as their own had been. Darling Frank! How deeply she loved him, would always love him, as he would always love her. She was for ever asking him for assurance that his love would not change even though the years should assail her face and figure. She picked up her hand-mirror and, staring into it admiringly, decided that nothing so disagreeable could possibly happen to her. Gradually, imperceptibly, as their children grew up, she would grow older, just a little older, but she would never seem old to him or to them. Frank sometimes laughed affectionately at her. 'Silly pet,' he said once, 'of course you can't help adding to your age, but you'll be nicer to look at when you're thirty than you are now, and by the time forty arrives you'll be perfect. And to me you'll always be the impulsive, beautiful girl I met at Dermot McGilray's before I went to the front. How I used to dream of you out there, so young and fresh, with all life before you! Do you know, darling, out there I never really had the nerve to think of a future together. In all that muck and blood and fear it just didn't seem possible that one day, if I came back at all, I should be your husband.'

'Oh, but I knew you would! I never thought of anything else the whole time you were away. And I used to pray for you to get wounded . . . oh, not badly, like you were, but enough to get you sent home,' she confessed serenely.

'Good God! Well, I certainly got a Blighty one all right, and here have I been blaming that Boche sniper, little knowing you were egging him on! Why, he might have shot my head off! Would have done, too, if his eyesight had been as keen as his ambition.'

'But I always knew you would come back safely. It was in the cards. Rosa used to read them for me, but I kept on praying for you just to make sure.'

As volume seven of Mr. Hall Caine was unfortunately downstairs, where Nurse Cowick took her afternoon rest, Hilda's thoughts turned to her wonderful friend, Rosa Johnston. Rosa, a mine of wisdom and endowed with tremendous courage, was a book-keeper at the place where Hilda had worked before her marriage. They had taken to one another at their first meeting despite the considerable difference in their ages, for Hilda, though unaware of it, longed for a more understanding affection than her aunts seemed able to give her, and Rosa lavished upon her young friend a wealth of interest and love which the other, though she affected to take it lightly, fully returned. Rosa was the only child of an old and beloved mother, and it was some considerable time before she could summon up courage to confide a secret, of which she was pathetically ashamed, namely that this mother lived in an almshouse in a poor and obscure neighbourhood. Life, she also confided, had once been very different. That, however, was long years ago, when her father was alive. After his death his affairs were found to be in such disorder and his debts so heavy that everything had had to be sold and they were destitute; but her mother had been given sanctuary in one of the almshouses to the upkeep of which her husband had always contributed generously, and with this tiny home there went a small income and a weekly allowance of coal. It was a rule of the Almshouses Trust that, except in case of illness, no relative might live permanently with an occupant, and Rosa, to be near her mother, had rented a room in the same poor neighbourhood. At twenty, untrained for any profession, she had been confronted with the problem of earning a living. Luckily she had a natural aptitude for figures and had managed to secure a post in a city office. But from time to time, until she obtained her present job at the Pierian Hall, she had been unemployed and had suffered intensely. She was a splendid person, and was herself more than a little in love with Frank, though Hilda was far too engrossed in her own happiness to perceive this, and would not have been at all perturbed if she had. Frank admired Rosa for her courage, and was profoundly grateful to her for the affection she gave to his wife. Hilda would have been not a little surprised had she overheard Rosa laughingly describing to Frank their first meeting in the cloakroom at the Pierian Hall:

'There she stood, bang in front of the mirror, smothering her face with make-up, oblivious to the fact that I too wanted to tidy myself. I watched her, and I don't know what it was, but when she turned round and smiled at me in that friendly way she has, I realized that she was terribly lonely. We lunched together in an A.B.C. and the more she tried to impress me with an account of her clever friends and her clothes and her bed-sitting-room, the more convinced I became that she was acutely unhappy. There was something missing. I remember saying to my mother when telling her about Hilda: "She makes up her face as if she was on the streets, and talks as if she was fifty, but I don't believe she knows a thing! What she needs is looking after." I couldn't make head or tail of that yarn she told me about her aunts, and leaving home, and so on. Now that I know her, of course, I can understand that she must have been a responsibility, but even so I think there was something lacking in those aunts, in Helen anyway. She never seems to have had any really *young* friends — girls and boys of her own age. Mother suggested that I should bring her home, and they hadn't been together five minutes before Hilda was confiding to her that what she wanted more than anything else was a baby. She didn't mention a husband! My mother's face was a picture, but all she said was "Yes, my dear, but hadn't you better find a husband first? It's usual." After she'd gone, mother said: "You were right, Rosa. She doesn't know anything. At her age she's no business to be living by herself and doing as she pleases. You must bring her to see me often. She's as good as a tonic." And that, coming from such an old Victorian, was pretty staggering.'

'What a friend you are to her!' Frank said gratefully. He paused, evidently pondering his next words. 'I wonder if some time you would have a heart-to-heart talk with her about money. She simply has no idea of it, which I suppose is natural, since she's never had any. I give her all I can, but it seems to vanish long before it should. Poor lamb! I'd cheerfully tackle the Boches all over again if that would bring in more.'

'She'll learn, Frank. She's inexperienced, that's all. I used to try and advise her not to be such a spendthrift when she was at Pierian Hall, but she never listened. When they started war savings in the office she was one of the first to come into the scheme, but no sooner had she saved up a few pounds than out it came for a new outfit! I can see old Thompson, the cashier, grinning about it to me now. In fact we all used to laugh at her. By the time pay-day came round she hadn't a penny, and she would either go without lunch or borrow from me, if I had a sixpence to spare. But you should have seen her on a Friday night, with a week's salary burning in her bag! She used to insist on standing me a good meal, and I do believe it was the only time she ever had one that really nourished her.'

'Well, see what you can do, Rosa. Until I'm demobbed I've only got my pay. I shall get a pension, of course, for this' — he shook his empty sleeve — 'and intend to commute part of it as soon as it comes through. That should give us about a thousand pounds to set up house on our own and leave a little reserve. I should like to get out of that damned suburb, but flats and houses in town are expensive and likely to remain so for a considerable period. At my last Medical Board, the MO. advised me to try sea air for a few months. My nerves are not right yet. I've terrified Hilda more than once when I've been dreaming — having a nightmare I should say — and cursing the Boches for the sons of bitches. I thought we might take furnished rooms in Brighton for a time. Hilda loves the sea, Brighton can never be dull, and there's a fine train service to London. I'm worried about my nerves, Rosa; I've got to make a good life for Hilda and the child.'

Utterly contented with things as they were, and supremely confident of a roseate future, Hilda continued to dream and to plan and secretly to enjoy enormously yet further volumes of the obligingly prolific Mr. Hall Caine, whose books were evidently part of the dining-room furniture. But her enforced idleness ended at last, and Nurse Cowick, having initiated her into the rites of tending the baby, announced her imminent departure. Husband and wife were overjoyed by this news, to celebrate which Hilda felt entitled to a present. 'Just look, Frank,' she exclaimed gaily as she pointed to an advertisement in a daily paper, 'quilted satin bed-jackets at half-price! I couldn't miss such a bargain, could I? Will you buy me a blue one to match my dressing-gown? You always say how nice I look in blue.'

'Of course I will, darling girl. You haven't had a really nice present yet. Everything seems to have been given to that little glutton in the cot. I'll get the jacket for you tomorrow.'

'Oh, thank you, Frank. But you are not to grudge baby anything at all. And you won't forget that you must give nurse something over and above her fee. Perhaps I ought to pay her. What do you think?'

'Leave it to me, pet. I'll make her a gallant speech – you know, expressing my gratitude for the way she's looked after you. I'll settle with her after breakfast. Then just think! Tomorrow I shall come home and have my two girls all to myself. What more could a man ask of life?'

'Nothing,' Hilda responded with fond complacency. 'Nothing at all.'

But the next morning, no sooner had Frank departed, than an alarming incident occurred. Hilda was standing at her bedroom window, waiting for Frank to wave before he turned the corner, when Nurse Cowick stormed into the room, shrieking: 'Three weeks I've been here and not seen a penny of my fee yet! And it's no use pretending to look so innocent, Mrs. Burton. You're not going to make me believe your husband didn't know that I was leaving this morning. He should have paid me before he went. He never meant to pay me! I can see that plain enough now by the way he sneaked out of the house after coming up here to you. It's shameful! That's what it is. Shameful to keep a hard-working woman waiting for what is her due. But I don't set foot out of here till I *do* get my money – no, not if I have to call in the police. And crocodile-tears won't help you, either. You're just as bad as he is. It was *your* business to see I was paid before he went. This hasn't been a straightforward case. I've been on the go from the first minute I arrived – and now no money!'

Nurse Cowick, red with anger, stood menacingly over her patient, who now sat by the fire suckling her baby. Hilda, thoroughly scared by this outbreak, did not know what to say or do. She held the child more firmly, afraid lest the nurse, in her rage, might do it an injury. Tears welled up and dropped on the baby's flushed little face as it pulled greedily at her breast. Gradually the tugging eased and the child drowsed off to sleep, but Hilda made no move to lay her in the cot. She held her still closer, and said appeasingly: 'I'm sorry, Nurse. You'll be paid as soon as my husband comes home. He must have forgotten that you were leaving this morning. Why don't you go now, anyway? I'll send him straight round to you the minute he returns. You talk as if we didn't mean to pay you,' she concluded with a fine attempted hauteur.

'Do you think I'd trust either of you once I was out of the house? A *furnished* house at that! What do you take me for?' Nurse Cowick almost screamed at her.

Hilda, her courage mounting, retorted angrily: 'Lots of people have to live in furnished houses while the war is on, but it doesn't mean that they can't pay their bills. And you ought to be ashamed of yourself for speaking as you have about Captain Burton. My husband is not a cheat. And what is more, he's done his bit for England, and you're a vulgar, bad-tempered woman. Calling yourself a professional nurse indeed! Why, when baby was born you thought everybody was too busy to notice you throwing the afterbirth on the fire. But *I* saw you, you dirty old woman. Yes — instead of taking it downstairs you threw it straight on this fire when Doctor Mallinson was putting those stitches in. That was a filthy, unprofessional thing to do. A horrible thing to do. The sort of thing the old Mrs. Gamps did a hundred years ago. I shall never forget it. And please go out of my room now. It's bad for me to be upset. It's bad for my milk. Baby will have convulsions or something. She might die! Such things can happen. I've read about them. And when my husband returns, I shall repeat everything you've said, and perhaps it will be *us* who will call in the police, you abominable old slut!'

Though inwardly quaking, she placed the child in the cot; and then resolutely faced the nurse, who stood there with her mouth half-open, her starched cap slightly askew on her greying hair, too astounded either to move or speak. For three weeks Hilda had been the most tractable of patients, and now here was this hitherto docile young woman suddenly rearing up at her like an angry snake!

'Go away!' she said commandingly. 'This is *my* house. Leave this room at once, I tell you!'

The nurse, not trusting herself to answer, went quickly from the room and slammed the door, which Hilda at once locked. From outside, the woman shouted viciously: 'Very well, Mrs. Burton. But I'm not leaving this place till I've seen the colour of your precious husband's money, and that's flat.'

Hilda, safely locked in with her baby, now felt herself a veritable Boadicea, and indulged in a final, childish taunt: 'You're a vulgar old midwife and I can't think why we ever engaged you.' To this there was no reply, and as she sat down again by the fire, she wondered if it would not have been wiser to have had her baby in a hospital or nursing-home. At least she would not then have suffered the indignity of seeing a portion of herself flung on to the fire, nor been left as she was now at the mercy of a virago whom she regarded as a potential murderess.

She and Frank had discussed this important question endlessly until, in the nick of time, Hilda recalled a story she had heard an Irish hospital nurse relate with great dramatic detail. At the time she had joined in the laughter when this young woman solemnly informed her listeners that one night, when there was an unprecedented number of maternity cases — 'one on top of another and that's the holy truth' — a flustered probationer had blundered so carelessly that all the newly-born babies had got thoroughly mixed up; and though each proud mother duly received a child to take home, to the end of their days they would never know that it might not have been the one born to them. Hilda, unaware that the story-teller was known among her friends as the Baroness Munchausen, had implicitly believed the fantastic tale. But when it came to *her* baby it was no laughing matter, and she gravely recapitulated the episode to Frank. He laughed, too, and entertained her with amusing sketches of once happy homes rendered desolate as the changelings, gradually developing sinister traits previously unknown in their families, progressed from the cradle to the gallows. But even Frank, though he dismissed the silly tale as just another instance of Irish embroidery, thought it no laughing matter for all that, and they had decided to take no chances.

Tiptoeing to the door, she could hear Nurse Cowick below, muttering and banging angrily about; she was evidently making herself some tea, of which she consumed extraordinary quantities at all times of the day and night. Oh, if only she would drink her tea and go for a walk! Once out of the house, Hilda determined, she should never enter it again unless Frank were there. For some minutes she stayed by the door, listening hopefully; but, comfortably ensconced by the sitting-room fire, enjoying her tea, Nurse Cowick remained too, waiting like an aged crocodile, so Hilda imagined miserably, to snap at poor Frank the instant he returned.

As she sat by the cot and adored the sleeping child, she wondered how Frank could have been so horribly forgetful about the nurse's fees, for no other explanation even crossed her mind. And what was she going to do until he came home? It was again a Saturday, and he had promised to be back about two o'clock; but until then that dreadful woman downstairs, whose anger she could feel swelling and mounting all over the house, would be immovable. What a mercy she was feeding the child herself, for the very thought of confronting the nurse again made her tremble despite the brave face she had managed finally to show. She busied herself about the room, and after that, with the timely help of Mr. Hall Caine, the morning passed slowly until lunch-time. She heard the nurse moving about in the kitchen, evidently getting something to eat. She, too, wanted her lunch, but she would have to wait until Frank rescued her. She posted herself at the window to await him, and her heart lifted when she saw, not Frank, but Rosa's trim little figure advancing determinedly down the road. Instantly Nurse Cowick became as naught, and she raced down excitedly to admit her friend.

'Oh Rosa! Rosa! Oh – how good it is to see you! That nurse! I've had to lock myself in with baby. Frank forgot to pay her this morning and she's been saying the most dreadful things about him. About me too. Send her away. She's like a black witch. She'll poison my milk if she stops a minute longer. I can feel her doing it!'

Nurse Cowick, contemptuously ignoring her recent patient, addressed herself indignantly to Rosa: 'I shan't need no sending, Miss, when I get my money. It's disgraceful that I'm still waiting for it. I might have known what was wrong when her husband went off so quietly this morning. If you ask me she's as artful as he is. I've another case to go to on Monday, and I need my rest.'

'Of course you do, nurse,' Rosa conceded quietly, 'and there's no question of your not being paid today. Captain Burton will be home between five and six o'clock. Will you take my word for it that I myself will come round to you this evening and settle up? It's only just after two now, and you won't want to stop here when there must be so much you have to do.'

Impressed by Rosa's authoritative air, Nurse Cowick,

after some hesitation, muttered that she supposed it would be all right, but that it seemed to her to be a very peculiar way of carrying on. 'It's the first time I've not been paid before leaving a case,' she said truculently.

'As I have just promised, nurse, there is no question of your not being paid today. I'm sorry for the little misunderstanding. You've done a splendid job here, and I know how grateful both Captain and Mrs. Burton are to you. Now don't let us waste any more of your time. I'll see you this evening without fail.'

Nurse Cowick looked closely at Rosa, so self-possessed and, if looks could be trusted, so truthful. 'Very well, Miss. I think I can take *your* word. Good afternoon, Mrs. Burton. I'm sorry if I upset you, but right is right, isn't it?'

'Goodbye, nurse, and thank you very much for all you've done,' said Hilda tactfully.

Rosa, now in complete command, saw the nurse to the gate, and on re-entering the house was seized by Hilda and whirled around the sitting-room in a mad waltz. 'One, two, three! She's gone, she's gone, she's gone! What an old pig she is! I feel as if I could dance for ever now she's out of the house.' Laughing and breathless, Hilda pushed her friend into an armchair. 'You stay there, Rosa darling, while I bring in something to eat. I haven't had any lunch, and I don't expect you have either. But what an extraordinary thing you should have come down today. Did Frank ask you to?'

'Yes. He phoned me this morning and said there was a bit of a hiatus about Nurse Cowick's fees and that he hadn't wanted to worry you about it. He was expecting to get the money this afternoon, though.'

'Oh, I see,' said Hilda thoughtfully; and then, dismissing the sordid topic from her mind, showed her friend the advertisement of the dressing-jackets. 'When Frank telephoned you, did he say whether he'd managed to get me the blue one I wanted? It's so ridiculously cheap, Rosa. *Half*-price!'

Rosa sighed. Would Hilda never begin to learn? This was evidently the opportune moment for that little talk which Frank had asked her to have with his wife, and as they ate a picnic lunch from a low stool before the fire she endeavoured to make Hilda realize that uncomfortable things were happening — an inflation was in progress, and money was purchasing less and less. She must try, therefore, as a loyal wife, to do all she possibly could not to embarrass Frank financially.

'I'm serious, Hilda dear. You know as well as I do that Frank grudges you nothing. But that dressing-jacket! Why do you want another when you already have several pretty ones? And baby's coming has been an expensive business. Surely you can see that? Frank has had to borrow to pay the nurse's fees. An old friend of his — and yours — is lending him a trifle this afternoon. That's why he isn't home yet. When the pension business is settled and he gets back on his paper, everything ought to go smoothly. But meantime it's up to you to help all you can by keeping expenses down.'

Hilda did not conceal her astonishment. 'But, Rosa, there's always been enough money, and Frank has never refused when I've asked him for more. If he can't give it to me one day, he always manages it the next. Of course, I shall help him all I can. Oh dear! I wish I hadn't worried him about the dressing-jacket. I only wanted it so as to look nice for him. He loves to see me in blue. "A Symphony in Blue." That's what he called me once. I know what I'll do — if he has bought the dressing-jacket, I'll ask the shop to exchange it for something useful. Something towards our own home, like a cushion or a coal-scuttle.'

Rosa smiled. 'I shouldn't do that, Hilda. Anyway, exchange will be no economy in this instance. You must try to be careful and go on being so until he's demobbed. Do you remember telling me at Pierian Hall about your Aunt Helen continually lecturing you about the virtues of thrift, and quoting: "Annual income, twenty pounds, annual expenditure nineteen nineteen six, result happiness. Annual income twenty pounds, annual expenditure twenty pounds ought and six, result misery." Well, it's quite true. The great thing is not to go buying odd things here and odd things there. That's the way the money goes!'

'Oh, for goodness' sake, Rosa, stop lecturing me! You're worse than my aunt! Of course I shall start being careful right away. Why, I would do anything in the world to help Frank, and if it wasn't for baby I'd go and find myself a job. Listen — here is Frank!' She ran out to greet him, and they came into the sitting-room arm-in-arm.

'Hello, old Rosa! Where's Nurse Cowick?' he inquired cheerfully.

'She's gone. Rosa made her go. Oh Frank, why didn't you explain to her about the money being late? She was horrible to me. I had to lock myself in the bedroom. She said she would fetch the police if I didn't pay her. Have you got the money for her? Rosa promised to take it round after tea.'

'Of course I've got it. And I've got something for a lovely girl as well.'

He gave her a bulky parcel, and she shook out the coveted dressing-jacket, azure blue, and shimmering as only expensive satin can shimmer. She gazed at it delightedly and then, to his amazement, began to repack it carefully.

'Why, sweet, isn't it the one you wanted?' he asked sadly.

'It's beautiful, Frank. Quite beautiful. But I've been thinking. I don't really need it, so I'm going to change it for something useful in the house. It was very wrong of me to ask you for it just now. Rosa's been talking to me and I've become a reformed character.'

'What nonsense are you talking, Hilda! Unpack it again. Here — let me see you in it.'

She slipped it on and looked weakly at Rosa; and she, thinking that the foolish girl had never looked prettier nor Frank more deeply in love, smiled and nodded indulgent approval.

CHAPTER III

NOVEMBER 11TH, 1918

FRANK and Hilda Burton were still in their quiet suburb when the Armistice came, for he was not yet free from periodical examination by Medical Boards. He fulminated against the doctors for keeping him hanging about in uniform, but to Hilda he looked so brave and splendid in this that she was in no hurry to see him in mufti. Within easy walking distance of the house there was a charming park, and on fine Sunday afternoons she loved to stroll there with him, the child in her arms, and display to all the world that she was the wife of a hero. When people perceived this fact by his empty sleeve she was secretly gratified by the admiration and sympathy which they showed, though Frank appeared not to notice their tribute; also he appeared to dislike any offers of help. Once, when he was fumbling with a shoelace, a man darted forward and tied it for him, only to be thrown a surly word of thanks. On another occasion a woman asked if she might strike a match for him, and moved hurriedly away with a burning face when he answered curtly that he could manage perfectly well for himself. Hilda, as embarrassed as the poor woman, remonstrated with him. 'She only wanted to help, Frank. I think it was kind of her. People like to do little things for you, and they'll think you're very queer if you snub them.'

'Let them think. I'm not an animal. I can still do everything for myself — except carry my own child. Curse that blasted Hun!' Then, disturbed by her bewilderment, he said penitently: 'I'll try not to be so damned ungrateful, pet. But I do wish people would leave me *alone*. Their well-meant offers only make me feel clumsy. Oh! I know it might be much worse. In a bus the other day I sat next to a poor chap who had lost both his arms. There we were — two of us with one arm between us! He had to tell the conductress where to find his money. And there are bloodier things — what I saw at Le Tréport for instance. Hilda, you must pull me up when I break out like this, but when I think of that poor devil in the bus . . . and those others in hospital . . .'

'*I* shouldn't have cared, Frank, how you had come back,' Hilda interrupted firmly. 'I should have loved you just the same, and I'd have worked for you, too, and done everything for you. Everything!'

'As if I should have let you! This' — he twitched his sleeve — 'is enough for you to put up with. When Mary was on the way I sometimes wondered whether this wretched stump would be transmitted. I even asked one of the MO.s, who laughed and told me not to be an ass. You used to wonder, too, didn't you?'

'No. I knew that our baby would be perfect. Poor Frank! Does it hurt *all* the time?'

'No. Only when there's frost or rain about. Then I feel like a victim of the Inquisition — as if red-hot pincers were nipping me. But the last MO. I saw said that this trouble would gradually go. The queer thing is that at times I forget the arm isn't there, and find myself reaching out and losing my balance. It's the rummest sensation — possessing a phantom limb. Thank God it won't affect my job if ever I get back to Fleet Street. And when they fit me up with an artificial contraption — kid glove and all — I shall be the finest tiger in all the jungle and not ashamed to walk abroad with my wife and child.'

'Frank, don't talk so wickedly! I don't want you to have an artificial arm. I want everybody to know that you were in the war. Why shouldn't they? And another thing — why won't you ever let me see it? I should like to kiss it.'

'If you ever do that, Hilda, I shall be either unconscious

or defunct. Don't be so morbid! This withered branch is not a sight for your beautiful eyes.'

'Husband and wife are one flesh', Hilda said solemnly, 'and I love your ghost arm even more than the living one.' The lengths to which he went to conceal his mutilation puzzled her. Even in the privacy of their bedroom he managed to hide it from her, though for all his care and contriving she had once caught a glimpse of it through the half-open door, and had longed to rush in and kiss the withered stump that looked so white and helpless and horrible. He would then know how deeply she loved him and would never again ask her what she could see in such a useless old crock. Why, until he had come so miraculously into her life, it had been as bleak as a Polar icefield. She looked fondly down at the white bundle she carried, and with a tender glance at Frank decided that there was not another family in the park as perfect as her own. The only flaw in her general happiness was the mortifying fact that little Mary had no pram worthy of the name. It was true that Frank's mother had given her one, but when it had arrived she had looked so disappointed that Frank had asked, a little brusquely, what was amiss with it.

'Everything! It's shockingly old-fashioned. It's obviously an old one that has been re-conditioned. Why, I wouldn't be surprised if it wasn't yours! I shall hate to take baby out in it. Other mothers will smile at it, and then look sympathetic. You've no idea!'

'I'm damned if I have! I thought all perambulators were alike, and now you're trying to tell me that they actually have fashions, like hats!'

'You don't understand, Frank. I want our baby to have everything as nice as other babies have. Can't we sell this horrid old thing and buy a new one? Baby's worth it, isn't she?'

'What a Scrooge you make me feel! If I had the money, you could buy a smart new pram tomorrow, and you know it. But we must try to go carefully till I commute part of my pension. Oh Hilda, don't you understand how much I want to give you? When this blasted war is over you shall have everything you deserve. Just wait and see!'

A few months later the war was over. The church bells were pealing madly, and the suburb, sloughing off in one bursting second its malaise and its snobberies, was transformed in a manner marvellous to behold. Mrs. Huntley, weeping happily, burst into the house with the tremendous news. 'It's over! It's over! And now we can all have a real good cry. I don't seem to have had the heart for a proper cry till now, if you know what I mean.'

Hilda flew upstairs to where Frank lay convalescing from influenza and flung her arms about him. 'It's over, Frank! Your war is over! You should just see them outside. Everybody's in the road, singing and dancing. Listen! They're singing "God Save the King". But what are you doing! You mustn't get up yet. You *know* you mustn't. It's dangerous after that 'flu.'

'Mustn't I?' Frank shouted excitedly. 'The devil himself couldn't keep me in bed today. We're going to town, my darling. I'm not spending this day in bed or in this benighted suburb either. We might as well be in the Sinai Desert. Off you go and make arrangements. Ask Mrs. Huntley if she can look after baby for the day. Don't look so scared! We *must* be in London today. I shall be all right. Now go and see to things. Telephone Rosa and ask if she can meet us at Victoria. She won't be working today. Nor will anyone else the world over. Get moving, my lamb. I'm going to Fleet Street if I perish as a result, so hurry, there's my girl.'

Hilda, delighted, despite her fears for Frank, rushed down to Mrs. Huntley, who was vainly endeavouring to get on with her housework.

'Of course I'll have the baby, Mrs. Burton. You and Captain Burton go and enjoy yourselves. What a day this is for him, though he shouldn't go out yet — but there, you'll never hold him back today, so it's no use trying.'

Laughingly, Hilda agreed, and holding the baby at arm's length she said gravely: 'Listen, Mary Burton. The war is over. Really and truly over. This is a wonderful, wonderful day for everybody all over the world. And your father was in the war, my darling. He helped to win it, and he was badly wounded. That's why he can't ever hold you up like this. Your father is a very brave man. One day, when you're grown up, you'll know all about it and you'll be so proud of him.'

The baby, staring at her with wide, serious eyes, began to chuckle.

'She understands, Mrs. Huntley! In her funny little way I do believe she understands!'

'Get away with you, Mrs. Burton! Give her to me and be off. I'll take good care of her.'

'Thank you, Mrs. Huntley, I know you will. But she does understand, all the same,' Hilda insisted. 'We'll be home by five o'clock.'

'No need, Mrs. Burton. I'll bring her back about then and put her to bed and stop till you get home. So don't feel you've got to hurry, though Captain Burton shouldn't be out in the night air.'

By midday they were at Victoria, where Rosa awaited them at the entrance to their platform. Hilda, kissing and hugging her, commanded Frank to do likewise, whereupon Rosa cried because, she explained, she was so happy to be celebrating this tremendous occasion with the two people she loved best in the world, after her mother. Victoria Station was a solid jam of deliriously happy people. Two girls, perceiving Frank's empty sleeve, boldly kissed him, and their escort, a young second-lieutenant, thereupon kissed Hilda and Rosa. Frank, announcing that strong drink was called for, began to push towards the refreshment bar, with Hilda clinging to his arm and Rosa to his Sam Browne. Men and women, close-packed though they were, made way for them, and soon they were up at the bar where Frank, without asking their preference, ordered double whiskies and sodas. He drank his at a gulp and promptly ordered another round, but Rosa protested that one was enough for her, while after a couple of sips Hilda poured hers into Frank's glass. He did not thereupon countermand the new order, but dispatched all three with astonishing ease. He was not allowed to pay for further drinks. Several civilians begged that they might have the honour, and Hilda, observing him proudly, saw him drink whisky after whisky to the damnation of Germany and the glory of the British Empire. She was charmed by the deference which all these smiling strangers were showing him, and more than content to remain there for as long as he decreed. Rosa, however, as she noted his mounting gaiety, became uneasy and whispered to Hilda that they ought to be moving. 'We must get him out of here,' she said urgently. 'He's ill and all this drinking and excitement won't help. And he's still in the army, Hilda. You don't want anything disagreeable to happen. We *must* get him away. Say you want your lunch. I want mine, anyway. He'll be all right after he's had some food.'

Hilda, only vaguely comprehending why Rosa was seriously worried, reluctantly agreed and could scarcely credit her ears when Frank, her Frank, who had never before spoken to her in a tone other than caressing, snapped: 'Lunch! You damned women are all alike. Always wanting to be fed. Oh, all right. We'll go if you insist. But first, one more for luck. Come on, Rosa. Drink up! And you too, Hilda. This is no ordinary day. But what are all these blasted civilians celebrating for?' He glowered at two good fellows who had just been standing him whiskies and sodas. They coloured, and one of them, but for Rosa's lightning whisper — 'shell-shock . . . pretend you haven't heard' —

would have turned nasty despite Frank's missing arm. As it was, with grave courtesy they made an opening for them through the crowd and out on to the station, There, after shaking hands with Rosa and Hilda, one of them said quietly to Frank: 'My boy was only drafted a few days back, and he's safe. That's why I happen to be celebrating, among a few other reasons.'

Frank, mumbling an apology, gave an excessively melodramatic salute and they made their way out of the station into crowds that were even denser. It was obviously impossible to secure a taxi and make for Fleet Street, where he longed to be, and Rosa sensibly proposed that they should, for the time being, retreat into the Underground, and go to lunch at Harrods. 'The place will be empty, I'm sure, for everybody's up here — all London I should think.' Hilda, thrilled at the prospect of gazing at beautiful clothes, persuaded her resentful husband that lunch at Harrods was the highest pleasure he could give her; and, fighting their way to the Underground, they were quickly in Knightsbridge, which looked like a deserted village. The great store, as Rosa had surmised, was empty, and in the restaurant itself only a few tables were occupied. At the next table to theirs Hilda observed two women, one elderly, the other no older than herself, wearing deep mourning, and as Frank spoke some endearment to her, which they plainly heard, the younger woman's eyes filled with tears. Glancing at her cautiously, Hilda noted the regimental badge at her throat, and perceived also that she wore a wedding ring. Instinctively she knew that the girl's husband had been killed in the war. What if it had been Frank instead? She found this thought so unbearable that when some hilarious subalterns and their girls began to dance she jumped up and urged Frank to dance with her, for she wanted movement, fun, excitement — anything to forget that sad-faced girl almost sitting beside her. But he was no dancer, so she seized Rosa and whirled her round the room, though all the time she could not keep her gaze from the two black-robed women, who were sitting absolutely rigid, staring at one another, as the laughing girls and boys swept past them. They were like figures on a cameo, or two persons who, embedded for centuries in a glacier, had been callously exposed in their bitter grief. Seeing them thus, Hilda released her friend and ran back to Frank, her heart exulting that he would always be there, always be hers, for ever and ever and ever. She tried not to look again at the two tragic figures who presently, looking neither to left nor right, walked stiffly from the room.

Frank now firmly decreed that they, too, must go. 'While you and Rosa are titivating yourselves I'll go and look for a taxi. I count on you, Rosa, not to let Hilda be too long about gilding the lily, and for heaven's sake don't let her dawdle round the showrooms. I'll meet you outside in ten minutes. So long!'

They were down on time, but there was no Frank. Five minutes, ten minutes, a quarter of an hour passed and still there was no sign of him. 'We must just wait,' Rosa said imperturbably. 'It might be ages before he finds a taxi.'

'But look at the empty taxis going by,' Hilda pointed out angrily.

'Probably all booked, my dear. You walk slowly up the street, and I'll wait here in case he comes from the opposite direction.'

Hilda, beginning to feel anxious in spite of her resentment, walked away. What if he had been knocked down? Killed? Taken to hospital? She was continually obsessed with this fear, for he might so easily overbalance, put out his ghostly hand to save himself, and be instantly crushed to death under a speeding vehicle. Whenever he was late coming back from town, she endured extremities of fear. She could not read, or sew, or even just sit still, but would stand for hours by the window listening for his step. As she continued hurriedly down the Brompton Road, her eyes anxiously darting from one side to the other, she noticed an empty taxi standing before a public-house, and somehow knew that it was waiting for Frank. It was a solid Victorian-built pub, and the lower half of its gigantic window was made of such thick frosted glass that even Sam Weller could not have seen through it. But by standing on tiptoe she was able to peer through the clear glass of the upper half and, heedless of curious passers-by, she did so. The place was crowded with beaming men and, standing at the bar, drinking earnestly with the taxi-driver, was Frank. Incensed by this cavalier treatment of Rosa and herself, Armistice or no Armistice, she raced back to her friend with the unflattering news. Rosa, however, received it with studied calm, and to the suggestion that they should forthwith proceed to retrieve the errant Frank presented a resolute 'no'.

'What's the hurry, Hilda? Isn't it natural that Frank should want to celebrate today? He'd hate us to go in and make him feel conspicuous. I don't imagine he'll be long. Look! I believe this is the taxi slowing down. Don't let him know you've seen him. Let's pretend we've only just left the store. This is very much Frank's day, Hilda. Try to remember that, because all sorts of things may happen yet. Now mind. Don't reproach him. If he's had a few drinks, you'll only irritate him, and in any case it won't do the slightest good.'

Frank, very flushed, jumped out, and said apologetically: 'I had to walk nearly to the Victoria and Albert before I found a cab.' Hilda gave him an angry look, but a warning pinch from Rosa kept her silent and, though profoundly shocked and hurt that he could lie so shamelessly, she loyally endeavoured to share Rosa's excuses for him. By the time they reached Hyde Park Corner she had almost forgotten her grievance and, catching the infectious gaiety of the crowds everywhere, suggested that they should have the taxi hood down so as to see better. In Trafalgar Square the crowds were so tightly packed that the taxi was scarcely able to crawl, and for long periods was at a standstill. It was an unforgettable scene of human happiness. In all those laughing thousands there were no strangers. All men were brothers. There was a long line of taxis in front of and behind them, and those that carried khaki-clad men were being mobbed. Hilda, eager for Frank to receive his rightful meed of admiration and gratitude, coaxed him to his feet, and immediately his empty sleeve was noticed there were spontaneous cries of 'Thank you, sir! Good luck to you! And to the ladies!' Frank saluted; Rosa cried a little; and Hilda smiled approval as men and women thrust up their hands and begged to shake the hand of a hero. The hero, meanwhile, kept muttering that it was a lot of damned hysteria, but she knew from his punctilious saluting that he was not displeased. She was tremendously proud of him; no greater or humbler deference was paid to the Duke himself after Waterloo than was paid that day to every member of His Majesty's Forces. Even their driver, arms folded patiently across his steering-wheel, and exchanging cheerful badinage with equally patient fellow-drivers, was heard to boast to a driver alongside who had only an elderly civilian in his taxi: 'Took me into a pub in the Brompton Road and stood me a couple of pints as if we was mates. That's 'is missus — the young lady. The other lady is 'er ma.' Rosa laughed, and Frank, at this revelation of his recent lapse from good manners, gave Hilda a comical look which she returned with a forgiving smile. Inch by inch the taxi nosed forward, through the Square, up the Strand, and into Fleet Street. And all the way they had an almost royal progress. Flowers were thrown into the taxi, and by the time they reached their destination they had acquired two extra passengers, a couple of young women who had contrived to perch themselves on the folded hood. When Frank paid the fare, the driver refused a tip. 'Not today, sir, thanking you all the same. I don't take no more than the fare today from a gentleman like yourself. The pleasure's been mine. Good afternoon, sir, and good luck. Good afternoon, ladies.' He clambered back into his seat, and with the two girls now sitting triumphantly inside, smiling and waving at the recent occupants, nosed away.

The crowds here were not so suffocatingly dense, and Frank managed to get them into a teashop and, by gaily saluting a harassed, middle-aged waitress, to secure two seats. 'You'll be wanting a cup of tea, I know, and this is as good a place as any for me to leave you for half an hour.' Hilda looked mystified, but Rosa nodded understandingly. 'I must look in on a few pals, Hilda darling, and it's no use taking you two with me. You'd only get bored and tired. Anyway, everybody will be working full tilt. There's never any armistice in Fleet Street. Stay here and enjoy your tea and I'll be back, by the look of this place, even before you get it. Save a cup for me. So long, dearest.'

After watching him speak to the waitress, turn round to wave, and then walk out, Hilda gazed blankly at her friend. 'What an extraordinary thing to do! Rosa! What a *rude* thing to do! I thought all of us were going to the newspaper office. I've never been in one, and Frank has talked to me so much about his that I was looking forward to seeing it for myself. He said it was shockingly grimy. What's the matter with him? Don't you think it's queer of him to leave us like this? Today!'

Rosa, astonishing woman, did not think so. 'Nothing is queer today, Hilda. I don't know anything about newspaper offices either, but obviously they'll be busier than usual today. Frank's quite right. We should only be in the way. He can just walk in and around, but with us tagged on to him people would have to be polite for a second or two even while they were wishing us at the North Pole.'

'You seem to forget, Rosa, that I am his wife,' Hilda retorted. 'He ought to want to take his wife with him wherever he goes today. You'd feel this way too if he was your husband, so it's no use your trying to make excuses for him all the time.'

Rosa diplomatically tried to switch to a less personal topic, but Hilda, full of grievance, sat glumly silent, brooding on Frank's second desertion of the day, and magnifying it until it became a major insult for which there could be no possible forgiveness. And why should Rosa, unmarried, feel so competent to advise her on the management of a husband? Rosa, sipping her tea, chatted brightly and did her utmost to distract her outraged friend, but as the half-hour lengthened into an hour she, too, fell silent. People were standing, waiting for tables, and casting aggrieved stares at them. At last, unable for very shame to sit there any longer, Hilda decided that they must wait outside, and thus, cold and miserable, they maintained their speechless vigil. Hilda by this time was feeling far too unhappy for anger. Some dire calamity must have befallen Frank, for how otherwise could he treat her like this? She began to make excuses for him. He was not really well enough to be out of doors, and she blamed herself for she knew not what. She was anxious, too, about her baby; but when Rosa suggested that she should go home, leaving her to wait for Frank, she refused. Then, again in a taxi, he arrived, and Rosa, after one quick glance, pushed Hilda into the taxi and followed her before Frank had time to get out. 'Victoria,' she called to the driver, and then whispered to Hilda: 'Be nice to him. Behave as if nothing unusual has happened. He's ill, and you must get him home and to bed. I'll see you to the train, and you must have a taxi at the other end. On no account must you let him walk home.'

She had seen instantly that Frank had been drinking heavily, and she was not surprised. She had been apprehensive all along — ever since he had left them in the tea-shop. Her heart went out to Hilda who, for all her self-confidence as a married woman, hadn't the remotest idea how to cope with the situation. She hadn't yet grasped what was really the matter with him. She meekly accepted Rosa's statement that Frank was ill, more so than she had herself thought, little guessing her friend's anxiety that he should do nothing to attract the attention of the military police. On such a day, perhaps, they might turn a blind eye, but Rosa felt that this was not a risk that should be taken. Frank, glaring at the singing crowds who still thronged the pavements, suddenly wrenched down a window and, leaning out, shouted: 'Shirkers! God-damned civilian scum! What the hell are you singing for?'

'Oh Frank! Don't!' Hilda pleaded as she pulled him back. He gave her a strange look, and lurched heavily against her, muttering: 'Bastards! Bloody civilian bastards. They ought to see the trenches. The dear bloody old trenches. Sweet home from home. One night a piece of ours caved in and showed up a corpse. We chucked chloride of lime over it. One good smell to cover up another. And one of our chaps went balmy and started singing:

> The springtime, the merry merry springtime,
> When birds do sing, hey ding a ding a ding,
> Sweet lovers love the spring.

Sweet lovers. That's you and me, Hilda. That poor sod. We gave him a lovely grave. A beautiful, beautiful grave. Awfully well done by the Pioneers; with a little cross on it and a bit of a Christmas tree too. Oh! It was a treat to behold. Here! I'll give them a song!

> What did we join the Army for?
> Why did we join the Army?

The next lines are for soldiers only, my Hilda. We used to

sing it to the Regimental March of the Manchester Regiment. In one way and another we saw a lot of the Second South Lancashires. The corpse was one of theirs. They were grand fighters. Never gave in. One time in billets I got to know one of their officers pretty well. Chap called Filmore. He said his men were absolutely fanatical — ready to commit murder in defence of their home town. Once when we were thinking up tortures for Wilhelm II if ever we got him tripped up, he told me how he had heard two of his men discussing the same fascinating topic. Said one: "What are they going to do with the Kaiser when this bloody owd war's ower?"

'"How should Ah know, tha' bloody fool. What they done to Napoleon, Ah reckon. Send 'im to St. Helen's."

'" 'Ere, steady on about St. Helen's. We don't want no Kaisers in St. Helen's. Ah wor raised there."

'"Sorry. Ah meant no injury to St. Helen's, but that's where they upended Napoleon." '

Neither Hilda nor Rosa even smiled. The taxi, with a suddenly clear patch of road ahead, shot forward, and again Frank lurched against his terrified wife. Her head was in a whirl. Could this aggressively muttering man, telling dull, meaningless anecdotes, really be Frank Burton, her clever, affectionate husband! She looked in bewilderment at Rosa, facing them bolt upright, rock-like in her steadiness. Frank, belching strange obscenities, and continuing to mutter irrelevant anecdotes, leaned heavily against her, and as he did so Hilda at last realized the truth.

'Why, Rosa! He's drunk! Dead drunk! Look at him! An officer and a gentleman! While we were worrying ourselves sick about him, he was merely getting drunk!' In a sudden fury she shook him. 'Frank, wake up! If you could see yourself! Wake up, I tell you!'

Rosa took Hilda's hands in her own and said sadly: 'I know, but he's ill, too, and losing your temper won't help. It's time you woke up as well, Hilda dear. In a way I'm almost glad this has happened while I'm with you, for you were bound to find out some time. You must help him. The important thing is to get him safely into the train, and then it's up to you to get him home. I wish I could come with you, but I must get to my mother. She's been alone all day. Hilda, you've got to be strong enough and wise enough for two.'

'For three,' Hilda exclaimed fiercely. 'I wouldn't have believed it of Frank. He's just a common drunkard. I'd like to hit him!'

'Pull yourself together, Hilda, and stop feeling sorry for yourself. As his wife, you have responsibilities too. Ah—he's waking up, and we're nearly at Victoria. Now be sensible, darling. A distressing thing like this won't happen again if you make up your mind to help him.'

Frank groped for her hand, and said drowsily: 'There's only you, Hilda. Never anyone else but you.'

'You see, it's up to you now,' Rosa whispered.

Hilda, flattered and excited by the challenge, rose to the occasion. Were they not husband and wife? For richer or poorer? In sickness and in health?

'It's all right, Frank,' she said stoutly. 'Everything is absolutely all right. Here we are at Victoria. We shall soon be home now.'

The driver tactfully helped him out, and, standing with poker-like stiffness, he made a tremendous and, so he thought, successful effort to appear normal, but to Hilda the brief walk to the train was the longest she had ever known. They found an empty compartment and Frank, the tension over, collapsed into a corner seat, again uttering strenuous imprecations on all civilian bastards. Hilda clung despairingly to her friend, loath to let her go.

'You're doing splendidly,' Rosa said encouragingly. 'He's relying on you. Don't lose your head. Don't say anything to make him realize the state he's in. Coax him to bed the minute you get home, and after a sound sleep he'll have forgotten the whole business. And you must forget it too. I'll come down as soon as I can. So long, my dear. So long, Frank, and thanks for my lovely day.'

Hilda, alone with her husband, who had relapsed again into a drowsy stupor, began to think and to remember. All manner of once shadowy warnings from friends and relations about certain mysterious habits of Frank's now took on a disturbing clarity. But her disquietude was only momentary. Had he not murmured, in the midst of his otherwise senseless ramblings: 'Only you, Hilda'? Was that not conclusive proof that he had no thought but for her? Of course it was. If he was weak, then, as Rosa had said, it was her appointed task, as his wife, to help him vanquish his weakness. By the time their station was reached she had worked herself into a state of martyred exaltation about the grave responsibility of wedded life; and as she gently shook her husband awake he stared at her in confusion and in terror as she quoted brightly: ' "Love is not love which alters when it alteration finds." Remember that, Frank darling, and now hold on tightly to me.'

There were no taxis in the station yard, but, unearthed for the day from some Augean stable, and drawn by a steed whose lean and melancholy aspect made Hilda think of Don Quixote's Rosinante, there was a sombre four-wheeler, which Hilda hopefully engaged. This moribund vehicle was icy cold and creaked alarmingly as it rumbled slowly along; but, close-pressed against her husband, she laughed at every jolt. It had been a marvellous day. A day full of warmth and colour and joy. A day to be remembered, with gratitude, for ever!

CHAPTER IV

WHISKY AND SEA AIR

THE Army authorities, blandly impartial, remained unmoved by Captain Burton's plea for his discharge. The doctors reported that he was still suffering from recurring shell-shock, and that therefore it would be some little time before his disability pension could be properly assessed. Meanwhile he continued with his work in a department of the War Office, but became extremely vague whenever Hilda questioned him as to what kind of work it was. He said that it was not of the slightest importance; that it did not even keep his hand, let alone his head, intelligently occupied; and he became so abusive about the mental shortcomings of certain high-ups that she wisely changed the subject — until the next time. She remained convinced, however, that this airy belittling of what he was engaged upon was merely natural modesty, and that when ultimately deprived of Frank's counsel one branch at least of the British War Office would inevitably collapse.

The year for which they had rented their furnished house would soon be up, and the owners had advised them that they would not be re-letting it; also that Mrs. Owen, the tenant, would be coming down upon a certain day to see if everything was all right.

'All right? Whatever does she mean, Frank?'

'I expect she wants to make sure that we haven't had more than our share of "fair wear and tear". Be nice to her, darling.'

'Of course I shall be nice to her, but don't you think you ought to see her as well, Frank? Surely for once you could arrange to be home at tea-time?'

'That's not a bad idea, Hilda. I'll manage it if I can, but there's no need for you to feel worried about Mrs. Owen. I'm sure everything looks none the worse for wear so far as we are concerned.'

'I should think not indeed. Why, we've been ideal tenants. She ought to be grateful to us for being here.'

'So she will be when she sees how nicely you've kept the place.'

Mrs. Owen duly appeared and, after a prolonged inspection of every room, pronounced herself satisfied, though Hilda was profoundly shocked when she asked to see the mattress of the big double bed in which she had been confined. Exposing it to full view, she said indignantly: 'When baby was born I had a rubber under-sheet, Mrs. Owen. I'm rather surprised that you should think I don't know how things should be looked after properly.'

Mrs. Owen blushed, and said apologetically: 'I'm sorry, Mrs. Burton, but you seem so young; after all, it is my home. My sister let her house furnished when her husband joined up, and the tenants were dreadful people, so you see. . . .'

Hilda did not see, but recovering her natural cheerfulness she brought in tea, and in her turn apologized for the cakes being shop ones.

'Oh, but I prefer shop cakes, Mrs. Burton. I never can make them to look as fancy as they make the shop ones, can you?'

'I've never tried to, and I've never before met anybody who preferred bought cakes to home-made ones,' Hilda answered severely, thinking that Mrs. Owen was a perfect fool.

'Oh well, it wouldn't do if we all thought alike, would it? These are nice enough for anyone. I hope you'll let me see your baby. I think she's waking up. I can see the pram rocking a bit.'

Hilda, delighted to show off her treasure, brought Mary

in, and said proudly: 'There! Isn't she a pet? Would you like to hold her for a minute or two?'

'Oh, please! She's lovely! I wish she belonged to me. We can't have any children, and we do want them so. My husband and I have often talked about adopting one. Do you think it would be just the same as if it was our own? Perhaps it would if we adopted one right from birth.'

Hilda, astonished that a woman so big and healthy could fail to produce her own children, nodded politely, though she knew that it would not be at all the same thing. Poor Mrs. Owen! How awful to miss the happiness of feeling a child growing within one; never to experience the ecstatic shock of the first fluttering; never to receive all those charming little courtesies and attentions that even total strangers paid to an expectant mother. Wrung with compassion for her unproductive guest, she pressed her to eat another cake and have another cup of tea.

'No, thank you, Mrs. Burton.' She glanced at the clock and then, giving the child back, said nervously: 'There's just a little thing . . . I was hoping to see your husband. Is he likely to be home soon?'

'He promised to get back for tea if he could. He said he wanted to see you; but it looks now as though he won't be back till the usual time, about seven o'clock.'

'I'm sorry to hear that. I don't like to bother you, Mrs. Burton; it's about the rent. It's two months' overdue. The agent says he's written several times to Captain Burton about it, and that he keeps on promising to send a cheque. Oh dear! I wish I could have seen him.'

'There's nothing for you to worry about, Mrs. Owen,' Hilda said with a brave attempt at nonchalance. 'My husband has a great deal of money invested in Russia, but of course he can't get any of it yet because of the war.'

Mrs. Owen, giving no sign that she disbelieved this extraordinary statement, answered quietly: 'It isn't *me* that should be worrying, Mrs. Burton.' She was older by some ten years or so than Hilda and, realizing that the news had startled her, was genuinely sorry for her. She looked so guileless as she fondled her baby, murmuring endearments to conceal her embarrassment, that she almost felt like asking her pardon for having mentioned the matter; but doubtless, now that she knew of the debt, it would be settled, though not, silly girl, *via* Russia.

'Well, I really must go. I know how difficult things are for most people just now, except the profiteers, but do ask your husband to let me have his cheque by the end of this week. I have bills to meet myself then, including, incidentally, the rent of this house.'

'Oh, I will, Mrs. Owen,' Hilda promised gravely. 'I'll see that the cheque is posted tonight. I'm so sorry there's been this delay. Goodbye, and thank you for letting us have your house.'

She closed the door thoughtfully. It was mortifying to be in debt for the very roof over their heads, and her face burned as she recalled Mrs. Owen's gentle reproach: 'It isn't *me* that should be worrying'; but as she bathed and fed the baby she made every conceivable excuse for Frank. Poor Frank! How worried and harassed he must be! It wasn't his fault that he was still entirely dependent upon his pay and allowances. Mrs. Owen had been really kind and understanding, and whatever happened that cheque must be sent forthwith. The matter thus settled, she cheerfully prepared the evening meal, and the instant Frank appeared requested him there and then to write the cheque and post it.

Frank, somewhat aggressively, asked what was the necessity for such haste. Couldn't a man come home and rest his eyes upon wife and child without being badgered about a little thing like the rent?

Hilda, shocked by this cynicism, exclaimed:

'But it isn't a little thing, Frank. We owe the money, and you must send it at once. I promised Mrs. Owen.'

'Damn Mrs. Owen! What does she want to come upsetting you for? And damn that nonconformist conscience of yours, too, my pet. The rent is *her* worry, not mine,' he continued banteringly. 'Now Hilda, stop looking so self-righteous. It isn't a deadly sin to owe a few pounds. And what was *her* husband doing while yours was sweating in No Man's Land? Sitting snugly in his reserved occupation. What inconvenience has the war meant to Mrs. Owen and her husband?'

'Ah! But they never once failed to buy a flag each on flag-days. Mrs. Owen told me this when I finished telling her about all those wretched months you were in hospital. She said it perfectly seriously, and it did sound so funny.'

'It *is* funny. And these are the people you are nagging me about. Yes, dearest, nagging! These good patriotic citizens who never failed to buy their little flags. I walk about for the rest of my days with this' — he moved his mutilated arm — 'and they, I suppose, will keep their dear little flags to remind them that they also served. Never mention flag-days to a fighting man, Hilda. If you could have heard the way we used to talk of such warlike activities over there, your ears would have dropped off. Cheer up, sweetheart, and forget Mrs. Owen. Don't let her spoil our evening.'

He went upstairs, whistling 'If you were the only girl in the world'. Hilda, though sharing his contempt for Mrs. Owen's flag-day sacrifices, could not forget that heartless: 'It's *her* worry, not mine.' It was all very well for Frank to chaff her about her nonconformist conscience, but a debt was a debt. She had given her word and she would keep it. If Frank hadn't got the money, then he must borrow it, as he had borrowed before, from their old friend Dermot, who always seemed to have heaps. She wished he would come down again to see them, for it was months since his last visit. Twice since then she had asked him to dinner, but each time he had sent her an affectionate letter pleading excess of work, and urging them to leave their arid suburb and return to civilization, which for him meant Chelsea. How, he asked witheringly, could they endure life in such a vacuum? If they had hired a furnished tent in the Sahara, he could not have been more horrified. Now she came to think of it, no one but Rosa had been to see them for ages; not even her aunts. They, at any rate, did not make fun of the suburb, and had seemed always to enjoy their visits. As she busied herself with the meal her uneasiness mounted, and out of it arose a chilling thought. Was it possible that Frank had borrowed money from her Aunt Helen and not repaid it? Horrid little suspicions arose as she recalled her aunts' last visit. Her shy Aunt Mildred was always quiet, but on that particular evening her Aunt Helen, too, had been unwontedly silent. They had left much earlier than usual and, when they were putting on their hats and coats in the bedroom, Helen, regarding her thoughtfully, had asked: 'Is everything going all right, Hilda, with you and Frank? I don't mean between you personally but . . . well . . . apart from his health, have you any worries? Any money-troubles, for instance?'

'Of course not, Aunt Helen. What do you mean?'

'Oh, nothing, my dear. Nothing really. I just wondered how things were panning out. It's expensive living in a furnished house, even a small one like this. I'll be glad when you're in a home of your own. Quite apart from the expense, there's no sort of anchorage in another person's house.'

'It won't be long now before we get our own place. Just as soon as Frank is able to commute part of his pension, we shall set up house properly.'

'And pay all your debts,' Helen said lightly.

'If we have any,' Hilda answered gaily.

'As you say, if you have any. But I hope you won't have.'

As she recalled this seemingly harmless conversation, her anxiety deepened into a certainty that Frank had borrowed from her aunt and, on the principle that it was her worry and not his, omitted to repay. There could be no other reason for her long silence. Did the same thing apply also to Dermot, and to other old friends? Was Frank in debt all round? She remembered how thoughtful he had looked when, only a short time ago, she had asked him to buy a white fur jacket for Mary. All the babies, she pleaded, were wearing them. He had argued that it was a fearful extravagance and that Mary, like herself, had no need of fine feathers. Both, he said flatteringly, could encase themselves in khaki and get away with it; but in the end he had yielded and even accompanied her to choose the little coat. And he had thoroughly enjoyed the spectacle of Hilda conferring importantly with the saleswoman. It seemed to him incredible that this simple transaction could involve so much activity, such peering into fur-filled boxes, such head-shakings from Hilda; while throughout the entire proceedings the child surveyed the scene with indifferent eyes. When the long counter disappeared from view under piles of snowy jackets, all looking to him exactly alike, Hilda made her choice and brought it to him to pay for. For such a mere handful of white fur it seemed to him staggeringly expensive; also totally unnecessary and only suited to a new-born Eskimo. But Hilda was so delighted with the garment that he managed to pay up with a smile. As they walked home, he told her how he longed to buy furs for her too, and sent her into fits of laughter by asking her if she would like sables.

'Oh Frank, how ignorant you are! Don't you know that sables are the most expensive furs in the world? Why, I've never so much as thought about them for myself, though I could wear them, couldn't I?'

'None half so well, my love. You shall have them one day. And jewels too. Of course I know sables are expensive. Imperial Russian sable — how smoothly it rolls off the tongue! I shall buy you a little one.'

'No, Frank. Not even a little one. It will have to be stone-marten or skunk. Skunk is very fashionable, and it never wears out. If only I could have a long, wide stole of skunk, and a huge pillow muff to match, I should never, never want you to buy me another single thing!'

She had to plead hard with Frank before he wrote out Mrs. Owen's cheque, and her conscience smote her when he said lightly: 'You know, darling, if you will buy expensive furs for that little perisher upstairs, somebody has got to suffer, but I'm sorry it has been Mrs. Owen. Now don't look so sad. She'll get her cheque in the morning, and you won't lose any sleep tonight, so all's well. I should have sent the cheque at the end of the week, anyway, but until our ship comes home no more gew-gaws for our unappreciative daughter.'

'Oh Frank, you make me feel awful — selfish and thoughtless. Talk to me. Tell me some more about those queer people you used to know — The New Bohemians. I had heard about them before I ever met you. Uncle Phillip was one; so was Dermot, and that young man, Richard Middleton, who killed himself. When some of them used to visit us Aunt Helen never let me stay in the room, unless it was a very special sort of party she was giving. What did they do? And where are they all now?'

'Where indeed, Hilda? But don't forget that I was one too. And always shall be.'

'It was a sort of club, wasn't it? What happened to it?'

'What indeed, pet! It was the war. Dermot, the truest Bohemian of us all, said that we died of it. As for what we *did*, how can I explain to you that we didn't do anything? We were nearly all journalists or authors or poets, and we used to meet once a month — in a pub, naturally — and, well, just drink and talk, and talk and drink; and we had an occasional sing-song; and we damned to perdition all Philistines; and we swore by the God of Battles that, drunk or sober, we would never lose our profound respect for the English language, even though all we had to write about for our various papers was a flat-iron. And how we talked, Hilda! It was the moon we tired with talking, and sent *her* down the sky. And we respected women. We were old-fashioned romantics, I know, but we were something more than just drinking pals. Where's a better word — "comrades" fits the bill, though we should have blushed to use it. Most of the time, no matter how hard we worked, we were broke to the wide. And we did work too, twenty-four hours straight off, when necessary.' He laughed. 'What a prig I must sound!'

'No, Frank, don't stop! Tell me more about them. I wish I could have been one.'

'It's lucky for this old Bohemian you weren't. What else can I tell you? Well, hard-bitten though we were, we believed in the Church of England, and the King of England; and we adored Ellen Terry and we loved Marie Lloyd. And once, when a brother of the coast fell so seriously in love that, to quote his own words, he decided to "take the extreme step of getting married", Richard Middleton, gloomier than usual, wrote a lament for the occasion, and we all made a copy of it. Let me see — how did it go — like this:

Pass me the cypress, hand me the rue;
Girls are too many, friends are too few:
As old as the stars is my story,
As old and as new.

Fill up the tankard, fill with brown beer:
Here's to the roses that grew yester year,
And here's to the eyes of the lady
That drew him from here.

Mop up your heeltaps, turn the pots down,
Ponder a little the man you have known,
Gone from the friendship and laughter,
Gone from the town.

Wish him good fortune, stars in his sky,
A headful of day dreams to pass the world by,
And say au revoir to the husband,
But "Comrade, goodbye!"

'The prospective bridegroom sobbed when we chanted it in chorus, and to sustain him we gave our solemn word that if, as a husband, he failed to spend at least four evenings a year with us, we would go in a posse to his house and collect him. As a matter of fact he married a very sweet and sensible girl, for he turned up every month to rub in what we were missing as bachelors. Comrades! That's what we were. And it was the same with the fighting men out in France. Do you follow me, dearest?'

'Yes,' Hilda answered gravely. 'And next time you stay very late in town I shan't mind a bit. I shall enjoy thinking of you having a good time with old friends, only I think you should let me know if you are going to be dreadfully late.'

'How like a woman to make conditions! That's the snag, Hilda. Fleet Street is so small, so self-contained. You can't walk five yards along it before running into a pal, and then the pair of you turn into the nearest pub for a drink and a chat, and sure enough there'll be another pal propping up the bar, and looking as if you'd kept him waiting; and in no time at all there are half a dozen of you. Sometimes a spot of trouble breaks out when we don't always see eye to eye. The other night, for instance, T. W. H. Crosland dropped in, and by an unlucky chance somebody mentioned Oscar Wilde. It was as if one had set fire to gunpowder! Poor Wilde! Crosland loathes the very sound of his name and it didn't help when Dermot McGilray, with malice aforethought, recited verse after verse from the *Ballad of Reading Gaol.* We all thought Crosland would tear him in pieces. The hours fly fast when a few friends are gathered together in a Fleet Street pub. And all the way home I curse myself for a callous brute, and hope you're sound asleep, but you never are. I feel I ought to be refused admission instead of being fussed over and given a wonderful meal.'

'But I like waiting up for you. It makes me feel important — a person of consequence. From the time you leave in the morning I look forward to your coming home, and I never feel bored or lonely. Mrs. Huntley says it puts new life into her to hear me singing about the house. She says she used to when she was first married, but hasn't had the time since! It's such fun being married, and having a baby. I never really think about anybody but you and Mary, because nobody else seems to matter, except Rosa of course. When we're rich, we'll make things easier for her. She's been so good to me, and she does have such a hard time.'

'Yes, Hilda. We'll do all sorts of things for Rosa some day, but it must be you and Mary first.'

Hilda smiled at him trustingly, and not for the first time, deep in love though he was, he half-wished that he had never set eyes on her. So implicit was her belief that he was capable of surmounting all obstacles to a shining future that he had not the courage to disillusion her; to confess his sickening fear that he was a long way yet from the sound health so essential for his civilian job. When black dejection swamped him, he would try to concentrate upon her eager face; assure himself that it was worth every sacrifice asked of him; but in the end it was easier to drink himself into hope and courage, though he had to do it secretly. He had managed to convince her — as yet he could always sway her by mere words — that his lapse on Armistice Day was the very first of its kind. She was alarmingly ignorant, but she was by no means a fool, and unless he could pull himself together a day of reckoning would come. She would not then smile at him as she was smiling now. Ah well! She could always blame the war. The good old war! Meantime he would do as the MO.s advised and get down to the sea. A few months by the life-giving sea ought to quiet his jangling nerves and make him his own man again.

A sudden cry from the child sent Hilda flying upstairs, and while she was away he drank deeply from a flask he always carried with him. Whisky! Wonderful stuff! Plenty of whisky and plenty of sea air — that was the perfect cure for all his ills, no doubt of it!

CHAPTER V

DOCTOR BRIGHTON

So it was that they went to Brighton, where Frank had engaged rooms in what he cheerfully described as a comfortable old-fashioned boarding-house, full of atmosphere. As he paid the taxi-driver, Hilda noted unhappily the dingy Nottingham lace curtains over the grimy windows; the yellowing 'Apartments to Let' card that obscured the fanlight; the general air of seediness that left her in no doubt of the 'atmosphere'. A sharp-faced little woman greeted her listlessly and led the way to an overcrowded sitting-room, veiled from the world by Nottingham lace; leading out of it, through yellow varnished double doors, was a bedroom, likewise overcrowded and shrouded in Nottingham lace. The domestic arrangements were explained to her. They were simple in the extreme. Hilda was to supply all provisions, and Mrs. Mingo would cook them in her kitchen below stairs. The only extra was a charge of eighteenpence a week for 'the cruet', and if by any mischance — here Mrs. Mingo glanced meaningly at the baby — the outsize white chamber-pot suffered damage, it was to be replaced by an exact replica. Hilda, fascinated, examined the 'cruet', a heavy plated Victorian one which stood on the mahogany sideboard. Of all the dingy articles in the dingy room it was this object that depressed her most, for it was full of filthy, solidified condiments. Finally she picked it up and swung it to and fro for a second, glancing at Frank as she put it down, and remarking inconsequently:

'This is the only "extra". Did you hear, Frank?'

Mrs. Mingo, after agreeing to provide them with dinner that night from her own resources, withdrew, and Hilda, her eyes again on the cruet, remained ominously silent.

'I know,' Frank said quickly. 'I know the place smells a bit stuffy . . .'

'Atmosphere, I suppose,' Hilda interrupted sarcastically.

'Cheer up, darling! We shan't be here more than a few weeks. I had an awful job finding these rooms. I saw plenty of others, but they were all so damned expensive. Think of the sea, Hilda, just round the corner. Think of my commutation being under way. After our meal I'll take you to the Old Ship for coffee and a drink, if Mrs. Mingo will keep an eye on Mary. Put that blasted cruet in the sideboard and concentrate on the bounding ocean!'

Hilda brightened a little. 'I ought to have been with you when you looked for rooms. You don't seem to have any sense sometimes. After seeing this cruet, I can't let Mrs. Mingo touch baby's food. I must manage up here, on a spirit stove.'

'All right, pet. Nothing simpler. I'll go and buy one right away. Now don't fret. I can smell the ozone even in here. Can't you?'

'No. I can smell cobwebs and cabbages and lodgers. I can smell "atmosphere". I should never have dreamt of taking rooms like these. Mrs. Mingo must have put a spell on you. I do think you might have picked somewhere cleaner. We aren't absolute paupers, are we? Don't stand there staring at me. Go and buy the spirit stove, a bottle of methylated, and two little saucepans. Nothing matters, of course, so long as baby is all right. I shall keep her out from morning to night, smelling the sea.'

Frank, astounded, continued to stare. Hilda, always so brightly acquiescent, was snapping at him, and making him feel such a brute that he could only mumble further excuses and hurry to do her bidding. Why hadn't he had the sense to tell the taxi-driver to take them along the Front before bringing them here? Hilda, with her passion for the sea, might then not have minded 'Catriona' so much. At the corner he had a glimpse of the Front, and vowed that the minute his commutation came along he would take her to the Old Ship or the Albion, where for a few weeks at any rate she should live gloriously. He made his purchases, added a bunch of white roses, and on the way back turned into the bar of the Albion to fortify himself against further reproaches, even, as he almost feared, tears.

Hilda, however, was very far from tears. Perpetually hopeful, she had made up the cot, given Mary her bath, borrowed milk from the landlady, and now, with the child on her lap, waited for Frank's return; and as she waited she heard the sea. The slap, slap of the breaking waves more than atoned for the dingy apartments, and she knew that heavenly days lay ahead. The clean, sweet air would work wonders for Frank, and they would be happier here, if that were possible, than ever before. When he came in, she was in the highest spirits. She placed the roses he had bought where the monstrous cruet had stood. Then, seizing a dusty bulrush from what appeared to be a section of drain-pipe, painted black and lavishly decorated with arum lilies, she waved it and cried: 'I am the Property Man. This is a beautiful room in a beautiful house. Our house! The carpets came from Bokhara. The furniture was created by Chippendale. The lawn beyond is smooth and framed by many flowers. And the child in this room is ours and the most beautiful thing of all. There, Frank darling, that's the kind of home I want and the kind we shall have one day. And all because I've heard the sea and you've brought me roses. I'm sorry I was so nasty about these rooms. They're not too bad after all, and Mrs. Mingo says she'll mind baby any time we want to go out. Whenever we want anything very badly, I'll be a Property Man — you know, like they have in the Chinese theatres. He points at nothing, gives it a name, and the audience immediately sees it.'

Frank, his spirits rising too, kissed her. 'Splendid! Go and tell Mrs. Mingo we shan't want her dinner. We'll dine at the Old Ship. We can't afford it, but we'll go, even if we have to eat stewed bulrushes for the rest of the week.'

While Hilda attended to the baby, she congratulated herself, for the hundredth time, on her good fortune in having acquired such an unusual husband; a husband who could talk absorbingly, as she thought, about anything and everything under the sun, and who now, as she rocked Mary to sleep in this ghastly parlour, evoked for her all the sparkling charm of the Brighton of the Regency. The child slept, but she continued to rock her lightly, and blushed for her silly play-acting when it was Frank who, by the magic of word and phrase, had transformed the room into the fantastic Pavilion, where, instead of a noisy gas mantle, there were thousands of tall, golden candles; and a great ball, and 'Prinny' himself; and Mrs. Fitzherbert; and Beau Brummel, and many other famous personages. She felt that she could sit there listening to him for ever. The baby stirred, and Hilda laid her in the cot. Frank came into the bedroom and, as together they gazed down upon her, Hilda turned to him and whispered: 'Who wants to be rich? I wouldn't change places with a Pierpont Morgan,' a sentiment which delighted him.

'Come on, Frank. I'm starving. After dinner you can show me Regency Brighton, and tell me more about it. You make me feel as though you had actually known the men and women who lived in it. You're so clever, Frank, aren't you?'

'No. Just a poor bloody journalist with the gift of the gab. After all, it's my job to make things interesting and alive and I'm not so sure that I do it all that well. I shall end up by boring you yet.'

'Never!'

'Flatterer! Come along. I'm hungry too.'

'Catriona', with all its drawbacks, did not subdue Hilda's cheerfulness. To Frank's relief she accepted it as a necessary interlude, a marking-time, and as such sensibly made the best of it. She made friends with Mrs. Mingo. Frank was given three weeks' leave. The sun shone. The sea was a never-failing joy, and by any post the news would come from the Ministry of Pensions that their financial troubles were over. Frank declared that his beastly nerves were steadying up; little Mary glowed like a rose; and Hilda, not unmindful of her own attractions, and very mindful indeed of Frank's obvious pride in her as they walked abroad, was enjoying life to the full.

Frank was not the only man still wearing uniform; there were hundreds of wounded 'Tommies' about, their hospital blue ironically making the gay Front appear even gayer. There was a deep bond of comradeship everywhere among the soldiers, and several times they invited a 'walking' hospital case back to 'Catriona' for tea, a little treat which they declared made a welcome break in the monotony of convalescence. In the evenings, when the child slept, with Mrs. Mingo on guard, they enjoyed themselves immensely. They went to the Hippodrome; and applauded Wee Georgie Wood and other engaging artistes. They took long walks by the sea as far as Black Rock; they sat in the lounge of the Old Ship or the Albion and revelled in the gaiety all around them. On one such evening when Frank, the box wedged between his knees, was about to strike a match, a man rose from a nearby armchair and saying shyly: 'May I?', struck a light for him. Hilda, apprehensive lest her husband should behave churlishly, was astounded to see him spring to his feet, salute, and say: 'Thank you very much, sir!' The stranger was hastening away when Frank said quickly: 'This is someone we both have a great admiration for, Hilda. My wife — Mr. Rudyard Kipling.' Hilda, almost paralysed with self-consciousness, managed to smile up at the great man, but as they shook hands she was totally bereft of speech, and blushed for her confusion. For a few minutes the two men talked together. Mr. Kipling inquired where Frank had got his wound, and how he was adapting himself to peace; and to her further astonishment Frank made light of his missing arm and said deprecatingly: 'It's nothing, sir. Only a Blighty one. I was one of the lucky chaps. Good night, sir. This will be an occasion to remember — eh, Hilda?'

Still speechless, she nodded and smiled, and Mr. Kipling, who seemed to be even more confused than herself, bowed gravely and went from the room.

'Well, Hilda, I wonder what he's doing here? If I wasn't always looking at you I'd have spotted him when we came in; there's no mistaking those extraordinary eyebrows. Poor fellow. The Boches got his only son.'

'Dermot McGilray makes fun of him. He says he's too jingoistic. He and Aunt Helen quarrelled once over one of his poems. When I first came to London she made me copy out poetry to improve my handwriting and my mind at the same time, so I know quite a lot of Kipling. I never could understand Dermot not liking him.'

'As an Irishman Dermot has one consuming passion, and it certainly isn't Rudyard Kipling! There's too much pink on the map of the world for Dermot, but for Kipling there can never be enough. And that goes for me too.'

'And for me, Frank.'

'And for Miss Mary Burton as well. One day you'll be able to tell her that Mowgli's creator once deigned to notice her benighted father who, for a wonder, had the savvy to comport himself like an officer and a gentleman — of the British Empire.'

'It was a lovely thing to happen, Frank. But wasn't he shy, though I think he was pleased to be recognized, don't you?'

'No, dearest. I'm quite sure he wasn't. When I think of

his son — half my age — I feel I've no business to have come through.'

'Now Frank! You're being melodramatic. *He* wouldn't think that way. I could see that he was really sorry about your wound, but I just can't understand a great man like him being so very shy.'

'Ignoramus! Next time you hear Dermot, or anyone else, belittling him, go for them hammer and tongs. Why — he's never written a line that isn't his own.'

A few days after this pleasing incident there came the long-awaited letter from Cox's Bank, and, passing it over to her, Frank said grandiloquently:

'Hilda, my best beloved, we are passing rich. We have one thousand pounds. Inform Mrs. Mingo immediately that we shall be leaving here tomorrow. I'm going now to book a room for us at the Old Ship. Then I shall go to London for a few hours. I must get to the bank before closing time. I shall be back about seven o'clock, and tomorrow you're going to have a mighty shopping spree. You're to buy whatever in the world you want; within reason I ought to add!'

Hilda, her heart bounding, read the coldly formal note from the bank many times. One thousand pounds! It was a fabulous sum. They could buy the earth with it. They could visit the moon. Frocks, hats, coats, furs. Visions rose before her radiant eyes. Visions of herself, marvellously dressed. Visions of little Mary, still more entrancingly arrayed. A new outfit for dear old Rosa. A wonderful present for Rosa's mother. And, most blessed, most wonderful of all, a home of their own in which to savour their wealth to the full. One thousand pounds! It would last for ever. They would never be poor again. They would never be in debt again. They could hold their heads high, the equal of any. She hugged Frank. She hugged the baby. She surveyed herself and Mary in the spotty mirror over the mantelpiece; she spun round to her smiling husband and hugged him again, and then poured forth such a cataract of immediate, absolute wants that he begged for mercy.

'I did say "within reason", pet. A thousand pounds is a lot of money, but it won't last for ever!'

'All right, darling. I'll be sensible — if I can. I'll begin straight away by stopping here until we leave for our own home. I don't want to go to an hotel. It will cost such a lot for three of us. I'd rather spend the money in other ways. Off you go to town and come back with a bagful of money — three bags full — one for each of us!'

She danced about, singing 'Baa Baa, Black Sheep' with such expression that Mrs. Mingo, who was dusting the hall, immediately divined that her ground floor had come into the fortune which she had so often talked about, and hastened below to impart the unwelcome news to Mr. Mingo.

Shortly after Frank had left, Hilda set out, with Mary, for a leisurely, preliminary survey of all the finest shops in the town. One immense, gleaming window, given over entirely to baby wear, she studied with absorbed interest. With its exquisite little frocks of blue, pink, and ivory crêpe-de-chine, it was like a summer flower garden, and it was marvellous to know that she could buy to her heart's content even if there was an inflation going on. One thousand pounds! Ten hundred pounds! As she moved, in a happy dream, from one lovely shop to another, she noticed an estate agent's window and stopped to study it, though there was no question of them seeking a permanent home in Brighton. Frank wanted to live in London — in Central London, or in Chelsea. Reading the various advertisements, which were chiefly of furnished houses and flats, her attention was arrested by one which ran:

> To be sub-let on long lease in quiet Square near Front giving on to well-kept private gardens for tenants only, beautifully furnished, self-contained maisonette. Eight

rooms. Complete home. Owner going abroad. Immediate possession. Inclusive price for furniture and fittings only £400.

Hilda read it again. Four hundred pounds for a home ready to walk right into! They were rich enough to buy it. No more furnished houses. No more dingy lodgings. If they both liked it, then all their troubles were at an end for, however Frank might argue, there really was no serious obstacle to remaining in Brighton. Far otherwise indeed, for Brighton had character, gaiety, charm and history; and in addition to all these attractions there was the sea, the Downs, and the lovely Sussex hinterland. As she stood there gently rocking the pram, her eyes glued to the little oblong of typescript, she decided that here was a heaven-sent answer to all her prayers. This, she told herself solemnly, was Destiny; for had not wealth been bestowed upon them only one brief hour ago, and her steps mysteriously directed to this magic window. Of course there was Frank to be thought of very seriously, for he had said so often that he could not bear to be long away from London, for which he had a passion equal to that of Doctor Johnson. In all their talks about setting up house he had always insisted that no journalist could survive at too great a distance from Fleet Street, which contained the three amenities necessary to civilized man — work, pubs and characters. It would be difficult to persuade him to the contrary; but it should not be impossible.

She pushed open the estate agent's door, and called to a woman sitting at a typewriter.

'It's about this advertisement,' she said, indicating the little card. 'Can you give me more information, please? Where is this maisonette? And is it really beautifully furnished?'

'Certainly it is. Mrs. Connell lives there. Her first husband was killed in the war. She has just married again — a

Canadian officer — and they are going to settle in Canada. But let me give you an order to view. It's in Princess Square. Why not go right away and see it?'

'I should like to, but will Mrs. Connell be at home?'

'Any day up to twelve o'clock, or after three-thirty. I'm sure you'll like the place. Princess Square is very select, and it's only a minute from the sea.' She darted into the office, and returned with the order to view. 'You keep straight on, then take the first turning to the left and you're there. I do hope you'll like it. It's a real snip.'

Hilda glanced at the order. 20 Princess Square. It looked nice and it sounded nice. Childishly jigging the pram up and down, she hurried off, oblivious now of the alluring shops. When she reached Princess Square she gave a little gasp of pleasure, surveyed it for a few seconds, and then walked very slowly round it. The tall houses, faced with cream-painted stucco, were charming; they had wide, nobly proportioned steps and pillared porticos, and on the first floor delightful balconies of delicate ironwork gay with pots of geraniums, trailing ferns, and lobelia. The Square gardens were enclosed by neat hedges of privet, and through one of the gates she saw children playing on the smooth lawns, and nursemaids wheeling prams on the gravelled paths. Her mind was made up. Unless the interior of Number 20 belied its shining windows, it was going to be her home. It was Destiny, and Frank could not argue about Destiny. She rang the bell and a handsome woman of about thirty-five opened the door, scanned the order to view, and asked her in. She showed her home confidently; undoubtedly it was well-furnished, as Hilda saw at the first glance. Everything looked *good* — carpets, curtains, coverings. There were several pieces of furniture which were too solid for her taste, but they could be sold and replaced; likewise the pictures and the too ornate china ornaments and immense vases. The whole place was well-cared for, and was a warm, living home that anyone could be proud of. At four hundred pounds it was a tremendous bargain — a real gift; and when, upstairs, Hilda stepped on to the balcony outside the big bedroom and looked down upon the trees and shrubs of the gardens, Frank's mind was made up for him; he hadn't a chance. From the bedroom she could hear the sea. What bliss to lie in that great bed and listen to it! To sit with Frank on summer evenings, on their own balcony, talking, laughing, reading — all to the sound of the sea. They would hear it in every mood; soft and lazy in summer; leaping and roaring in winter. And how pleasant to have relatives and friends to visit here! How her Aunt Helen would rhapsodize over the comfort and convenience of the place; and how Dermot McGilray would complain that the geraniums were too red, and the lawns too green! She and Frank and Mary would be so happy here; and as fixed as the Pole Star, for Frank need not always earn their bread by journalism. Some day, he had assured her, he was going to write the play of the year, and make their fortune. He had indeed written the first act and read it to her. Like everything that he wrote, she had pronounced it to be a work of indisputable genius that would certainly make him both rich and famous. When that glorious day dawned they would of course have to buy a house in London in which to entertain other geniuses, but they would always keep 20 Princess Square, to refresh them whenever they grew weary of being famous. Enraptured by these prospects, Hilda informed Mrs. Connell that her husband would certainly take the maisonette over, and asked if she might bring him to see it that evening.

'Of course, though I can't guarantee not to sell if anyone else wants it in the meantime.'

Hilda, alarmed by this awful possibility, said naively: 'Oh, please don't do that! My husband's been wounded, and this is our first chance to get into a home of our own. We haven't been able to afford it until now. Until today in fact. He's commuted part of his disability pension. It only came through this morning and he's gone to London to see his bank. We'll give you a cheque tonight. I promise.'

Mrs. Connell looked at her curiously, then smiled. 'All right. If anyone turns up during the day I'll keep the matter open until tonight. You can call any time after eight o'clock. Your husband will have to see Mr. Cohen, my landlord, about taking over the lease. He's a good landlord, by the way.'

Hilda thanked her and returned light-heartedly to 'Catriona', there to make the hours fly faster than ever until Frank came back. Every afternoon she had been taking Mary along the Front, but today she went instead to Princess Square and circumambulated it many times; and each time she came to number twenty she gazed upon it enthralled. Her home! It was no mirage created by wishful thinking. There, behind those pretty curtains, was everything she had so longed for. Her own household gods. Her very own.

Dinner-time came at 'Catriona', but Frank was not back to share it with her. Hilda, her eyes riveted on the gargantuan marble clock, waited miserably. Half-past eight! He could not be back now until after ten o'clock, and there was Mrs. Connell expecting them at Princess Square. She went in to look at Mary. Poor little baby girl. What a father to have! He was behaving as selfishly as he had done on Armistice Day. It was, of course, a fact that he knew nothing about the maisonette, but even so he should have come straight home after seeing the bank. He was spending the evening with his friends in Fleet Street, drinking, neglecting his wife and child, and throwing away a chance that would never come a second time. Rosa's golden advice about not reproaching him was forgotten, and Hilda vowed angrily that this time she would not forgive him. He was cruel. He was a drunkard. He was a bad husband and a bad father. The thought of Mrs. Connell's anger as she, too, waited vainly made her feel quite ill. Supposing he didn't come back at all that night! They would lose the maisonette, for during the afternoon Mrs. Connell must have seen a dozen would-be purchasers. She went to meet the ten-thirty train and returned alone to 'Catriona' to wait wretchedly till midnight. The house was absolutely still, for everyone but herself was in bed. She stayed by the open window, and when at last she recognized Frank's step she did not run to the door to greet him. He was full of the most abject apologies. There had been so much to do, he explained. People to see. He had tried his damnedest to be home earlier but hadn't been able to manage it. Would she ever forgive him?

'No, Frank Burton, I shan't. How could you be such a pig! I've been crying. And now I've got a headache and it's all your fault. You don't love me, and you don't love baby. And something marvellous happened this morning. But now it's too late. We've lost it.'

'Darling! Don't be so mysterious. What have we lost? Calm yourself and tell me about it.'

'I won't calm myself! I can't. We've lost a home. You're always saying what a shame it is that I haven't got a proper home, and now, when there's a lovely one all ready and waiting for us, you go and lose it through enjoying yourself. Other girls don't have to live in furnished rooms for years. I want my own home. I saw it this morning, and only four hundred pounds. Such a bargain! And we could have afforded it easily.'

'Dearest, darling girl, what *are* you talking about? Sit down. Here — a cigarette. That's better. Now stop being cryptic. Tell me all about it, and *don't* look at me like that. I'd as lief you stuck a knife into me. Now, just tell me quietly, pet.'

Soothed by the cigarette, Hilda dabbed at her eyes and described, in glowing terms, her visit to Princess Square.

'But, of course, we've lost it while you were getting drunk.'

Frank, his blue eyes glinting strangely, said angrily: 'I'm not drunk, you silly girl. Only astonished by your extraordinary news. It needs some thinking about. And four hundred pounds. . . .'

'Just wait till you see it. We can walk into it and feel as if we'd been there for years. It's that kind of a home. Oh, I know it's not like having chosen everything ourselves, but everything in it is good. I promised Mrs. Connell that you'd give her a cheque tonight. If she's sold it I'll never forgive you.'

Frank laughed. 'That settles it, Hilda. We'll go round first thing in the morning, and don't fret any more. It won't have been sold overnight. Brighton isn't bursting with nocturnal house-hunters as impulsive as you are. Everything was all right about the pension. For one sound right arm, one thousand pounds. Not such a bad exchange in the circumstances.'

'Oh Frank, I do wish you wouldn't say such horrible things. I'm sorry I was nasty about your being so late. I really will try not to worry about you. It's only because I get so frightened in case you've had an accident. I imagine such dreadful things happening to you.'

'Well, don't, dearest. Harden your heart, then I need not worry either.'

'If you *do* worry,' Hilda answered lightly, with a tinge of malice that surprised him.

A few hours later, scarcely giving him time to eat his breakfast, Hilda was showing him round 20 Princess Square, and he could not deny that it was all she had described. He still had many qualms about settling down in Brighton, much as he liked it; but as Hilda moved excitedly from room to room, her whole manner expressive of one already in possession, he had not the heart to refuse what was, after all, her right. It was now merely a question of their being approved as tenants by the landlord, after which, Mrs. Connell said, there was no reason, as far as she and her husband were concerned, why they should not enter into possession by the end of the week.

Mr. Cohen received them graciously; decided that people with four hundred pounds at their command must be eminently desirable tenants; gave them, with upturned hands, his blessing, and sent them back to Mrs. Connell, after which they were to conclude the tenancy agreement with the estate agent. Hilda, with studied nonchalance, watched Frank write out the cheque for four hundred pounds; nor did it escape her that he wrote it with a matching nonchalance. When Mrs. Connell in her turn wrote out a receipt, Hilda held her breath, then, her eyes roving possessively around, burst out impulsively: 'It's ours, Frank! Our own home at last! And such a lovely one, too! Oh, Mrs. Connell, thank you, thank you, for letting us have it.'

A week later they were in, and Hilda, intoxicated with the joy of possession, laughed and cried and sang impartially as she again ran from room to room, caressing the gleaming furniture, and shouting greedily: 'All ours! And all so exactly right!' And certainly, for a modest family, it was just that. There was a fine big sitting-room; a pleasant dining-room; the big bedroom with the delightful balcony; a dressing-room which Frank thought must have been a powder-closet in the house's palmier days; another bedroom for guests, and a smaller one which Hilda decided to use as a play-room for Mary.

'Oh no, Hilda. Mary must have the powder-closet. We shall want this small bedroom for a maid.'

Hilda opened her eyes very wide indeed. 'Don't be so absurd, Frank! We can't afford a maid. We don't want a maid. You mean a charwoman.'

'You are going to have a maid, my pet. We can get a

good general maid for forty pounds a year. With Mary to look after, and myself away all day, you'll be tied hand and foot unless we have someone living in the place. And don't forget the week-ends. I shall want to take you out then, so it's essential for us to have some nice, sensible girl whom we can leave in charge when necessary. I'm not going to let you subside into being merely a mother, or to spend most of your time in a damned kitchen, either.'

Hilda, though charmed by this loving consideration, protested: 'It's not a damned kitchen. Come and look at it properly.' It was a spacious, old-fashioned kitchen, with a red-tiled floor, a huge dresser that took up nearly all of one side, and a rapacious-looking black-leaded range. Leading out of it there was a scullery, with a gas stove and sink; and beyond that an enormous larder with wide slate shelves and a stone-paved floor. There was no garden, merely a long, narrow, brick-paved yard surrounded by white-washed walls, but against one of the walls there was a magnificent japonica, and at precise distances all round there were green tubs containing dwarf evergreens.

Surveying the immense black range in the main kitchen, Frank remarked: 'Isn't this the sort of kitchen that cries out for a real, old-fashioned servant? I don't imagine it will ever see such a legendary being again, but at any rate we can look for an amiable young woman, neat and clean and smart in her cap and apron.'

Hilda, in whose bosom the teachings of her radical-minded Aunt Helen were still firmly embedded, was genuinely shocked. 'Why, Frank, I believe at heart you're a snob! What would my Aunt Helen think! She and her suffragette friends say that a cap and apron is a badge of "servitude" which no right-minded woman should wear.'

'That's as may be, but I'll bet she won't object to the "servitude" when she visits us. Now I'm going out for a few minutes. See if you can find some wine glasses. When a man sets up hearth and home, he must do the business properly.'

In a happy dream Hilda roved around, still scarcely believing that she was home. What was it Frank had asked for? Wine glasses. She found them in an old corner-cupboard in the dining-room. Lovely glasses of all shapes and sizes, glittering icily as the sunlight struck them. She was tapping them with her fingers, enjoying the bell-like fluting, when Frank came back, calling gaily: 'Champagne, Hilda! "The Widow" herself and blow the expense. I was lucky to find it.—Jerusalem! What a publican's dream! Let me look. Here we are.' He carefully extracted two champagne glasses, unwrapped the bottle, and gravely saluted it.

'I asked the chap to draw the cork for me—one of the civilized pleasures that blasted Hun has done me out of. Here's to him burning in Hell, and here's to us three, my darling.' They drank, to each other, to Mary, to every friend they could remember, and to the future, Frank insisting that there must be no heel-taps. Hilda, her senses floating deliciously, said warningly: 'I have to think about things, Frank. Lunch for instance. I daren't drink any more. I must go shopping.'

'Nonsense. Drink up.' He re-filled the glasses. 'I'll do the shopping. But what is this town crammed with hotels for? We'll go out to lunch.'

'But baby?'

'There you go, Hilda. Now perhaps you can see why a maid is necessary. Come along. They'll find something for Mary at the hotel. And afterwards you're going out to spend money while for a change I take my responsibilities as a parent seriously and look after our daughter. I expect we shall both go to sleep, so we shan't bore each other. These are for you, and if there are not enough I dare say I can manage a few extra.'

He handed her a wad of crisp five-pound notes, at which she stared bewitched. There were ten of them. Fifty pounds, and all for her and baby.

Frank, trying not to look as pleased as he felt, was astonished to see her place the notes in a bureau. 'But, Hilda, I want you to spend the money, today. You've had to wait long enough for it. Don't be a zany. Put it in your bag.'

'You needn't worry, darling. I shall spend it all right. But not today. I'm going to be sensible and make a list of what baby wants, and what I want. Then I shall shop wisely.'

' "There are more things in heaven and earth . . .",' he said laughingly. 'If that's the way champagne takes you, then it's not a luxury after all. Let's finish the bottle. What a surprising girl you are! Stay like it for ever.'

CHAPTER VI

'THE JINGLE OF THE GUINEA'

STANDING before the full-length mirror in her bedroom, Hilda was admiring herself unreservedly and reflecting that life in Princess Square was sheer heaven. She was trying on a navy-blue coat and skirt that had just come from the tailor, and had cost more than any garment she had ever possessed. She was naturally slim, but its severe classical line made her appear even more so; perhaps, she thought, too much so, for as a young matron she ought not to look quite so boyishly flat. Her furs, however, would conceal this defect, and from a nest of tissue paper she reverently withdrew a long stole and a huge muff of dark, lustrous skunk. These she laid upon the bed, smoothing them with sensuous pleasure, her heart brimful of tenderness for Frank, who had so generously bought them for her in London a few days earlier. He had tried to smuggle them upstairs, as a grand surprise, but she had intercepted him and divined instantly what the box contained. 'My furs! Oh Frank! My furs!' For some minutes she was too excited to touch them. They were the first she had ever possessed, and she was almost afraid of them.

'Are they all right, pet? The kind you wanted? I got them at Harrods. And who do you think helped choose them? I should never have dared on my own.'

'Rosa, of course.'

'Yes. I asked her to get time off for something terribly important. She was dead against my buying them just yet, and gave me a little homily on the virtues of thrift at this stage in our affairs; but all the same she thoroughly enjoyed selecting them, and she's coming down for the week-end to see you in them. Well, what do you think of our choice?'

'How can I think, darling! I can only look. Oh, but they're beautiful. They must have cost an awful lot of money, Frank.'

'Not as much as you're worth, Hilda. Don't be frightened of them. Put them on for me.'

She did so, draping the stole in a wide arc across her narrow shoulders, and holding the muff loosely as she turned triumphantly towards him.

'You look absolutely marvellous!'

'Thank you, Frank. Thank you, again and again and again. I'll take such care of them. They'll last me all my life. Let's try them on baby — against her face. Come and look.'

She dropped the stole like a coverlet over the sleeping child, and carefully arranged one small hand upon it. All mothers, Frank supposed, doted upon the perfections of their children, but at times Hilda really went to extremes.

As she stood now, posing in her furs, she congratulated herself yet again upon the unparalleled happiness of her lot. Frank's health was undoubtedly greatly improved. The 'nerve exhaustion' seemed to be disappearing and, although the Medical Board remained obdurate about issuing the final 'all clear', he continued in the, to her, somewhat vague work for which he had such contempt, while occasionally contriving to augment his income with articles in the daily papers. He had also begun to write a short book which he proposed calling *Twenty-four hours in Battle*, a minute realistic description of one day's events at the Front, written from one soldier's standpoint — a literal, not literary, bold, bone-truth account. The French, he explained, had done one or two good studies in the same vein, but there had been nothing so far in English. He had sent an outline of the book to a famous publisher, whose most distinguished reader had reported on the project so favourably that the publisher had sent him an encouraging letter telling him to go ahead, whereupon the author had immediately requested a royalty advance of ten pounds, which came by return of post. He had read his first chapter to her, and she had marvelled that men could be so brave amid such horrors; and marvelled, too, at his genius in making the dreadful scenes come so hideously alive.

'There shouldn't ever be a war again, should there? How can God let such things happen, Frank?'

'Well, I don't see that it's His business to rectify our folly, though out there, after a particularly bloody onslaught, I thought how pleasant it would be if things went as they did in Old Testament days with the Israelites. If all Governments, for instance, talking more bloody rot than usual, were suddenly struck sideways, silent and grinning, and the arms manufacturers and the press lords with them. What a simple way of keeping the world sane. It's rum, isn't it? that God could do it, but very properly won't, while we, who could too, don't dream of it. We deserve all we get, and perhaps we shall wake up to the fact one day. I'm no crusader, but I am trying to do my bit with this little work, and it will bring some grist to the mill into the bargain — at least I hope so. "Wisdom is a defence, and money is a defence", so says Ecclesiastes.'

'Money is a defence.' As Hilda put away the furs, she suddenly realized how much they were going to need to economize in future. Something that should have happened had not happened. She consulted a miniature calendar kept secretly in her handbag, and made a precise calculation. She was going to have another child. A son, of course! She was enraptured and, as for Frank, he would be wild with joy. 'Money is a defence.' He would have to make pots of money now, for it would cost so much to educate a boy. She returned to the mirror, wondering for how long she would be able to wear her beautiful new clothes. As if it mattered!

What did matter was that she couldn't possibly wait until Frank came home before telling him the news. She must telephone him at once. His voice sounded anxious as he asked: 'What is it, Hilda? Are you all right?'

'I should just think I am! I'm going to have another baby, Frank. Isn't it splendid? And it's sure to be a boy. I've only just found out.'

There was a silence and Hilda, faintly aggrieved, asked impatiently:

'Aren't you pleased, darling?'

'Yes, yes. Of course I am, though I don't think it's true, and I ought to know.'

'It is true, and you don't know. We'll call him Nicholas, shall we?'

'Anything you say, Hilda, but don't get over-excited. It could be a false alarm.'

'All right. I'll try to keep calm, if I can. But there's no doubt about it. So long, Frank, and will you telephone the news to Rosa?'

'I will, dearest. So long.'

Hilda walked towards the Front in search of Mary, who was taken for an airing every afternoon by their neat, pretty maid. In answer to an advertisement in the local paper she had received at least a dozen replies, from which Frank had selected three candidates for an interview, thereafter refusing all further aid despite her extreme nervousness at conducting such an important affair by herself. Of the three, Dorothy was by far the easiest to look at and Hilda, as yet naively influenced by external charm, had chosen her in spite of having been made to feel that it was rather a step downwards for Dorothy to become a general maid after working in a doctor's household on 'parlour work' only; a doctor, she had subtly managed to convey, being far higher in the social hierarchy than a mere temporary officer. Hilda, duly humbled, recalled how, as a girl of fourteen, she had energetically and successfully set at defiance all her elders to escape the lowly fate of Dorothy; and because of this tremendous fight so far forgot her status as mistress of a household as to feel quite sorry for the girl; indeed she found herself hoping that she would refuse the job. But when she showed her the little bedroom which she had delighted in making so pretty; and when she informed her that every afternoon she could take baby for an outing; and when she explained that, being the most modern and enlightened of mistresses, there would be no hard and fast rule about 'free time'; and that, furthermore, she could always ask a friend or two in for the evening, Dorothy, though obviously regarding her as somewhat weak in the head, had shown herself eager to enter this paradise of social justice. In the mornings she was trim and fresh in a cotton dress and a starched cap, while from lunch time onwards she looked even more pleasing in a black dress and the frilliest of white pinafores. She was a very pretty girl indeed and had patently been made much of in the doctor's establishment, for one morning, as she was clearing the table, she said astonishingly: 'Do you know, madam, I've been here for over a month and Captain Burton has never taken the slightest notice of me?'

'Hasn't he, Dorothy?' said Hilda, so startled that she could only repeat stupidly: 'Hasn't he?'

'No, madam, not once.'

'Well, it shall be rectified. I'll speak to him about it this evening.'

'Thank you, madam,' said Dorothy, gratified.

Hilda duly repeated this exchange verbatim, and Frank, laughing, asked what he ought to do about it. 'Ought I to kiss her, do you think? I suppose she is rather an attractive girl, but with you around I just don't see her, that's all. Tell me what to do.'

'Well, perhaps you should show a little interest in her. I

talk to her quite a lot, and she's very good with Mary. We talk about all sorts of things.'

'That's different. Two girls together, you know. All right. We can't have her nursing resentment. I'll mend my ursine ways at once.'

After this all was well, for though Frank never contrived to get beyond: 'Good morning, Dorothy. Everything all right with the world today?', he asked it with such concern that she and Hilda became as one in their belief that no man deserved better of his King and country than Captain Burton — a belief which he also shared.

Feeling that she would burst if she did not discuss her glorious discovery with someone, Hilda searched everywhere. Where could Dorothy have taken baby? Surely not to her home, for that had been expressly forbidden. Disappointed and angry, she at last went to the girl's home, and outside it saw the empty pram. The door was open and crowing merrily on the hearthrug was Mary, but of Dorothy there was no sign. Shaking with nervousness, Dorothy's mother mumbled that this was the very first time the baby had been there, and that her daughter had only slipped out for a few minutes.

Hilda, picking the child up, said coldly: 'Please don't bother to explain any further. Dorothy gave me her word that she would always take baby by the sea or in the park. It's unhealthy for her to be cooped up indoors, and it certainly won't occur again. Will you please ask Dorothy to come and take away her things this evening? I dare not think what my husband will say when he hears of this.' She walked out with a fine air of grandeur; but when Frank that evening heard the tale of Dorothy's misdeeds, although indignant, he cautioned moderation and advised that she should not be sent packing until they had replaced her. 'I hate to see you working like this, Hilda. There's no need for it.'

'Don't be silly, Frank. I'm not made of sugar. I won't have another maid in the house. I'll find a charwoman for the cleaning, and I'll manage the rest.'

'No, Hilda. I won't have it. Besides, if it's really true about this other matter, you can't manage the rest. You're quite, quite sure, sweetheart?'

'Quite sure. Aren't you thrilled? You've always said how wonderful it would be to have a son, but now you're going to have one you don't seem all that pleased about it. Did you tell Rosa?'

'No, darling. I thought . . . well . . . it might be a false alarm. But if it isn't, then of course I'm thrilled. You know I am. Now be nice to Dorothy when she turns up. You're going to have adequate help as long as ever I can manage it.'

'As long as you can manage it, Frank. What do you mean? Is anything wrong? There is. I can feel it. Tell me at once.'

'Well, I'm now on Civvy Street again — a free man!'

'But I thought that was the one thing in the world you wanted. Now you can go back to your paper again.'

'That's just the trouble, pet. The job isn't there any longer. They've been damned good about things, and they've promised me the next job going, but meantime I'm at leisure, so to speak. We shall be all right for quite a while yet, and something's bound to turn up, but this post-war world is in such a mess. We seem to be whirling into an even worse barbarism than the war. Everybody's grabbing for himself. The civilian bastards made the most of their chances while we silly mugs were at the Front. Can't blame them, of course. Ah well, as long as I can hold a pen I can make a living, but I want it to be a first-rate living for you and ours.'

Hilda, to whom it was inconceivable that it should not be so, kissed him and said gaily: 'Cheer up, darling. I'm not worried, so why should you be? Let's talk about young Nicholas. He's going to be such fun; and how Mary will adore him. Think of them growing up together! Be like me and concentrate on that. And no more Dorothys until you're safe in a good job. You've no idea how economical I can be if it's really necessary.'

Frank, however, persuaded her that this immediate sacrifice was not necessary, and the penitent was reinstated on giving her word of honour not to take her charge visiting again. Moreover, his gloomy fears of being unable to provide adequately for his wife and family proved to be unfounded, at least temporarily, since he almost at once obtained press propaganda work for Government Bonds and Hospital Appeals. Hilda sometimes suspected, when he came home very late, that he had been drinking heavily, but she was much too absorbed in the coming child to let this disturb her seriously. In his sleep he still fought bloody battles and, wakened by the tumult, she heard language that both appalled and fascinated her. In the dead of night, against the murmuring of the sea, these strings of curses were bizarre and terrible, but they did not puzzle her nearly so much as the quotations from various mighty poets that followed. At breakfast she sometimes repeated a quotation, but Frank was always sceptical about having uttered them in his sleep. He said she must have dreamt them.

'We didn't spout much poetry in France, Hilda. We talked mostly about food, and Piccadilly Circus, hot baths and good beds. All the time I was there I only came across one other chap who had a volume of verse with him. I had the Milton you gave me, and this fellow had a Wordsworth. He was a lawyer and I've often wondered what he's up to now. But you ought to wake me up if I do make a shindy. I'm not a professional quoter like your Aunt Helen. She'll be remembered by it.'

Aunt Helen, who never refused an invitation to 20 Princess Square, quoted all day long when there; and when it was borne in upon her that not only her carefree niece, but the intelligent Frank also, were bored by this excess of culture, she feared that they were in grave danger of turning into Philistines, and expressed the hope that they would ultimately return to London and salvation. Hilda she deemed to be especially in peril, for she did not appear to be interested in anything or anyone but her husband and her daughter and her charming home. 'And very properly too,' Frank remarked loyally. 'I also used to think London was the only possible place for civilized life. As far as my work goes I still think so, but what do you get out of it, Helen, that's so eminently desirable?'

'Theatres. Cinemas. Lectures. Meetings. And people. Whom do you know down here worth talking with? And what on earth do you *do* with yourselves — at week-ends, for instance?'

'Nothing, Helen, except enjoy them. As for people, don't be such an ass. As far as I'm concerned, the week-ends simply fly.'

'It's true, Aunt Helen. It's true of every day for that matter. I never seem to have enough time for all I want to do. And anyway, London is so near that it doesn't really matter about not actually living there, does it, Frank?'

'No, darling,' he lied stoutly.

'Well, I'm disappointed, Hilda. I'd love to see you settled in a nice flat in London, knowing lots of interesting people; giving "evenings" like Phillip and I used to do before the war; like Dermot does still. You used to be so go-ahead, Hilda; interested in all the newest books and plays. And now . . . Oh well, it's your life, and you certainly seem to be enjoying it.'

Rosa was of the same opinion as Hilda. She came down for occasional week-ends, and showered affection on Mary, and gave further sensible advice to Hilda on how best to manage Frank when his nerves were on edge. Fortunately she was there one week-end when Frank had an appalling fit of depression, and sat moodily for hours at his writing-table, screwing up sheet after sheet of his manuscript — *Twenty-four Hours in Battle*.

'The blasted thing's gone dead on me,' he exclaimed savagely. 'I think I'll go out for a spell. A good walk might put things right. You don't mind, Hilda?'

'Of course not, darling. But don't be late for dinner. It's rather special, because of Rosa.'

When they were alone, Rosa, deeply perturbed, inquired if he was often as dejected as this.

'No. It's only occasionally that he's like he is today. It's the war, isn't it?'

'I'm afraid so. He's not really well yet. Is he drinking very much? You can talk to me, child. Tell me whatever there is to tell. Life hasn't gone as smoothly for me as it has for your Aunt Helen. I've had to live it, not get it out of books, so perhaps I understand it better.'

'I don't think he drinks such a lot, Rosa; but he gets dreadfully irritable with people, though never with me. Sometimes he doesn't come home until the last train. He likes to have a night out with his old Fleet Street friends, but he always tells me where he's been and who was there. It's fun really for me, too, because he always has such interesting things to tell me. I quite enjoy waiting for him and looking forward to his news. But I've never seen him like he is today. Look at all these wasted sheets. He usually writes straight on with hardly an alteration. But look — whole pages criss-crossed.'

Rosa turned over the sheets curiously. She felt extremely uneasy about Frank, and when he did not return for dinner she became seriously alarmed, but she concealed this from Hilda.

'He must have gone for a really long tramp. Probably on to the Downs. I don't think we ought to wait for him, but see that Dorothy keeps his meal hot. And try not to upset yourself, Hilda. Remember there's someone else to think of now.'

The hours dragged on and, in spite of Rosa's comforting presence, Hilda was in a state of near panic when Frank had not returned by midnight. Even Rosa now seemed a little less calm, and readily agreed to Hilda's suggestion that they should go out and look for him; this at any rate, she reflected, would keep her quiet. They were putting on their coats when Hilda heard a key being turned very cautiously; then Frank walked into the bedroom and, without apparently seeing them, lay down, as if in a trance, on the bed. He looked absolutely rigid and, forgetting Mary sleeping so peacefully, Hilda cried out: 'He's ill, Rosa. Very, very ill. We must fetch a doctor. I'll go. Doctor Cresswell — we've booked him for my confinement — lives across the Square. He'll come at once.' Before Rosa could prevent her she was gone, and in a few minutes was back with the news that the doctor was following. By this time Rosa knew what was really the matter with the recumbent Frank, and was cursing her slowness for not having seen it the instant he came in. He was dead-drunk, so drunk that he didn't look drunk. There seemed to be no life in him at all, and it was miraculous how he had managed to reach home safely. There was a slight tap on the outer door and Rosa hastened out, hoping to have a quiet word with the doctor: to ask him, in fact, to conceal the truth from Hilda. But Hilda, her hearing inconveniently acute, overheard their whispers and turned angrily on her friend when, followed by Doctor Cresswell, she came back into the room. 'How dare you say such a thing, Rosa? My husband is *not* drunk, doctor. He's very ill.'

The doctor nodded, felt Frank's pulse, lifted up an eyelid, and said reassuringly: 'There's no cause for alarm, Mrs. Burton. Your husband is certainly not himself, but he's in the best place and will be perfectly all right in an hour or two. Loosen his things, and put a blanket over him. Now don't get agitated. You might bring on a miscarriage.' He was so astounded at her ignorance, and so sorry for her, that he gave no sign of his annoyance at being called out in the middle of the night to examine a drunken man. As he was leaving he said generously: 'Don't let him know you called me in. I'll make it a courtesy visit. Poor chap. He must have been through a good deal. Now, you ladies, take my advice and go to bed. Good night. I'll let myself out.'

A glance passed between him and Rosa as he walked out, a glance which caused Hilda to redden. 'So Frank *is* drunk! With you here, too, and me going to have another baby. Oh Rosa, how could he? I'd like to . . . I'd like to . . .' She rushed to the bed and shook it fiercely. 'Wake up, Frank. Wake up and look at yourself. You're drunk! Rosa! Whatever can Doctor Cresswell have thought?'

'Bless you, Hilda; nothing. It's all in the night's work for him. Pull yourself together. Remember what he said about a miscarriage. You really must keep calm. And you must stand by Frank. Supposing he'd walked over a cliff or something.'

Hilda trembled. She covered him up quite gently, put a pillow under his head, and they left him. Back in the sitting-room, soothing themselves with a smoke, they talked and talked, for neither felt as if they could sleep.

'What I can't understand, Rosa, is how Frank can be as drunk as he is and not look it. He was very strange when he came in, but he certainly didn't look drunk.' She was reflective for a few seconds, and then suddenly went into peals of laughter. 'It's all right, Rosa. I haven't lost my wits; but Frank once told me of a very queer thing that happened to a friend of his, and *now* I know it didn't happen to his friend at all! It happened to himself. At Victoria Station. He said his friend, a dramatic critic, was going to Folkestone to see a play there prior to its London production;

that he had an attaché case with him containing his things for the night; that he put this down while he bought his ticket, turned to pick it up, and found it gone. The station policeman was called, and this is how Frank described to me what then happened:

'Policeman: "You say you put the case down while you got your ticket, sir."

' "That's right, officer."

' "And what did the case contain, sir?"

' "Pyjamas, shaving tackle, etc."

' "No money? No valuables?"

' "No, officer."

' "Now sir, was the case like the one you are carrying?"

' "Own twin to it, officer."

' "I see. Well, we'll do our best for you, and let you know. It was exactly like the case you now have?"

' "Exactly, officer." '

Rosa laughed. They both laughed. 'How Frank took me in over that! If it hadn't been for tonight, I should never have tumbled to it. Of course it happened to Frank. I don't wonder the policeman looked thoughtful.' She laughed again, and Rosa beamed at her. 'Good girl! That's the way to take it. What fools we are to get flustered because a man has a few drinks. I don't know about you, but I should welcome a cup of tea.'

'Lovely. Let's go into the kitchen. It's warmer there. Go and have a peep at Frank while I make it.'

As she made the tea Hilda sang to herself. She had already forgiven her husband and was, as usual, blaming the war for his lapse. It wasn't his fault at all. It was the war that was responsible.

Rosa came in, with a half-bottle of something in her hand.

'I found this on him. Whisky. There's still a little left.'

'Pour it down the sink. That's the best place for it. Give it to me.'

'Don't be so childish, Hilda. Pour good whisky down the sink! Let Frank finish it when he wakes up. He'll need it.'

'Rosa! You surprise me. What I've got to do is to make Frank loathe the stuff, not encourage him to drink it. Give me that bottle.'

'No. Now Hilda, listen. Don't go getting romantic notions about reforming Frank. If I know anything at all about men, that's the surest way of heading for the rocks.'

'Indeed! And what *do* you know about men? You're not married. Surely I ought to know what's best for my husband.'

'As you say, I'm not married, but I've been in this world twenty years longer than you, and I've learnt a few things on the journey. You have a long way to go yet, Hilda. What has happened tonight can happen again, and you won't always have a friend at hand to help out. You must face up to this. It's the war. Keep that well in mind.'

'I wonder, Rosa, if it really is the war.' As she poured out the tea, she related to her friend all she could remember of the hints and warnings she had received about Frank before they were married.

'I know all that, Hilda. But all the same it is the war,' she repeated. 'Frank has talked to me freely about himself; about the hopelessness he sometimes feels. He adores you, but he once cursed himself to me for having been such a swine – his own expression – as to marry you. You've got to take him as he is, and count your blessings. And you've got a good many to count, my dear. The husband you wanted; Mary; the coming baby; this lovely home. What more could you want? There! What a speech to make at two o'clock in the morning!'

'Isn't it, especially as you haven't told me a thing I don't know? But listen. I can hear him moving.'

They sat motionless, straining to hear. They heard him curse as he walked to the bathroom, then water splashing and more curses.

'Ought we to go and see if he's all right?' Hilda whispered.

'No. Wait. I think he's coming in here.'

The door opened violently and Frank stood glaring at them as if he had surprised them in plotting his murder. Hilda, her heart shaking, looked quickly away.

'Well?' he said aggressively. 'Well, Hilda! Now you know what a rotten swine I am. Go on! Say it!'

He swayed, and she ran to steady him, but he shook her off. 'Don't come near me. I'm not fit. Hello, old Rosa! You been comforting my wife? Good friend. Good old Rosa.'

'Drink this, Frank,' and Hilda poured out for him the remainder of the whisky, but he stared at it angrily and made no move to take it.

'Drink it up,' Hilda coaxed, 'and then have some tea. Everything's all right between you and me, Frank. Everything.'

There was such deep shame in the look he gave her that to conceal her embarrassment she busied herself with the tea until she could repeat steadily: 'Everything is just as it was.'

'You mean that, Hilda?'

'Of course I mean it. Cut my throat and pierce my heart if I don't speak truth!'

She drew a finger across her throat, and laughed. 'Come on, Frank Burton. Tea? Cigarette?' She lit one for him and, when he began to stammer further apologies for whatever beastliness he had committed, she placed a hand over his mouth and commanded him to stop. 'It's over and forgotten, darling. Damn that old war to eternity. It's Sunday and we're all going to have a happy day. We'll take Rosa on to the Downs this afternoon. Poor dear, she has to go back early in the morning. Drink your tea, Frank. Good night, Rosa. Breakfast in bed for you today.'

Rosa jumped up and kissed them both, giving Frank an affectionate shake as she said brightly: 'Next time you go on the spree, old boy, think of others. We might all have been together and had a high old time. Good night, and God bless us all. You haven't drunk your pick-me-up. Down with it, Frank.'

Hilda, madly hoping that he would not touch the wicked stuff, looked at him appealingly. He hesitated, then, with a self-assuring laugh, drained the glass, drew her arm through his, and marched her off to bed.

CHAPTER VII

THE SECOND HOSTAGE

So far as Hilda was concerned, life became ever sweeter, for had not Destiny ordained that she was to be such a tower of strength to Frank that he would never again forget his dignity as a man, a husband, and a father? As she went about her absorbing preparations for the new baby, even the departure of pretty Dorothy, who was to be married, failed to disturb her serenity. They parted with every mark of mutual esteem, Frank surpassing himself on her last morning to the extent of hoping that she would make her prospective husband as happy as he was himself. They replaced her immediately by Millie, a solid, round-faced girl of eighteen, who, try as she would, never succeeded in looking tidy. Her cap sat crookedly on her abundant brown curls and made Hilda think of a toy yacht riding out a squall. Her black woollen stockings were never quite unwrinkled. Her capacious, embroidered white pinafore, though clamped on fresh from the laundry, achieved in the space of five minutes a limp and faintly spotted look. The top of her stays protruded like an iron palisade, and altogether she was the greatest possible contrast to her predecessor. She more than compensated, however, for these drawbacks by displaying the same gratifying interest in the military achievements of Captain Burton as Dorothy had shown, and her brown eyes sparkled with interest when Hilda gravely informed her about the coming child. After hearing this important news she would tumble forward eagerly to save Hilda the slightest exertion, and was continually asking if she was feeling all right. Did she desire hot milk? Could she fancy a cup of tea? Hilda, who had experienced no pregnant 'fancies' with

Mary, now developed an extraordinary passion for poached eggs, even getting up in the small hours to appease this powerful craving; whilst throughout the day Millie, humble before the mysteries of pregnancy, would bring in a succession of poached eggs and watch earnestly while they were consumed.

After Dorothy's pre-occupation with her own indisputable charms, Hilda found such selfless interest highly agreeable, and she was profoundly flattered, too, by Millie's assumption that as a married woman and a mother she was a tremendously important person. They became great friends, and on fine afternoons walked up and down the perpetually fascinating Front, Millie wheeling the pram and Hilda indicating that its beautiful occupant belonged to her by keeping one hand possessively upon the handle. And when Mary, beaming upon the passing world impartially, drew forth little cries of admiration here and there, Millie beamed too. She was deeply interested in everything, no matter how crass, that Hilda chattered about, and although Hilda's favourite topic was the Burton family of three, and their immense good fortune in being those three, she never seemed to be bored and heartily concurred that as a united family they were unique. Hilda went about with her chiefly because she liked her, but also because, during week-days, she had no other companion. Frank, who feared that she might be lonely, had urged her to see more of young Mrs. Stockell, the wife of a British ex-Intelligence officer with whom he had fraternized in the bar of the Albion, and whose hair-raising accounts of his exploits throughout the war made him a welcome visitor anywhere.

The Stockells were still without a home of their own, and lived in a furnished flat in Kemp Town. They were the first acquaintances in Brighton to come to Princess Square for a meal, and Hilda worked thoughtfully to achieve a dinner that was gastronomically perfect. Irene Stockell was beautiful, far more so than herself, but as chilling as frozen snow. She was spoilt and petted by her husband, but Hilda perceived no answering warmth, and decided that she was a person who would always take and never give. She had two small boys, for whom she had a nurse, and she frankly regarded them as a mortal nuisance. She was a fearful snob and did not conceal her astonishment when Hilda informed her that not only did she do everything for Mary, but that she found it inexpressibly dear to do so. Mrs. Stockell would have let her own children wilt like plants in a sunless room rather than do anything so 'common' as to take them out for walks herself. She was discontented because they were still, according to her standards, comparatively poor, though for one pretty dress that Hilda possessed she had half a dozen far more expensive ones. Frank suspected her of being a nagger and said brutally that the kindest thing she could do for her husband would be to elope with a rich lover and leave him to the warmth of the two little boys. Hilda tried valiantly to like her, but it was embarrassing to hear her exclaim enviously as she looked about her: 'How lucky you are, Mrs. Burton, to have your own things around you!' Julian Stockell flushed, and Frank said banteringly: 'For one complete home, one complete limb. That was the price, Mrs. Stockell, and I know which I'd rather have. Do you mind carving, old chap? Hilda is no great shakes at it as yet.'

The evening was not a success, though Frank talked well, as did Julian Stockell. Hilda shivered as he described, for her entertainment, some of the narrow escapes he had had from falling into the hands of his opposite numbers in German Intelligence; and when he recounted how one night in Hamburg two of these officers, who were looking for him, actually slept in the next room to his own, she could have shaken Mrs. Stockell for her indifference. Irene did not even share Frank's and her own indignation when Julian remarked that the only thing he had never enjoyed about his war service was being presented with white feathers by patriotic women on his brief returns, in mufti, to England. He said he had carefully preserved them all, with the date and place of presentation. Hilda, frankly in love with her own family, could make no contact at any point with the bored young woman, and their acquaintance died of malnutrition, though Frank and Julian remained on the best of terms and occasionally spent an evening together in one of Brighton's cheerful pubs.

Mrs. Stockell was certainly no loss, for Hilda had never before felt so contented with her lot, so much so indeed that, when Frank broke the news that once again he was a 'free' man, she laughed and advised him to count his blessings. Now, she pointed out cheerfully, he would be able to finish *Twenty-four Hours in Battle*, and afterwards write the wonderful play that was to secure their children's future.

'Don't look so solemn, Frank. We've still got something left from the commutation, and we can always economize. For one thing, I can do without Millie. I've got everything I shall need for Nicholas, and I shan't want anything for myself for ages. Something is sure to turn up. You're so clever, darling. Why — you look as if we hadn't got a penny in the world!'

'That's just it, dearest. For all practical purposes we haven't, except for my truncated pension. It's rotten of me to have let you in for this just now. I've kept it dark for some time, hoping another job would come along. I've pulled every string I could, but there's nothing doing yet.'

Hilda, startled out of her complacency by his grave matter-of-factness, exclaimed: 'But all that commutation money! Hundreds and hundreds of pounds! We can't possibly have spent it all. Why — you let me go on buying whatever I wished for and you said there would be plenty over for my confinement. Oh Frank, it was such a lot of money!'

'It wasn't a fortune, Hilda, though it seemed so at the time. But I had some personal loans to repay; and it did me good to see you spending on Mary and yourself. The trouble . . . well — apart from personal debts to friends like Dermot — there was something else, a preying mantis in Regent Street — to be precise, a money-lender. I must sound like a character in a melodrama talking to you about money-lenders. He used to cash post-dated cheques for me. That, of course, was when I was still drawing army pay. I had to cut free of him at any price, and it was a heavy price, damn his eyes!'

'Oh Frank! A money-lender!' Hilda, recalling her own brief, abortive encounter with one of these sanguinivorous beings, was shaken and stared at her husband as if he had just escaped a violent death. 'You must never go to a money-lender again, whatever happens. Promise me you'll never go to one again.'

'You bet I won't. But I've got to find money somehow until a job comes in. We can't live on my pension, that's certain.'

'But your book, Frank? Aren't you going to work on that? It's sure to bring in plenty of money. And what about all those articles you wanted to write?'

'Yes, yes, of course. But we must live meanwhile, and there's this baby so near. We have one substantial asset, though. Now don't get upset. It's only a temporary measure. All this good furniture — we can . . .'

'Sell our home? Oh no! We can't do that. Where's my baby to be born? In the workhouse?'

'Hilda, that's hitting below the belt! He'll be born here, in your own bed, and you shan't go without a thing. It's all quite simple. I've been to see Cohen, the landlord, and he's willing to take out a bill of sale on the furniture. You don't know what that means, but I assure you it's nothing very terrible. The furniture will raise enough to see us through very comfortably till I get straight, and we shall still be at home and nobody a penny the wiser. I wish to God you wouldn't look at me like that. I shall pay Cohen off in no time once some work rolls in. I'm not the only one out of work in a land fit for heroes to live in. These last few weeks I've lain awake at night wishing I was lying safely over there with a little wooden cross above me.'

'Frank! Who's hitting below the belt now? And you're being melodramatic again, too. I believe you say these things on purpose, to make me feel sorry for you. I don't mind a bit about the wretched bill of sale. What is it? What happens?'

Frank smiled with relief. 'Nothing you need fret about, dearest. As I've told you, we shall carry on here just the same. If I could have seen the business through without your knowing, I would have, but Cohen may want to make an inventory first.'

'Is *that* all?' Hilda also smiled with relief. 'What a fuss to make about a little thing like an inventory! All right, Frank. You can tell Mr. Cohen to go ahead, and I'll talk to Millie. I can manage perfectly without her. Doctor Truby King says the best exercise for pregnant women is ordinary, everyday housework.'

'Does he indeed? Well, I don't agree. You are not to dispense with Millie, especially just now. There's your nurse to be waited on, and there's Mary to be looked after, and there's me, and — most important of all — you. God! If only I had two hands. I'd find a job as a labourer.'

'Now Frank, don't go all melodramatic again. It gets on my nerves. And you'd be no good as a labourer if you had a dozen hands. I know more about labourers than you do, don't forget. You have to be born one, like my poor foster-father was. Shall I come with you to see Mr. Cohen? He might lend us more money if I do.'

'Cohen is a business man, pet, and not even your bright

eyes would induce him to give us a penny more than our things are worth. I'm off. Wish me luck.'

She waved to him encouragingly as he looked back before turning the corner. A bill of sale? It sounded a little sinister, and its full import was only now beginning to form clearly in her mind. She was not an absolute cretin and the more she thought about it the clearer it became that it was a very serious matter indeed. Once the bill of sale was 'taken out' their entire home would belong temporarily to someone else. She believed Frank implicitly about their present circumstances being transient, but this knowledge did not compensate for having her home mortgaged before her eyes, and she was dismayed to find herself peevishly criticizing her husband. He couldn't help his awful luck, and it was infamous that a man of his experience should be compelled to pawn his home while younger men remained safe in their war-time jobs. What worried her was her ever-growing perception that he was not always above playing to the gallery about his wound. He talked about it more than he should; drew attention to it at every opportunity, so it seemed to her. After all, she reflected, there were thousands of wounded men still in hospital in far worse case than he was. She had accompanied him once on a visit to an old comrade at Roehampton, and there she had seen things that had made her feel ashamed of her own splendid health. And what of those men who had not come back at all? She gave herself a little shake. She was being disloyal to her husband. That was a dreadful thing to be. She began to make excuses for him. It was only his way. His melodramatic harping on his wound was a kind of defence against continuing bad luck. She must play her part as an understanding wife. Economy was the watchword until they were out of the wood. A fierce yearning assailed her for a poached egg, but she sternly repelled this. There must be no further yielding, between proper meals, to such a ridiculous craving. She felt the child within her flutter as if in protest.

The craving mounted and would not be subdued. Poached eggs she must have, and going to the kitchen she solved the problem with Jesuitical logic by ordering them legitimately for lunch.

Frank returned in apparently good heart from the all-powerful Mr. Cohen, who did not, he informed her, think it necessary at this juncture to make an inventory, a curious omission which conveyed nothing to Hilda. What he did not tell her was that Mr. Cohen had only seen fit to advance a comparatively small sum upon their goods and chattels, a tithe, in fact, of their value, with the proviso that this sum must be repaid, with interest, at a certain date. Failing this, Mr. Cohen, with upturned palms, had pointed out that it would be his regrettable duty to sell their possessions, take his pound of flesh, and of course give back any money that might be over. It was, therefore, a dreadful shock to Hilda when, with Christmas almost upon them, Frank miserably confessed that, apart from the sum he had set aside for the expenses of her approaching confinement, Mr. Cohen's largesse had been swallowed up.

'Oh Frank! What are we going to do? Christmas without any money! It won't be Christmas at all, will it?'

'Well, darling, I was wondering if . . . well . . . if you could be a pal and lend me your engagement ring. I could raise quite a respectable sum on it, and you shall have it back quite soon.'

Hilda, deeply wounded, stared at him. 'My engagement ring? Oh, Frank, isn't there any other way? Can't you borrow some money? From Dermot perhaps?'

'It will only be for a few days, Hilda. You shall have it back on Christmas morning. Honest.'

Hilda went to her room and took out the tiny leather case containing her treasure, a slender marquise of diamonds surrounding a dark blue sapphire. Weeping, she recalled the marvellous day when Frank had taken her to choose it.

She had tried on a dozen rings, all of them the traditional half-hoops of diamonds, but she had wanted something different, lovely though they all were; and it was Frank who had suggested that only a marquise ring would be perfect for her. The salesman at once produced such a ring, all of diamonds, but, haunted by a line from she knew not where — 'Sapphires from the Kashmir Hills' — and scornful of tradition, she insisted that her ring must be of sapphires and diamonds. With great severity she had informed the salesman that if he could not give her such a ring, she would seek it elsewhere. Whereupon he had said quickly: 'We can design exactly what you require, madam. We can set the stones in wax, and you can choose from several designs. I know we can please you within a few days.' A week later she and Frank went again to the jewellers and there, glittering in its waxy bed, was this perfect ring, this marquise of diamonds with the sapphire smouldering darkly at its heart. How proudly Frank had placed it on her finger, and how childishly she had gloated over it. Even her austere Aunt Helen, though uncompromisingly plain-spoken about its cost, had admired it. She slipped it on and held her hand before the mirror. Her one beautiful jewel! How could Frank ask it of her? And was not an engagement ring sacrosanct? For a few days only, he had promised. She could not refuse. If she did, then he would have no alternative but to break into her confinement expenses, and that was unthinkable. She replaced it and took the little box to him. With a shamefaced mumble of gratitude he slipped it into a pocket and went out, presumably, she reflected mournfully, to pawn it.

When Christmas morning came she waited confidently for him to keep his promise, and searched the breakfast table with expectant eyes. He had several little gifts for her—scent, gloves and a copy of Pepys's *Diary*, but she could not see her ring. She looked at him wistfully, and said quietly:

'Give me my ring, Frank. You promised, you know.'

He coloured. 'Listen, pet. I couldn't manage it, but it's safe enough. You shall have it as soon as my cursed luck changes. You *must* believe me. Something's bound to turn up in the New Year. . . .'

'Don't talk to me,' she said savagely. 'You never meant to give it back today. You must have known you couldn't.' She began to cry. 'I'm all upset. I expect I'll have a miscarriage. Then you'll be a murderer as well as a liar and a thief. Perhaps I'll die, then you'll be a double murderer! I don't want your presents.' She pushed the packages viciously across to him. 'You can go and give them to the nearest barmaid. All I want is my ring!'

'Christ! Do you think I like doing this? As if I wouldn't give you the earth if I could!'

'I don't want the earth. I want my ring. I wish I'd never lent it to you. I wouldn't have, either, if I'd known you were going to cheat me like this. I'd be ashamed to make a sacred promise and not keep it.'

'I am ashamed. Damned ashamed,' he said so quietly that Hilda, jerked out of her self-pity, stared at him, and instantly the ring was forgotten. She didn't care if she never saw it again. She didn't care about anything but that Frank should never again look so wretched. She felt mean, and vulgar, and guilty.

'Oh Frank! I didn't mean it. I'm sorry. I know it isn't your fault. Thank you, darling, for all my lovely presents. And see — I've got a pipe for you, and a fountain pen as well. We'll have a wonderful Christmas!'

'That's my Hilda! What about sending young Millie home for the day? Be on our own, eh? She'll love it, and so shall we. You just sit quietly in the kitchen and give me your orders. It's high time I learnt how to cook a meal single-handed.'

Hilda laughed. 'This isn't a meal, stupid. It's our Christmas dinner. We've got a turkey. All right. Millie can go quite soon. But I must give her her present.'

'Right, then I'll start in. Christmas Day in England, with wife and child. What more can any man want?'

Hilda was enchanted. The work would fall on her, but Frank could keep an eye on Mary and amuse them both with delightful nonsense. Such talk there would be of 'Shoes and ships and sealing wax; of cabbages and kings'. Such a re-telling of old tales. Such comforting anticipation of the day when their ship came sailing home. Such exciting plans for the future of Mary and her brother. Nobody, seeing them so happy in each other, would have guessed that their ship had not even a home to sail to.

Millie entered, and Hilda, more than usually amused by her plunging cap and aggressive stays, had to make an effort to uphold her dignity as mistress of the household. She handed the girl a parcel, and told her that she might go home almost immediately. Millie, overjoyed, blushed her gratitude and Hilda, unable to keep her eyes off the jutting whalebones, expressed the hope that she would like her present.

'I thought you would prefer to have something useful, Millie. Open it and see if it's what you want.'

Millie eagerly did so, and revealed three snowy aprons, lavishly embroidered, and three jaunty caps that matched them. It was now Hilda's turn to blush, for in a rare flash of comprehension she realized, from Millie's guileless face, that she had blundered. Frank, equally perceptive, but mercifully quick-witted, said casually: 'Don't forget Mary's little gift for Millie,' and calmly handed her the flask of perfume he had just given to Hilda.

'Of course. I nearly did forget. It's Lily of the Valley. It will last for ages. You only need the tiniest drop on your handkerchief when you're going anywhere special.'

Millie, transformed, gave a gasp of pleasure. The aprons

and caps, she said tactfully, would come in very useful, and as for the scent, she would treasure it above all else. The two young women smiled at one another appreciatively, their self-respect restored, but when Millie had gone from the room Hilda said gratefully: 'That was splendid of you, Frank. Poor Millie! I've never felt so ashamed in my life. I can't imagine why I was such an idiot as to think she would like uniform for a Christmas present.'

'You aren't an idiot, Hilda. They're very pretty aprons. Now I shall have to replace that scent.'

'Well, I'll never do such a thing again. I'm surprised, though, that she was so pleased to have the scent, because she's a very religious girl. She always goes to a Salvation Army service on Sunday nights with her mother.'

'I never knew that. Good for Millie. I have a great respect for the Salvation Army, though I can remember the time when they were hooted and jeered at. But what a sad waste of good perfume! She won't dare to go home smelling of it.'

'It doesn't matter if she never takes out the stopper. What a man of the world you are, Frank! You make me feel wise, too. We'll have a wonderful Christmas, darling, even if I haven't got my . . .' She stopped herself, and repeated gaily: 'A wonderful Christmas. I only hope everybody, everywhere, is as happy as we are.'

Hilda, full as ever of hopeful friendliness, welcomed her nurse warmly, for she was young and smart and altogether different from the horrible old midwife who had attended her with Mary; while Millie, awed in the presence of authority, and put to shame by the glossily starched uniform, made superhuman efforts with her own appearance, and tumbled around generally in a fervour of good will. The memory of that first somewhat unusual confinement had vanished completely, and Hilda was determined to endure, and to enjoy, the birth of her second child in a manner appropriate to the wife of a hero. She was in bed, laughing over the engaging absurdities of Samuel Pepys, from whose *Diary* Frank was reading to her, when the first signal appeared. Nurse Swallow, hastily called, took one look at her and exclaimed peevishly: 'Well, I did think I might have had at least a couple of days free. You young women are always in such a hurry. Captain Burton, will you go and tell Doctor Cresswell we shall need him some time in the early morning, but that I shan't call him before it's necessary. That's right, Mrs. Burton, walk about all you want to.'

She bustled forward with her preparations and Hilda, bereft of Frank's sustaining presence, gazed into her mirror and was mortified to find that she looked exactly the same as usual. She ought surely to look pale and strained, but her eyes were shining and her cheeks were flushed. She surveyed the meagre appointments of her dressing-table, and wished that they were of silver instead of modest ebony. To create an illusion of opulence for the occasion she had placed at each end of the table a handsome leather-covered case, securely locked. One case contained a dozen fish knives and forks, the other a dozen tea-spoons, both of them being wedding presents. They looked well, and she fondly hoped that Nurse Swallow would conclude that they contained her jewellery. She thought sadly of that jewel which would have been such a comfort to her now, not only for its intrinsic beauty but as a very material sign that all was well with the Burton household. She longed for Millie, and timidly suggested that she ought perhaps to be wakened up.

'Certainly not,' Nurse Swallow snapped. 'What do you suppose I'm here for? She'll be needed in the morning. Ah, here is your husband. He can stay until the doctor comes.'

Hilda held on to Frank desperately, but after a time commanded: 'Go away! You're no help at all. I'd rather be by myself.'

Frank, very white, stood there uncertainly, but the nurse motioned him out. Everything thereafter proceeded normally, and poor Frank, waiting anxiously in the deserted sitting-room, was forgotten, the blessed nepenthe of chloroform being a far greater comfort than the tenderest husband in the world.

'Is it a boy?' Hilda asked drowsily as her mind began to clear.

'It is, and a fine little chap too.'

'Thank you, doctor. I'm afraid it's been a very ordinary case for you. No interesting complications like I had last time.'

The doctor smiled. 'We don't welcome complications on a job like this. Now, no more talking please. When nurse gives the word you can see your husband for a minute or two, and then you must go to sleep.'

When at last Frank was sent for, Hilda announced the sex of their new treasure with such triumph that everybody laughed.

'Isn't it marvellous, Frank? We have a son!'

'I know, sweetheart. I've been listening outside for the last few minutes. I heard the little beggar cry and it sounded like a boy. But how about you, darling? How do you feel?'

'Wonderful, but as empty as a blown egg. What time is it?'

'Six o'clock.'

'Then I'd like a jolly good breakfast.'

'Can she have it, doctor?'

'No, but a cup of tea won't hurt. I wouldn't say no to one myself.'

'It's on the way, doctor. Here it is, in fact.'

Millie came shyly in with a tray, and stood abashed before the busy spectacle, scarcely knowing how or where to leave the tray in her anxiety to appear proficient. She perched it awkwardly on the washstand and was tiptoeing nervously away when Hilda called excitedly to her and announced, for the second time, that she was the mother of a son.

'Oh madam! And I never heard a sound. Fancy me being asleep while you were having a baby! I'll never get over it. Why ever didn't the master wake me up earlier? I know I could have helped. Shall I see to the tea now?'

'No. Clear the court,' Doctor Cresswell said brusquely. Millie fled and Frank, receiving permission for a few more minutes, walked over to see his son, while Hilda lay watching proudly.

'I want to look at him, too, Frank. I can hardly believe it till I've seen him.'

Frank came back to her. 'It's a boy, all right. I must go, pet. Doctor Cresswell's looking very professional. So is nurse. Drink your tea and then go to sleep and dream of young Nicholas.' He kissed her and, exchanging a friendly grin with the doctor, slipped out, his happiness at the birth of a son mingling with a sickening fear for the immediate future. He had pulled every available string, but it would appear that the last recommendation for securing a decent job was a sound military record. The editor of one prosperous weekly journal, seeking an assistant editor, had even gone so far as to turn him down quite frankly because of his wound; two hands, apparently, being more essential for the post than one experienced brain. Then he had been offered a good job in Bombay on an august English newspaper published there. He had discussed this very gravely with Hilda, who had been eager for him to take it, saying that she would follow when she was safely through her confinement. Knowing nothing whatever about it, she had earnestly pointed out to him the indubitable advantages of life in India . . . the sun . . . the colour . . . Mother Ganges, and the Kashmir Hills. She had assured him confidently that she was perfectly capable of managing for herself until the child was born, but in the end her very eagerness had decided him against taking the work. He had no right to leave her at such a time, though he was wise enough not to say so. He had therefore lied and told her that on making inquiries he found that women were still forbidden to travel the seas because of the danger from unaccounted-for mines. She had of course believed him, but had still besought him to go, arguing that out of his handsome salary he could well afford to keep their home in Princess Square until such time as she could cross the seas. Furthermore, she emphasized that by remaining quietly at home for a while she would be able to save money, enough at any rate for her passage. The vision of Hilda saving money filled him with a fearful wonder. She had never yet had any to save, poor girl, but he knew her nature well enough by now to realize that she would be no better at the business than he had ever been.

At length he had managed to dissuade her from the Indian project, and now here he was, dependent on precarious free-lancing and what remained of his pension; their possessions mortgaged, and the expense of this second child to be met. The book, *Twenty-four Hours in Battle*, had gone sour on him, and he knew that it would never achieve completion; the best he could hope for out of it would be a few newspaper articles. It would not, in any event, have produced a fortune, though it had been uphill work convincing Hilda of this. She had a naive belief that he had only to work at it assiduously and it could not fail to set them afloat again. Every article of his that was accepted she read with flattering interest, and reviled all editors as employers of sweated labour when they did not pay what she thought such brilliance merited.

'If you had one article published every day, darling, we should be all right,' she had said to him encouragingly. 'Surely you could manage to write one every day; you always find something so unusual to write about.'

'If only it were as simple as that, Hilda! As a matter of fact, I'm lucky to get as many taken as I do. Spare a thought for the poor bloody editor, my lamb. He gets shoals of stuff loaded on to him every day — every day, mark you! Digest this and you'll begin to understand something about free-lancing, which is no job for a married man. If I don't land a worthwhile job on a paper soon, I shall have to look for something different. Advertising work, maybe. It's well-paid and I could do it, though I'm not what you might call enthusiastic about it. Still, when the devil drives, you know.'

Hilda, ignorant of the gravity of their plight, made rapid and normal progress, and longed for Nurse Swallow to be gone. She felt aggrieved that she had been unlucky with both her nurses and, wrapped up in her own engrossing affairs, never perceived that her present nurse, like the previous one, had observed various portents indicating that things were rather shaky with the finances of the Burton household. She was also apprehensive about her fees. But Frank, desperate, had mortgaged his diminished pension for some time ahead to the obliging money-lender of Regent Street in order to pay her fees and meet immediate household expenses.

When the time came for the nurse to leave, he made her a gallant little speech of thanks for her services, and then he and Hilda waited politely for her to announce that the taxi should be called. But Nurse Swallow sat on and on and on until even Hilda became aware that something was wrong; that the hot-water bottle she had given her as a present was not enough; that Frank must only have given her the bare fees, and that she was now waiting expectantly for the customary present of a few extra pounds. All Hilda's sympathies were with her husband, moodily smoking his pipe, and obviously very much alive to the humiliating situation. The atmosphere grew progressively strained, the conversation more monosyllabic and forced, until Nurse Swallow, accepting the fact that they had nothing extra to give her, coldly asked Frank to call a taxi. He raced to do her bidding, and their last memory of the disappointed woman was a piercing stare that ought to have killed them stone dead.

'Damn her! I know I ought to have given her something over, but I simply dare not. Don't let it worry you, Hilda. She shall have it at the first opportunity. It's a lovely afternoon. What about a drive along the Front in an open landau, you and me and ours? Wrap up well. You need fresh air, my sweet.'

Hilda was delighted at this suggestion and, snug in her furs, her son upon her lap, and Frank by her side with Mary on his, they bowled along in the mild February sunshine. The Front was a model of winter decorum; there were no boisterous holiday crowds; no alien sounds to spoil the music of the sea. The sky was a placid blue, and the trim lawns of Hove were green as Irish bogs. Mary, when first introduced to her baby brother, had smacked his face in a frenzy of jealousy, and had brooded darkly ever since on this red and crumpled intruder. As the nurse had brought him, so she had hoped that the nurse would take him away; but as this was evidently not to be, she now began to display a friendly interest in him. 'Nicky!' she shouted. 'Nicky!' and before Hilda could prevent her had given him a sharp little poke to remind him of her existence. He gave a whimper and, filled with consternation, Mary clung tightly to her father, who was laughing.

'Naughty girl!' Hilda admonished. 'You must never hurt your little brother, darling. He belongs to you, too. Kiss him better like a good little sister.'

Mary, after some reflection, did so, and, as further evidence that she bore him no ill will, thrust upon him her battered fairy doll and waited with quivering excitement for his response to this sacrifice. When nothing whatever happened she was about to administer a second poke, but Hilda stopped her.

'Good, generous Mary. Nicky can't say "Thank you" yet, darling. He's very little, like you were once, and he has to learn, like you have. But soon you'll be able to play with him, and then he'll give you *his* toys. You'll see.'

Mary, deeply impressed, nodded sagely, and, comically proud of the new addition to her vocabulary, continued to enunciate at intervals, loudly and proprietorially, 'Nicky.'

Nobody could have guessed that they were not on top of the world: that in sober fact there was less than a five-pound note between them and absolute want. 'Something will turn up,' Hilda assured herself. 'Something *must* turn up,' Frank silently echoed. 'Nicky,' Mary called out to a passer-by as she pointed a possessive finger at the sleeping bundle.

'Our Nicky,' Hilda corrected softly, and then, to herself, 'Our Mary and our Nicky.' As she looked out to sea she wondered, a little wistfully, how long it would be now before Frank could take her across the Channel for that postponed honeymoon in Carcassonne; how long before she could savour the magic of 'abroad'. She gave a little laugh. Why, life with Frank and Mary and Nicky was going to be all 'abroad'. How, indeed, could it be otherwise?

'A penny for them, Hilda,' Frank offered as he heard her laugh.

'There's good news on the way, Frank. I can feel it in my bones. It's that advertising job you've applied for.'

'Let's hope you're right, dearest. Oddly enough I was thinking of it too. We'll get to Carcassonne yet. You're not the only one who can feel things in your bones. I knew you were thinking of that ancient wonder when I saw you looking out to sea, though I'm blessed if I know what we shall do with this pair when we go junketing.'

'Oh, we'll find someone to look after them. Rosa perhaps, or Aunt Mildred. Not Aunt Helen! She only likes children when they're old enough to be instructed. Rosa would come like a shot if she could. She thinks there never was, and never can be, such a marvellous being as the one on your lap.'

'I see you've got it all worked out but for the missing link — the cash! Well, that's up to me, so here's hoping.'

'Cash! Link! Nicky!' shrilled Mary, swelling with pride over her mastery of these fascinating new words.

Frank hugged her. 'That's the way of it, old lady. Cash and lots of it for you and Nicky and Mummy.'

'Cash!' the child shrilled again, and then, remembering something she had once overheard as her father tried to do with one hand what could only be accomplished with two: 'Can't be done, hang it. Simply can't be done!'

CHAPTER VIII

THE GLITTERING REWARDS OF COMMERCE

HILDA's bones had spoken prophetically, for a few days later, when their entire worldly wealth consisted of only a few shillings, and Millie's dismissal became an obvious necessity, Frank's luck turned and he received a letter which sent them into transports of hope. It was from a world-famous pottery in a provincial town, and it requested a preliminary interview with him in London; after which, if this proved satisfactory, a second interview would be required at the pottery, an interview at which, if he was a married man, his wife would be expected to attend. All expenses of course, would be refunded, and the post, that of assistant advertising manager, carried a substantial salary. Furthermore, the letter proceeded, when their present advertising manager retired, as he intended to do within the year, his second-in-command would naturally step into his shoes. But, lest hope should mount unduly, the letter continued cautiously with the announcement that a final choice lay between those two of the many applicants who had been singled out for the preliminary interview, Frank and one other. Hilda, who had not the slightest doubt that Frank would be the lucky man, began at once to make exciting plans for future gaiety.

'We'll go to France on your first holiday, Frank darling. I shall be able to shop in Paris. Every girl dreams of doing this. Why, even Aunt Helen went raving mad in Paris and bought three expensive feather boas, two for herself and one for Aunt Mildred!'

'Here, not so fast, Hilda! I haven't got the job yet. The

other chap may be streets ahead of me as far as experience goes. I've never done this sort of work except for Appeals propaganda, though I don't imagine it's difficult; but it frightens me to see you so confident.'

'Well, I'm not frightened. Of course you'll get it. They've only to see and hear you. Besides, how can they help choosing you when they realize how much you have suffered because of the war?'

'That's about the last thing that would influence them, but I suppose it counts for something to have worked for a decent newspaper. That's what decided them to see me.'

'But I wonder why they want to see me, too.'

'Oh, that's simple enough. Working and living in a small provincial town is a very different matter from working and living in London. We should have to fit in socially. I wonder how we should like provincial life, Hilda. I've always hated the idea, for it can be pretty dull and narrow.'

'Frank! With all that salary how could life ever be dull? And just think what it will mean for Mary and Nicky. Besides, we needn't live in the town. We can have a house in the country. I shall keep my fingers crossed till you've got the job. I'll ask Millie if she'll come with us to Batsford. She's so devoted to Mary that I'm sure she will. What a blessing you didn't go to India! It was Destiny. This wonderful post was waiting for you all along. And they seem to be such kind, thoughtful people, wanting to see me and paying all the expenses.'

'That's only businesslike, dearest. You ought to know that. And for heaven's sake don't say anything to Millie, or to anyone else, just yet. I've got to beg, borrow or steal a few pounds from somebody at once, and I don't know where to turn for it. All will be easy if I get the job, but meanwhile the Burton family must live; and if we are summoned to appear at Batsford I can hardly ask for our expenses in advance. That would absolutely sink us.'

'There's always Mr. Cohen,' Hilda suggested brightly. 'Go to Mr. Cohen. When he learns that our ship has come home, I'm sure he'll lend us whatever we need until we can pay off the bill of sale. Shall I go and ask him? I don't mind at all,' she urged, confident that she could charm the needful from that gentleman, and ignorant of the fact that in addition to the bill of sale Frank was now badly in arrears with the rent and lived in constant dread of eviction. It was this that had made him turn to other fields than journalism, and if he did not pull something off quickly he dared not imagine what they were going to do. Looking now at Hilda, so supremely assured that nothing could possibly go wrong, he was infected by her enthusiasm. He agreed that Mr. Cohen would doubtless, at a price, advance a still further sum upon their belongings, but pointed out that such an astute man of business would not do so without tangible evidence that he had in truth secured the appointment in Batsford. The problem was how to find a few pounds meanwhile. Had she any further helpful ideas? Could she ask her people for a small loan? Failing this, would she let him raise the wind on such trinkets as she still possessed? It would be for such a little while, he pleaded, and then all would be well for ever.

Hilda's gaiety diminished somewhat, and she felt slightly sick.

'You mean that you want to pawn everything that I've got, Frank? All right. I'd rather this than ask Aunt Helen to help us out. You owe her quite a lot already, don't you?'

Frank reddened. 'Yes, but she'll get it back, and with interest if she wants that. What about your uncle? Wouldn't he help you? Your aunt need not know anything about it. You could telephone him at his office.'

'I could, but take my bits and pieces first, and if they don't bring in enough then I'll ask Uncle Phillip. At any rate he won't quote Polonius at me, as Aunt Helen would.'

She collected all her trinkets and gave them to him, wondering if she would ever see them again should the momentous interview go against him. But it was not going to go against him. That was out of the question, and anyway these oddments were not dear to her heart as her beautiful lost ring had been.

'I feel a swine,' Frank muttered, 'but bear with me a little longer, Hilda, and when we're respected citizens of Batsford you'll see what a grateful husband can do for a sweet wife. I shall become a reformed character. I shall wear a bowler hat on Sundays and take you to church. I might even be elected, after a decade or two, as a churchwarden. And as the son of a clergyman, should this notable fact ever leak out, I shall be regarded as a social asset. And you'll have to go to tea parties and bazaars and jumble sales, God help you! I wonder if we shall be able to stick it.'

Hilda, doubting her ears, said sharply: 'Don't talk like that, Frank. Of course we shall. There are two very important people whose whole future depends on our sticking it.'

'All right. All right, darling. I was only chaffing. But let's go out and have at least one drink to our future in Batsford. The gods demand it, and I certainly need it. Don't look so thoughtful, Hilda. I know we can't afford it, but come on.'

They went; and then, late though it was, walked along the Front to Hove, laughing and joking about the grand life ahead. Hilda had so many plans that she could scarcely get them out fast enough, but before the glorious façade of Brunswick Terrace they both fell silent. Against the darkness it was bone white, its long line jewelled here and there by the amber of a lighted room. As they gazed at it, enthralled, they knew that they would be sorry to leave this civilized town which, even on a winter night, was so rewarding to look at; so full of a past loveliness which yet carried no dead museum flavour about it, for it still flowered, still teemed with life. The grey streets of industrial Batsford would be different indeed, but as they walked homewards Hilda spoke again of the perfect home she would create there, a home in which, at last, they would strike abiding roots. They would not live in Batsford itself, she decreed, but in the country; in an old house that looked as if it had grown out of the earth. In this house Mary and Nicky would spend their lovely childhood; and in this house, when they were out in the world with homes and families of their own, she and Frank would live to a warm old age; and from this house, years and years and years ahead, they would end up like good Christians in the village churchyard, sincerely mourned by their children and their grandchildren, upon whom they would bestow the final benison of their Batsford gold.

Sitting by the open window of her sitting-room, listening to the murmuring sea, Hilda's dreamy, tender thoughts were upon her husband, hurrying home to her from the interview in London upon the result of which so much was at stake. Dusk had almost fallen but it was not yet too shadowy for her to distinguish a young woman of about her own age who was walking slowly past, gently pulling along a small girl, a year or so older than Mary. As they drew level the child, announcing that she was tired, sat down upon Hilda's doorstep, and not all her mother's coaxing could get her to budge. The two mothers exchanged a smile, and realized that they knew each other quite well by sight from perambulations along the Front.

'I'm waiting for my husband,' Hilda volunteered, selfishly hoping that they would move on and leave her to this enjoyable occupation. 'Your little girl seems to be very tired. I do hope you haven't far to go.'

'Not very. You have a little girl too, and a baby. I've seen you with them.'

'Yes. I have a son.' There was a pause, and then the stranger said diffidently: 'Perhaps we ought to introduce ourselves. I'm Marjorie Edmonds, and this is Stella.'

'I'm Hilda Burton, and my little girl is called Mary and the baby is Nicholas, though we always call him Nicky. Nicholas seems such a mouthful while he's a baby. Do you live near the Square?'

'About ten minutes' walk from here. I've been out all the afternoon looking for a flat. A furnished one. We're in apartments at the moment, and we don't like them. My husband is still in the army, though he's expecting to be demobbed any time now. He's a Canadian — at least he lived in Canada for a long time before he joined up. But I'm a real Canadian. I expect you guessed, though.'

'Well, when you spoke I thought perhaps you were an American, but I suppose it's the same thing.'

'It isn't! We're quite different from the Americans.'

Hilda apologized for her ignorance and was about to say 'Good night' when Mrs. Edmonds, who seemed in no hurry to go, asked somewhat wearily: 'I suppose you don't know of a furnished flat to be let where it isn't considered criminal to have a child?'

'I'm afraid I don't. I'm so sorry. But wait. Give me your address. We expect to be leaving this maisonette quite soon and going to live in Staffordshire. I'm sure our landlord would let us transfer the lease if you care to take it over. Unfurnished, of course. The rent is modest for these days, and it's awfully pleasant living in this Square.'

Mrs. Edmonds looked her astonishment. 'But how wonderful of you, Mrs. Burton! How kind of you! We're at 'Belmont', Pavilion Gardens. It's so stuffy, and our landlady detests children and doesn't care how often she says so. Oh, it would be heavenly to be in a place of our own.'

Hilda, remembering the cruet, the bulrushes, and the peculiar smell of 'Catriona', found herself much drawn to this attractive girl with the husky voice and interesting accent, and wished they had met earlier. She was just the kind of girl that she would have welcomed as a friend, such a contrast to the freezing Irene Stockell, who would have perished rather than speak to a stranger without a formal introduction.

' "Belmont", Pavilion Gardens. I won't forget. I'll drop you a line immediately our own arrangements are made. Goodbye. Your little girl is very pretty.'

'So is yours. Goodbye, and thank you very, very much indeed.'

Hilda resumed her vigil and even spared a few moments from Frank to muse upon her new acquaintance and memorize her address; certainly she would do all she could about transferring the lease. This would be a kind of thank-offering for all the happy days she had spent in Princess Square, and the even happier years she was going to spend in Batsford. It was quite dark now and, though she could not see Frank as he turned the corner, she heard him. She couldn't wait till he came in, but leaned out and whispered excitedly: 'Is it all right, darling? Tell me quick.'

'It's thumbs up, Hilda! Let me in, pet.'

She flew to the outer door. 'Quick, Frank, quick. Tell me all about it!'

'Let a man come in first!' They were now in the sitting-room and, assuming an air of consequence, Frank said gravely: 'You see before you, my best-beloved, the future Advertising Manager of Messrs. Mossop & Company Limited. It's all settled. I saw Joseph Mossop, the Managing Director, together with the present Advertising Manager, a fellow with a "damn'd disinheriting countenance" who is, nevertheless, the apple of the Mossop eye and the power behind the throne. Luckily, I think he didn't absolutely loathe me and believes me to be capable, when he's licked me into shape, of succeeding to the dynasty. For once, my missing arm has served me well. Joseph Mossop expressed the greatest interest in my military career and I know it was this empty bag' — he touched his tucked-in sleeve — 'that did the trick, plus one or two other things, of course. The pottery business is a wonderful set-up. A genuine old family concern. Employees been with them man and boy, girl and old woman, all their working lives. Everybody happy. Everybody good. The Mossops are powerful Radicals and dyed-in-the-wool Nonconformists. One of the family — there are several brothers — wrestles in the streets every Sunday night after chapel for the immortal soul of Batsford. I gathered that the rest of the family suffer over this zealot, but that it is against their principles to interfere. They're all right, Hilda. Solid, good-principled middle-class folk who have risen through honest work from the artisan class, but whether because of their principles or in spite of them I shouldn't like to say. Joseph Mossop — Jos to his workpeople — is a man of considerable charm. All through lunch at the National Liberal Club he never once referred to the job. He talked mainly about Charles Stewart Parnell! He's been reading a book about him. Well, every Fleet Street man can talk about Parnell too, and how! I've drunk many a toast to the sacred memory with our old friend Dermot McGilray, who sometimes has the grace to blush for some of his compatriots.'

'I know something about Charles Stewart Parnell too,' Hilda said modestly. 'It was my grandfather who brought the news to Moss Ferry that the forger, Pigott, had killed himself. Aunt Helen told me about this. She remembers my grandfather riding through the village on his great black horse, waving his hat and shouting for all the people to hear: "Pigott's made away with hissel! Pigott's made away with hissel!" She said women came running from their kitchens and men from the fields to hear the news. They were all Parnellites then in Lancashire. My Aunt Helen's one to this day, and so am I, just like Mr. Mossop.

'And there's another thing I've forgotten to tell you before — it's Mr. Mossop being a Liberal that's reminded me of it now. When Aunt Helen was a child on holiday with some relations who lived near Hawarden, one day she held open a gate on the moors for a coach to pass through and a gentleman leaned out, thanked her, and threw down a shilling. You don't need to be told who that was! When she showed her uncle the shilling, he exchanged it for another one and had Mr. Gladstone's mounted in gold and hung on his watch-chain!'

'History, Hilda! When you meet Jos be sure to tell him of both incidents. They'll delight him. They want to see you, by the way. They'll be confirming my appointment by letter, and will then fix a day for us to meet Jos and his wife in London — they seem to come down about once a fortnight — go back to Batsford with them and stay a couple of nights at an hotel there. I put out a few tactful feelers about Batsford society, and it seems to have its proper share of "characters". There's a retired minor canon living in the town who is an acknowledged authority on Georgian poetry; there's a retired civil servant who is terribly learned about the Paleolithic Age, and has no time for anything that's happened since; and there is a Peer of the Realm, genuine old vintage, living quite near the town in a Palladian mansion of which Batsford is extremely proud. It doesn't sound too bad, does it? Jos, by the way, doesn't think we shall have any difficulty in finding a house in the country if you are still set on it. In fact he mentioned one a few miles out that he thinks he could get for us. He lives in the country himself.'

'Oh Frank, it sounds absolutely wonderful! But what about the other man — your rival for the job!'

'That fellow? Oh, Jos said he was a good man but just a little bit too much of a live wire. Apparently he kept harping on what an excessively live wire he was. I rather think that Mrs. Jos felt he was altogether too "live" for Batsford. He's much younger than me, and not married. They prefer to have a family man, who'll settle down and not yearn for fresh fields and pastures new, which they thought might be the case with the other chap.'

'Poor man!' Hilda exclaimed disingenuously, having spent most of the day wishing the live wire was not alive at all to compete with Frank, although she had never been in any serious doubt of the issue. Frank *looked* so distinguished: so quiet and so gentle. It was inconceivable to her that anyone should ever hold a contrary opinion. There were, of course, those dark periods when he became arrogant and offensive through drinking more than was good for him, but, if he were firmly established in a worthwhile job, such grievous lapses were quite unlikely to recur.

She told him about Mrs. Edmonds, and he agreed that it would be a civilized act to give her the chance of taking over the maisonette. 'But don't be too impulsive, Hilda. From what Whateley, the advertising manager, said, I go to Mossops more or less on probation for three months; then, if I turn out all right, I shall get a yearly agreement. It's a mere formality and means nothing, but we mustn't leave here until the three months is up.'

'How ridiculous, Frank! They ought to give you a proper agreement at once.'

'Well, as I've said, there's nothing to it. What's sending me groggy is the problem of our immediate day-to-day living expenses. We go to Batsford for the "once-over" next week, and it will be plain sailing after that. Mr. Mossop suggested I should stop at the Railway Hotel till the probationary set-up is over; and the firm will pay half my living expenses. They'll also pay half the cost of our removal expenses when we go to Batsford for good. The salary is paid monthly, thank God! I only hope Cohen will advance a bit more on our stuff. I think he will when he sees the confirmatory letter, but he certainly won't let us move our furniture until he knows that I'm permanently fixed up with Mossops. We might do a moonlight flit, though.'

'Frank!'

'I'm not serious, darling. As a business gentleman I can't afford to be anything but a model of rectitude from now on, heaven help me!'

The confirmatory letter arrived two days later and, armed with this and accompanied by Hilda, he went yet again on a begging expedition to their landlord. Hilda had earnestly suggested that they should take little Mary with them, arguing that as Mr. Cohen was also a parent his heart could not but be moved by her infantile charms. She had been quite huffed when Frank had laughed at her, and it had taken all his tact to smooth her down and convince her that Mr. Cohen was unlikely to be moved by anything but the safe return of his money. Hilda thought that this attitude to their benefactor was both prejudiced and ungenerous, and retorted that, but for Mr. Cohen, they might now be in the workhouse. In the end, however, she conceded that Frank knew best, and they set out bravely on their unpleasing errand, each endeavouring to conceal from the other just how unpleasant it was. Suddenly, giving Frank's arm an affectionate squeeze, she said fiercely: 'Damn Mr. Cohen! He can't eat us. Cheer up, Frank. If he says "No" we can get to the Promised Land without him. I can always sell my furs. With prices still going up, they're worth three times what you gave for them. Here we are. Do I look all right?'

'Beautiful. Who would ever guess that you have two children! Well, here goes, and may the Lord, through his servant Cohen, have mercy upon us!'

The trim parlour-maid showed them into a richly furnished room where an enormous fire was blazing, and said that Mr. Cohen would not keep them waiting more than a few minutes. Hilda subsided into a princely armchair from which it seemed impossible she would ever rise without the aid of pulleys, and looked interestedly about her. Could this really be a house in England? Externally, it was just an ordinary, substantial, middle-class villa, but the room they were in might have been in the heart of an Oriental palace. Everything in it was expensive and everything was ornate; rich velvet curtains, a carpet so thick and soft that it was like a giant cushion, massive and glittering silverware, immense footstools and pouffes all over the place. It was so suffocatingly hot that she gained the fantastic impression that the furnishings were sucking up the air and that all was coalescing into a gigantic ruby-red sea anemone, into the mouth of which, if help did not come quickly, she and Frank, sacrificial victims, would disappear for ever.

'Help me up before he comes,' she appealed, and grasping Frank's hand she managed to get out of the chair and on to her feet.

'My word, Hilda! It's tremendous. Unbelievable, if we weren't actually in it. What a room! I'd like to see Balzac let loose on it. But sit down again, dearest.'

Unwilling to sink into another upholstered bog, Hilda looked about for something hard to sit on, but there wasn't anything. Even the fender had a plumply padded top of soft scarlet leather.

'I'll sit on this, where I can at least see all round me. If I sink in too far you must pull me out.' She perched herself circumspectly on a velvet pouffe, and had just removed her furs when Mr. Cohen came briskly in. He greeted them with charming courtesy, inquired after their health, asked about the new baby and then, after vainly urging Hilda to take a more comfortable seat, turned to Frank and inquired what he might do for him.

Frank produced Messrs. Mossop's letter, and explained, though not in the least humbly, his immediate difficulty in regard to ready money. Hilda, watching far too anxiously, suffered with him, for it was a horrible ordeal, amiable though Mr. Cohen was.

The financier read the letter thoughtfully, handed it back,

and said: 'I see. All right. All right,' meanwhile jerking his right hand up and up, palm uppermost, as if inviting Frank to place a coin upon it. 'We must not let you lose the ship for a ha'p'orth of tar, must we, Mrs. Burton? But I should not do it; really I should not. It is not good business. How much, sir, do you need? Twenty pounds? Yes, I think it can be arranged. I will include it with the other. It means that I lose my tenants, but it is not to be missed, this splendid opportunity. Oh no! It is not to be missed. Everybody knows Mossop & Company. Very excellent people indeed. I will attend to the matter. Come this evening, sir, at eight o'clock, to sign. Thank you. Good morning to you, Mrs. Burton. Good morning to you, sir.' He bowed them courteously out, and once clear of the villa they halted, took several deep breaths of cold, stinging air, and laughed. They were saved.

'There, Frank! Didn't I tell you that Mr. Cohen was a good man? You'd have thought we were doing *him* a favour!'

'So we are, innocent. His money's quite safe, and he jolly well knows it. What better security could he have than our entire home and the knowledge that I've a fine job with a world-renowned firm? But even so we're not out of the wood yet, darling. Don't forget that Cohen has got to have all his money back, with interest. In the long run it might be cheaper to let him stick to the furniture. But there's daylight ahead. A couple of years and we'll be squarely on our feet again. God bless Mossop & Company Limited!'

'And God bless Mr. Cohen of Brighton!' Hilda added fervently.

'Amen to that,' said Frank, punctiliously raising his hat. Then, pulling out a few pieces of silver: 'Just about enough to go and drink old Cohen's health. Come on, Hilda. It's the least we can do, don't you agree?'

CHAPTER IX

PROVINCIAL INTERLUDE

A FEW days later, fortified by their borrowed money and exhilarating prospects, Hilda and Frank were in a third-class compartment of the evening train to Batsford. They had this to themselves and were anxiously debating the pros and cons of their agreeable situation as guests of Mr. and Mrs. Joseph Mossop for dinner on the train. Frank was for boldly seeking out their hosts at once, but Hilda argued that, in view of their humbler status, it behoved them to remain where they were until dinner-time. This delicate problem was, however, happily solved by Mr. Mossop himself, for he and his wife, in their first-class compartment, had been discussing the same point, which she had settled by bidding him seek them out. Hilda, to her intense annoyance, blushed as Frank introduced her, a sad failing which, try as she would, she had never been able to conquer; but in her smart navy suit, grey hat and grey suède shoes she knew that she was looking her best and that Mr. Mossop, elderly though he was, seemed aware of the fact. She blushed even deeper when presented to Mrs. Mossop, who awaited them in the dining-car, but here again the knowledge that her clothes were right gave her confidence, and soon she was chatting away quite unselfconsciously. Mrs. Mossop, a round little woman with benevolent eyes, had an extraordinarily sweet smile, and she possessed to a marked degree the art of drawing people out by sheer receptivity. By the time they arrived at Batsford there was remarkably little she had not discovered about her guests, for Hilda, encouraged by her flattering interest, prattled away happily about her husband, her children, and her plans for a stimulating social life in Batsford.

'I'm afraid you'll find us rather staid, my dear,' she remarked softly, with a glance at Hilda's delicately varnished finger-nails, 'though we do let our boys play tennis on Sunday afternoons now. It was an uphill fight getting my husband to agree to this. He personally was not against it, but some of his family were afraid of "talk", though we live two miles from the town, have our own court, and can neither be seen nor heard by the most curious busybody. Provided one doesn't neglect church or chapel, I can't see any harm in a Sunday game of tennis. You'll find us a very mixed assortment, Mrs. Burton. Some of the Mossops go to church, and some to chapel — Methodist, Baptist and Congregational. We ourselves are church people.'

'So are we,' said Hilda promptly. 'My husband's father was a clergyman.'

Mrs. Mossop smiled, and glanced at her husband, who was deep in conversation with his new employee about the respective claims of the Tory and Liberal parties. Frank, a staunch Tory, keenly defended his political faith, and Mr. Mossop as vigorously extolled the virtues of the Liberal party. But he did it with such easy friendliness that Hilda, her head full of splendid dreams, knew that the Burton family had come into its own; that Batsford, which they had now reached and which mercifully she could not see, was their spiritual home. A luxurious car awaited the Mossops, and it was arranged that next morning this car would take Hilda and Frank to the Pottery, after which Hilda was to lunch with Mrs. Mossop at her home while Frank lunched with the Mossop brothers and the various heads of departments in the dining-room adjoining the offices.

A room had been reserved for them at the station hotel, and immediately they were alone Frank turned to his wife: 'Well, my darling, what do you think of Mr. and Mrs. Jos?'

'Oh Frank, they're lovely people! They couldn't have been nicer, could they? I feel as though I'd known Mrs. Mossop for years. I wish my Aunt Helen was like her. You seemed to be getting on famously with Mr. Mossop, too.'

'Jos the boss is a fine chap — plenty of brains. I hope all his brothers are as easy to get on with, though I'm a bit nervous about Geoffrey, the holy one. My God! It's cold in here.'

'Well, dearest, let's go to bed and snuggle up. It's half past ten and we've had a very long day. I do hope Mary and Nicky are all right. I don't think Mrs. Mossop approved of my leaving them with Millie when I told her she was only eighteen, and now I keep worrying about them. We must go home tomorrow.'

'Hilda, *stop* worrying! They're quite safe with Millie, but of course we'll get back tomorrow if you feel we absolutely must, though we shall give young Millie a blue fit waking her up at midnight.'

Hilda laughed. 'A girl who could sleep through a confinement is hardly likely to be wakened by a latch-key.'

'As you like, pet. But what about going down to the lounge and having a drink, by way of celebration? There's sure to be a fire there still.'

'But we don't *need* a drink after that wine we had at dinner! And whatever would Mr. Cohen say?'

'There you go again — worrying now about that damned Jew! It's our own money we're spending even if he has advanced it. I'm going to have to pay dear enough for it. Come along, darling. Just one little drink and then bed, eh?'

'All right, Frank, just one,' she stipulated, reflecting, with unusual sagacity, that it would never do for Frank to be seen celebrating, as he called it, on their very first night in Batsford. But it would be mean not to humour him, and it was such fun being with him in this enormous old-fashioned hotel — this gateway to their future Lovingly she slipped an arm through his and they descended to the vast lounge, where a fire still smouldered.

'Now, my sweet, what would you like? A whisky and soda? Why don't you try it? It's the best thing to sleep on when it's as cold as this.'

'You know I don't like whisky. Will it look common if I ask for some tea? I'd like that better than anything, but it's an odd time to ask for it.'

'Silly girl, of course you can have some tea! You must never be afraid to ask for what you want.'

He pushed the bell and a very old waiter shuffled in and peered at them through steel-rimmed spectacles which were mended across the bridge with shiny black thread.

'Yes, sir?'

'A double whisky and soda, please; and could you manage some tea for my wife? We've been travelling since early this morning, and she has a bad headache.'

'Certainly, sir, if the lady doesn't mind waiting a few minutes. Thank you, sir.'

'Thank you, waiter. We're very much obliged.'

'There, Hilda, what could be simpler? And let me repeat — never be afraid to ask. I'm surprised you were not taught that by your Aunt Helen.'

Hilda, full of admiration for the easy, authoritative manner in which Frank had secured the tea, smiled. What a marvellous thing it was to be married to a real man of the world! 'My Aunt Helen doesn't ask', she said solemnly, 'she demands. There's a difference. And I haven't got a headache, and I don't feel tired.'

'Don't be so literal. As far as that old waiter is concerned, you're absolutely dead-beat.'

Returning with the whisky and a syphon, the old man said comfortingly: 'The tea won't be long, madam. I'm seeing to it myself.'

Hilda murmured her thanks and, picking up the whisky, Frank cried gaily: 'To your beautiful eyes, my darling, and to happy days in Batsford.'

'Years,' she corrected quickly.

'Aeons, please God!' He took a good drink and Hilda wondered that the fiery stuff did not leave him breathless, for he ignored the soda water. He took a second drink and his glass was empty while her tea had only just arrived. As the waiter turned to go, Frank handed him the glass and requested the same again. Hilda gave him a disapproving look and then poured out her tea. Ought she to remonstrate? Rosa would have counselled her against it, and perhaps for this once, as they were by themselves, it didn't really matter. It was, after all, a unique occasion, but, meeting her eyes as he drank the second whisky, Frank coloured, and said with a grin: 'Now Hilda, stop thinking hard thoughts of your wedded husband. A man must let himself go at times, and you can't say this isn't one of them. I am now a business man and can afford a little extravagance. Besides, don't forget that our expenses here are being paid by the firm — my firm, I should say. Enjoy your tea and don't look so critical.'

He strolled around the room, examining the sporting prints that covered the walls, and Hilda endeavoured to banish her disquietude. But a horrid phrase kept nattering at her — 'no sense of responsibility, that's the trouble with old Frank'. She had unwittingly overheard it before they were married, and had laughed at it scornfully. 'No sense of responsibility!' Was that, she now wondered, the reason why he had never re-joined his paper? That had been a very mysterious business and, in spite of Frank's explanation that his shattered nerves were responsible, some glimmering of doubt had filtered through her indignation at the newspaper's scurvy treatment of him. Ignorant though she was, she did not think it was the kind of journal to serve an old employee unjustly, particularly in view of his war service. Putting down her cup she called out impulsively: 'Frank! Have you got a sense of responsibility or haven't you?'

He spun round and stared at her; then, realizing that she

was perfectly serious, burst out laughing. 'Hilda! What an odd question! What bee have you got in your bonnet now?'

'That is not an answer. Have you, or haven't you, got a sense of responsibility? I want to know.'

Frank, disturbed by her serious gaze and unusual pertinacity, pointed to his empty sleeve and asked resentfully: 'Why do you suppose I got this?'

'Yes, I know, darling, but that was before we were married, so it doesn't count as an answer. Have you got a proper sense of responsibility towards your wife and children?'

'It's time we went to bed, sweetheart. What are we in this damned town for? The question answers itself, you silly child.'

'But it doesn't. Can you be relied upon, or are you unpredictable?'

'What a big word, Hilda! Come along. Let's go to bed and dream of our babes, which is more than those perishing little egotists will be doing for us. We have a strenuous day ahead. A quite unpredictable day. It's a good thing Joseph Mossop doesn't think I'm unpredictable. Reflect on this undoubted fact, Mrs. Burton. Sense of responsibility indeed! Another drink is indicated to salve my wounded feelings.' He was about to ring the bell when Hilda seized his hand. 'No, Frank. It's too late, and you can't possibly need another drink, anyway. I've sorry if I was ridiculous. I suddenly thought of that attractive long word and wanted to sound clever. That's all.'

But that was not all, for the accusing phrase continued to worry her long after Frank had fallen asleep. Ah well, she must count her blessings; after all, perhaps it didn't really matter how much whisky Frank consumed provided it did not affect his work.

Although Batsford High Street presented a dreary spectacle the next morning, they had no time to feel depressed, for soon after breakfast Mr. Mossop's gleaming car called for them. Hilda, sensitive to Mrs. Mossop's obvious disapproval of nail varnish, had not only removed this but had dispensed with all her cosmetics in to the bargain. This was a fearful sacrifice, but she felt that a perfectly natural complexion might sustain her better through the ordeal of meeting the various important people with whom Frank was to spend his working life. They were all older than himself and all of them, she fondly imagined, approved to the full their Managing Director's acumen in having secured Frank for their own. When the introductions were over, she sat among them self-effacingly, trying hard not to blush when spoken to and assuming an air of profound intelligence to compensate for her unpowdered nose. She was especially interested in Mr. Geoffrey Mossop, the itinerant Methodist preacher, who appeared to be equally interested in her. Frank was making a splendid impression and she was listening earnestly, congratulating him with her eyes, when, leaning across the wide mahogany table, Mr. Geoffrey, in a penetrating whisper, gravely asked her in what faith she and her husband satisfied their spiritual needs. Silence fell round the table and then Frank, quick to cover her embarrassment, began talking again to Mr. Jos and she managed to say shyly that she had been brought up in the Methodist faith; she was about to add that she had long since abandoned it for the less exacting Church of England when Mr. Geoffrey, his eyes gleaming with gratification, exclaimed: 'Ah! True believers!' and, before she could retrieve her position, was informing her where to find the chapel at which he was the lay preacher. Hilda, now totally unable to think at all, looked exceedingly wise and glanced at her husband. He gave her a smile which said: 'The old boy's crackers. Humour him.' Sensibly she did so, though she had no intention whatever of accepting Mr. Geoffrey Mossop as her spiritual mentor.

Fortunately for her, the meeting now broke up, and under the guidance of Mr. Jos and a workman called Jim she and

Frank were shown round the Pottery. It was a fascinating experience and she was surprised not only by the number of women workers, but also by the fact that most of the employees were old people. Indeed, engaged on the more decorative work, all of which was painted by hand, there were men and women who must certainly have been grandparents if not great-grandparents. Everybody was busy; all looked happy, and, although there were hundreds of workers, Mr. Mossop appeared to know every one of them intimately. When they had been right through the Pottery, he said something quietly to Jim, who left them but returned in a few minutes with a tray containing a charming early-morning tea-set. Hilda recognized the design as one that had particularly enchanted her on their tour of the works, for she had cried out in admiration at the skill of an old woman who was painting tiny moss roses all over a similar set. With a smile Mr. Mossop turned to her and said: 'I could see how much you liked this design, Mrs. Burton, so I want you to accept this set as a memento of your first visit to our Pottery. We'll have it sent down to you.' Hilda, her eyes lingering on the dainty china, felt her simple thanks to be totally inadequate, but Mr. Mossop appeared to be gratified by her response; and as she picked up one of the fragile cups Frank's smile seemed to say that although he had come a long way from Fleet Street there were less rewarding ways of using his pen than by furthering the sale of such fine craftsmanship as this.

As Hilda, anxious about the children, pleaded that they really must take the afternoon train back to London, it was decided to abandon the original plan for Frank to lunch with the directors; instead Mr. Mossop took them both to lunch at his home. The countryside through which they drove, though not to be compared with Sussex, was undulating and pastoral, embossed here and there by woods and copses. These were now black and delicate traceries against the cold, clear sky, but Hilda, deep in country magic, knew that almost overnight the sheathed buds would unfurl to reveal myriads of wary, round bright eyes; there would be primroses too, and windflowers; and after these mists and drifts of bluebells. What glorious fun life was going to be! She wondered if Frank had guessed her thoughts, and whether he, too, would be as happy here as herself and the children. He surely would, for, if she was content, how could he hanker for the stony paths of Fleet Street? Beneath the car rug she took his hand, and from its warm pressure knew that he had read her thoughts and that all would be well.

On the home-bound train, utterly satisfied with the outcome of their visit, they were again having dinner. Frank, enormously pleased with himself, banteringly requested her to be more respectful to him in future, and expressed sincere approbation of all the Mossop brothers with the exception of Geoffrey. For Geoffrey, he warned her, was a simple fanatic, and such men were dangerous. Had she not observed, he asked, how afraid the rest of the brothers had been of him. Hilda had to admit that she had not, having been far too engrossed in appearing intelligent before them all.

'Well, we shall have to watch our step with Geoffrey. He's a rabid teetotaler, and that didn't exactly make me warm to him. And he's got his fanatical eye fixed firmly on you, a daughter nurtured in the true faith. He'll never rest until he has you chained up as a member of his congregation. The only one of the family who doesn't seem to give a damn for him is little Mrs. Jos. She thinks he's nothing short of a calamity, and admitted as much to me when we walked round the garden after lunch. She's a very charming woman, don't you agree, Hilda?'

'Of course I do. I think she liked us too. But I've been trying to puzzle out what was so odd about their house — inside, I mean — though I think it's odd for people with all that money to live in such an ugly new house, when we saw so many lovely old houses about. Didn't you notice anything queer about the rooms? They all looked like specimen rooms in an exhibition of modern furniture. Surely you noticed?'

'I did. And you're dead right about the specimen look. As for the house, I expect they had it built for them — nothing very odd about that. Then I imagine they gave a furnishing and decorating firm a completely free hand with the rest. I couldn't see a single piece of furniture that looked as if it had been inherited, or hunted for, or sacrificed for. There was no "junk" acquired on the way. No mix-ups. It was all brand-new and it all matched. But the pictures were the worst. All those damned German colour prints, all of equal size, all in natural oak frames, and all, so far as I could see, of wild geese flying over snowy landscapes. Just you think, Hilda, what one good contemporary painting could do for that dining-room, for instance. The life it could give to it. Why don't these merchant-princes learn how to spend their money? There was a time when the aristocracy could do it, and by God didn't they know how! When we know her well enough, I shall have to talk to Mrs. Jos. I believe she'd see the point. After all, Mossops are artists too, in their fashion.'

Hilda, deeply interested, recalled how dreadfully she had once been snubbed in a contemporary studio, by a contemporary artist, for venturing to admire anything but contemporary paintings. The woman had been a pig, but she now saw that there was much to be said for her point of view if nothing at all for her manners. And this being the case Mrs. Mossop was committing no solecism in preferring contemporary furnishings, a fact which she diffidently pointed out to Frank. He admitted the truth of this but argued that if Mrs. Jos had chosen things for herself, and taken her time about it, her rooms would have life and warmth instead of being flat and impersonal. She might have made mistakes but they would not have mattered: in fact they might even have helped.

'Yes. I see what you mean, Frank. I must tell you about the paper roses. They were in her bedroom, so I know you didn't see them.'

'Paper flowers? I'll bet they didn't come from the store. Go on.'

'Well, they were in a little recess all to themselves. They were quite dreadful; made of red crinkled shiny paper, and they were very dusty — like the bulrushes in "Catriona". And the vase was ugly, too — dark green blotchy glass. And yet somehow, awful though they were, they were not depressing. I know this sounds silly, but after the first shock they began to look real!'

'I can smell a "story", Hilda! Carry on.'

'You look like an old war-horse, darling. Yes, there is a story. Mrs. Mossop saw me looking at them. She isn't a bit snobbish, although she's so rich. She told me that when she was first married they didn't have much money. Mr. Jos's father, who started the Pottery, believed in making all his sons work, and until they were gradually taken in as partners he didn't pay them any more than he paid his ordinary work-people. She said they set up married life in quite a little house, and she couldn't afford to buy fresh flowers in winter, so she bought paper ones. And the artificial roses now in her bedroom are the last paper flowers she bought; and when they could afford to have their present home built and furnished she made a solemn vow that she would always keep those paper roses in her own room to remind her that she was once poor and had no taste at all!'

'And that's why they didn't bowl you over. Because she'd chosen them to please herself. I wish I could have seen them, keeping their fallen day about them. Here's to Mrs. Jos, and I hope we shall see much of her when we're established as country neighbours. Incidentally she'll warn off Brother Geoffrey if he makes too big a nuisance of himself.'

CHAPTER X

A TEMPORARY SEPARATION

FRANK, his great gifts indubitably appreciated at last, wrote to inform Hilda of the fact, but added that he found the separation from home harder to endure than anything he had ever experienced in France. He had been in Batsford for exactly two weeks, and at the end of a further two weeks would be home for a week-end. He would have come home every week-end had she not firmly counselled thrift until he received his first month's salary. They had parted sorrowfully, as if oceans were to surge between them for years instead of a few counties for a few weeks. They wrote to one another every day, Hilda detailing all her small domestic happenings — Mary's expanding vocabulary, her increasing passion for her brother, and that person's astounding capacity for slumber, which was broken only by meal-times. She also related proudly that every night she read a little of *Paradise Lost* or some other mighty work to guard against deteriorating, during this cruel separation, into nothing but doting parenthood. Frank wrote that Batsford was even duller than it looked, but that he had dined once with Mr. and Mrs. Jos and had asked to see, and been shown, the pathetic vase of paper roses; he had also had the felicity of hearing Brother Geoffrey preach, at a street corner, an impassioned sermon on the evils of strong liquor, and had been so depressed in consequence that he had crept away and made a tour of the little town, wet Sunday night though it was, until he had discovered a low but human pub, before the blazing bar-parlour fire of which he had passed the rest of the evening thinking of his beloved, and drinking, of course in moderation, not whisky but honest Staffordshire beer:

For beer does more than Geoffrey can (with apologies to
Housman)
To justify God's ways to man.

He had also been one Saturday afternoon on a pilgrimage to the native town of a great man. How many people in Batsford, he wondered, had ever heard of him? Certainly not Mr. Geoffrey, who would have gone down very badly with Doctor Johnson, and still worse with Mr. Boswell. He asked her to send him the immortal biography to sustain him against the hebetude of Batsford until he saw his family again. He urged her to take the greatest care of herself, sent his devoted love, and asked her not to commit herself irretrievably with Mrs. Edmonds over the maisonette. It would be time enough for this, he pointed out, when they themselves had settled on a house near Batsford.

For Hilda the days vanished in a whirl of small activities, but once the children were in bed she found the evenings lonely in spite of her books, and sometimes she would take her sewing into the bright kitchen and chat with Millie for an hour. It was on one of these occasions that she made the acquaintance of Millie's mother, who was as plump, round-faced and aggressively corseted as her daughter. The pair of them were drinking tea and eating fluffy little cakes, and there was an awkward silence as she stood hesitantly in the doorway. She decided that it would be inconsiderate to intrude, and was about to retreat when Mrs. Timms shyly asked if she would not try one of her cakes, freshly made that afternoon. Hilda accepted gratefully, and fully cognizant by now with the mystery of birth, sat entranced, though devoutly wishing she had not eaten the little cake, as Mrs. Timms expatiated, with fearful authority, upon the mystery of death. For Mrs. Timms, it transpired, was a professional 'layer-out', and had come round to inform her daughter of the death, early that morning, of their neighbour, Mr. Flint. Hilda, remembering how delighted Frank had been with the story of Mrs. Mossop's paper flowers, encouraged Mrs. Timms to talk that she might have another 'story' to send him. She was a Devonshire woman, born and bred in Plymouth, and her speech was racy and illuminating.

'What did Mr. Flint die of?' Hilda inquired gravely.

'Consumption, madam. 'E was only fifty, but 'e'd been going downwards for years. It's 'ere you can tell when it's going to 'appen.' Mrs. Timms, who had never heard of William Shakespeare, pinched her fat little nose and said dramatically: 'Sharp as a pin. You can always tell. I've never been wrong yet. Mr. Jessop — 'e's the undertaker — always likes to 'ave me lay out 'is "parties" — that's what they calls them — because I sets their shoulders in so nicely. It's a gift. Everybody 'asn't got it.'

'And have you always done this sad work, Mrs. Timms? Doesn't it upset you terribly?'

'Well, I must admit I didn't like it at first. The smell used to worry me and I always took plenty of peppermints to suck. They 'elped. But since I 'ad my accident I've lost my sense of smell and that's a very good thing in my case. It makes it easier and I don't need the peppermints. It don't mean a thing to me now, not even with a respected neighbour like Mr. Flint as I'd known for years. Poor Mr. Flint. 'Is feet was spotless, and they didn't 'ang over like some does. They stuck up stiff as ramrods. 'E was clean all over, just like a scraped bone. Shall I tell 'ee what was the biggest part of 'e? 'Is 'ands! Never seen such long ones. Of course I knowed directly what it was when 'is boy come for me. Half-past six this morning it was. 'E wanted me to go straightaways — they all does — but I said 'e wouldn't 'urt for three-quarter of an hour. It's not wise to leave them for more than that though.'

'Ah,' said Hilda wisely, 'I suppose that's because of *rigor mortis*?'

Mrs. Timms, profoundly shocked, protested: 'Oh no, madam. Nothing like that! It's because they sets so quick.'

'Oh yes. I see. But do go on, Mrs. Timms. I want to learn all I can, and you are so clever at expressing things. What do you have to do first of all?'

'I 'as to 'ave three clean towels. Oh — and if the party's lying on a feather bed that won't do in case of accidents. 'E 'as got to be on a hard mattress. Well, as I was saying, three clean towels, one clean white handkerchief — a big one — a clean white shirt, or a nightgown if the party's a woman, a pair of clean white socks if it's a man, and white stockings if it's a woman, and for a man a pair of pyjama trousers. My mother — she was a layer-out and taught me my trade — always kept a drawerful of white socks and stockings just in case the relations 'adn't got none. We puts them on for the undertaker's men. They'd shudder at the cold else, as you can imagine, madam.'

Hilda could not imagine, and furthermore did not want to. Neither she nor Millie were in the least disturbed by Mrs. Timms's revelations. *They* wouldn't be needing white stockings for some aeons yet. Both girls sat with their eager eyes riveted on the speaker but suddenly, feeling that perhaps she had gone a little too far, Mrs. Timms threw up her podgy arms and said regretfully: 'Well, that's what a layer-out 'as to do, madam. But you've only 'ad one of my cakes,' and she tendered the plate invitingly.

'No more, thank you,' Hilda said resolutely, but Millie, desirous of keeping her mother as long as possible, said coaxingly: 'Tell madam about that old lady, Mum. You know — old Miss Anson.'

'Oh, please, Mrs. Timms,' Hilda encouraged, thinking of the marvellous letter she would be able to write to Frank, so dull and miserable without her in Batsford.

'My word,' Mrs. Timms obligingly continued, 'that *was* a business. Some folks 'ave no sense at all. Not a grain. She'd been "set" for two mortal days and nights before 'er sister even 'ad the sense to fetch the doctor, she was that frightened. She couldn't seem to take it in that the other one had gone. And there was the poor dead soul with one leg doubled under 'er and 'er shoulders as wide as an armchair. My! What Mr. Jessop said to me on the quiet! We nearly 'ad to 'ammer 'er into shape, and then I never got 'er to set proper. Oh! 'Tis very important to get them nicely set. Very important!' Mrs. Timms paused, and then, flattered by the rapt faces of her audience, continued impressively: 'Of course, the laying-out isn't all. It's my job to do all the duties. I arranges the flowers in the room where the party is, and on the day of the funeral I 'as to be at the house early to take all the gentlemen's 'ats; and then I 'ands the wreaths to the undertaker's men, and when they've all drove off to church I draws the curtains and airs the 'ouse and gets the refreshments laid out. Mr. Jessop's very open-'anded and always gives me a bit extra to what the relations gives me because I gets their shoulders in so nice — like this.' She requested Millie to stand up, laid a hand upon each shoulder, and with a quick forward movement narrowed them until they almost met across the girl's chest. 'And the elbows is important too; they mustn't stick out.' She took Millie's warm red arms and folded them neatly, then turned to Hilda: 'There, madam. That's what a party ought to look like if 'e's properly set — all neat and close — not like a battleship.'

'And the white handkerchief?' asked the insatiable Hilda. 'What is that for, Mrs. Timms?'

'That, madam, is to tie up the chin. Poor Mr. Flint. 'Is 'ad dropped right on to 'is chest.'

'And tell me, Mrs. Timms, do dead people always have pennies put on their eyes to keep them shut? When I was a child I saw an old lady in her coffin and she had pennies on her eyes.'

'Pennies! 'Er relations must 'ave been very poor, madam! They should 'ave been 'alf-crowns! But mostly their eyes stay shut without such bribery. Oh, excuse me, madam. I was nearly forgetting to tell Millie about Mrs. Gabb — that's my next door neighbour. She come in with a bunch o' flowers and asked if I'd take them to Mrs. Flint as she didn't want to upset 'erself — she's carrying 'er first — so of course I runned along with them straightaways, and when I got to the 'ouse I could 'ardly believe my eyes! Every window — *every single one* — was wide open! The curtains was drawn of course, but every window wide to the world! Would you believe it, Millie? Robbie let me in and I said, "Whatever are you all about in 'ere, Robbie Flint? 'Ave you all gone soft upstairs opening all the windows? Why, you'll 'ave your poor Dad turning black as an 'at! Mr. Jessop's very particular you mustn't let a breath of air touch 'im. Go and shut them all at once!" Poor Robbie, 'e did look scared. Of course they didn't know no different. I didn't see Mrs. Flint so Robbie asked me to take the flowers into the front room. "No, Robbie. I'll take them up to where your Dad is." "But 'e's in the front room, Mrs. Timms. Mum thought 'e'd lie more comfortable there so Uncle Stan and Uncle Fred brought 'im down on the mattress." ' She addressed Hilda directly, divining that here was a true seeker after knowledge. 'That was a terrible thing to 'ave done, madam. You would think people would know better than do a thing like that, wouldn't you?'

'But what harm could it have done to the poor dead man?'

'Oh madam! Why, it would upset all 'is inside. Shake everything up. Oh! There's things I could speak of. Things that should never be. But there — I've got used to it and it don't mean a thing to me now. I just 'andles them natural, like as if they was still breathing. But my, I shouldn't 'ave talked so free to you, madam. I shouldn't like you to be upset, and with your 'usband away too. It don't mean a thing to me or my Millie, but you're different.'

'Not a bit of it,' Hilda protested. 'Thank you very much

for telling me what you have. And do come and see Millie any evening you like,' she added cordially, for provided she need not eat cakes made by a 'layer-out', here were riches indeed to cheer the exile in Batsford. She returned happily to the sitting-room and wrote many pages to Frank, giving him a verbatim account of Mrs. Timms's grisly operations, and promising that there would be more to follow.

But Destiny decreed that Hilda should not trifle further with the secrets of the defenceless dead. There was to be no repetition of that morbid evening which she and Millie had so thoughtlessly enjoyed: in which Mrs. Timms, glorying in her role as narrator, had delighted. A few nights later as, long past midnight, Hilda lay reading in bed, she was startled by the loud ringing of the doorbell, and instantly presaged some disaster to Frank. The bell rang again, and there was a sharp knocking also. Pulling on her dressing-gown, she ran to Millie's room, called to her to wake up, and then fearfully opened the street door. There was no policeman standing there to give her bad news of Frank, but a huge burly man who scowled at her and said bluntly: 'You Mrs. Burton? I've come for Millie. It's 'er mother. Go and fetch 'er.'

'Yes, of course. Is it very serious, Mr. Timms? Will Millie be coming back?' Hilda asked stupidly, an immense relief flooding through her.

Mr. Timms scowled again. 'No. Millie won't be coming back. 'Er mother won't be coming back neither. Never 'ad a thing wrong with 'er and now . . . But what's that got to do with you? Go and fetch my girl instead of standing there staring.'

Terrified, she fled back to Millie. It was fantastic, incredible, but the girl had gone to sleep again. Hilda shook her violently. 'Get up, Millie. Your father's here. You're to go home with him. Your mother's been taken ill. Do be quick.'

She went back to the door and timidly asked her formidable visitor to come in and wait, but he shook his head.

'Well, she won't be a minute, Mr. Timms. I'm dreadfully sorry. If there's anything I can do . . .' she ended lamely. Mr. Timms continued to glower, and Hilda, growing colder and colder, waited miserably for Millie. At last she came, her dark eyes anxiously searching her father's grim face. He took her arm roughly: 'Come on, Millie. I'll fetch your things tomorrow,' and without so much as a 'good night', he strode off, literally hauling Millie along.

Hilda, chilled to the bone, went back to bed and lay there in a passion of longing for Frank. Poor Mrs. Timms! And poor, dear Millie! All the ghoulish 'duties' at which she and Millie had laughed only a few nights before now haunted her. Poor Mrs. Timms! Who would draw in her plump shoulders, 'set' her nicely, tie up her rounded chin, and smooth on the white stockings? When, with such pride in her 'gift', she had described all these necessary rites in the gay, warm kitchen, they had seemed a thousand years away not only from Hilda and Millie, but from Mrs. Timms as well. Suppose it had been Frank who was 'never coming back'? Or one of the children? It was unthinkable. She lit a candle and went to the children's room, kissed them, and then tried to sleep, but Mrs. Timms would not let her. Her round face, bound in its white handkerchief, seemed to be floating about the room, and Hilda had to fight down the impulse to go out and telephone to Frank for comfort. Finally, amazed that she had not thought of this solace at once, she carried Mary into her bed, and Mrs. Timms troubled her no more.

When he heard her sad story, Frank wrote to insist that she must replace Millie, but Hilda pointed out that it was hardly worth while for the few weeks that remained before they were settled in Batsford. To please him, however, she compromised with a morning charwoman; this arrangement worked well, but her evenings were lonely in the extreme, and when the bell rang one night about eight o'clock she answered it eagerly, delighted at the prospect of a visitor. It was Captain Edmonds, sent by his wife to inquire if there was any hope of the tenancy being transferred. Hilda compared him immediately, and unfavourably, with Frank; but he made himself very agreeable and drew such a sad picture of his wife's sufferings with their child-hating landlady that, partly out of genuine sympathy for Mrs. Edmonds, and partly out of a silly desire to appear as a trusted wife whose every action would be approved by her husband, she calmly suggested that he should move his family into Princess Square forthwith. He gave her rather a queer look, scarcely believing that she could be serious, but she showed him round the maisonette and then, thoroughly enjoying her role of benefactress, talked of how they could best share it.

'It's staggeringly kind of you, Mrs. Burton. Marjorie will be beside herself. But are you sure that your husband won't object? Hadn't you better consult him first?'

'It will be perfectly all right. My husband won't question any arrangements I choose to make,' Hilda assured him. 'Of course, there's the landlord to be approached, but I don't think he'll raise any difficulty.'

'No need to tell him yet, is there? Possession is nine points of the law, you know.'

'Oh, I'm quite sure Mr. Cohen will be all right.'

'It sounds too good to be true,' Captain Edmonds said with a smile. 'But we must get down to brass tacks — I mean . . . well . . . what are we going to pay you for all this comfort?'

'Oh, that!' Hilda replied airily. 'Suppose we leave that part of it for my husband to deal with. We haven't got any money at all, but we soon shall have. He's just accepted a splendid post in Batsford.'

'Lucky chap,' said Captain Edmonds with cheerful envy.

'I wish I had something decent in view. I'm due for demob. any day.'

'You're not a Canadian, I believe?'

'Rather not, though I've lived over there. I was farming when the war broke out. Chucked it, of course, to join up. Marjorie came over with me to take up Red Cross nursing. If things don't turn out too well, I wouldn't mind going back to Canada, but my wife isn't keen, especially as she has no people there now. But to revert to those brass tacks, Mrs. Burton? I'd like to get everything as clear-cut as possible.'

Hilda, offended by this harping on brass tacks, was beginning to feel uneasy. What madness had possessed her to make the extraordinary offer to take this unknown family into the bosom of her own for even a few weeks? Certainly Frank would not take to this brash young man as she had taken to his attractive wife. She sought for some way out of her foolishness and said diffidently: 'I think perhaps you are right, and we ought not to settle matters finally until I've consulted my husband. He'll be home this next week-end. Yes, I think really we should let him decide.'

She looked anxiously at her visitor, but he was far too astute to let her get away with this change of front. With great eloquence he again appealed to her sympathies on behalf of his wife and little girl. She began to waver and, perceiving this, he extracted from his wallet a newspaper cutting, which he asked her to read. It was from a weekly journal which specialized in advertisements for property of all kinds, and this particular advertisement read: 'To let, in quiet road, Brighton, furnished flat. Four rooms and kitchen. All conveniences. Reasonable rent. No Jews, animals, children or likelihood.' Hilda was so indignant at the insolence of this that her misgivings vanished and she informed Captain Edmonds that he could move in immediately. She would make it all right with her husband, who would be equally indignant when she showed him the infamous advertisement.

As regards payment, she opined that if Captain Edmonds paid half the rent and shared the gas and electricity bills, that would be fair enough. Overjoyed by his phenomenal luck, Captain Edmonds protested that this was not sufficient: he pointed out that there would be the wear and tear of furniture, and that she must therefore make some charge for this. Hilda, reflecting that for the time being the furniture was the absolute property of Mr. Cohen, refused further payment, whereupon Captain Edmonds gave her another queer look, saluted smartly — too smartly, she decided — and took his leave.

Within five minutes of his departure Hilda realized clearly that she had made an abysmal fool of herself, and for the first time she felt apprehensive of Frank's reaction to something for which she alone was responsible. What on earth would he say about her folly? She need not, however, have worried. When he did come home, and she poured out her news in one agitated, self-excusatory rush, he was so happy to be with her again, to be out of what he described as the howling vacuum of Batsford, that he only commented rather drily that he supposed it was a little unusual for a man to leave a family of three and return to find it expanded into six; and that anyway, after the shock of losing Millie in such circumstances, it was good for Hilda to have companionship and interest. They spent a hilarious week-end laughing over the vagaries of Batsford society, and Frank warned her that the only people there whom she was likely to appreciate, always excepting himself, were Mr. and Mrs. Joseph Mossop. These two, he said, were real human beings, as were also the working men with whom, from sheer ennui, he spent his evenings in the little pub he had told her about. It was the one spot in Batsford, he explained, that moved him to nostalgic yearnings for Fleet Street, an unguarded admission that Hilda did not care to hear. One of its regular patrons was a Cockney printer who owned his own modest printing works in the town but who had, until setting up for himself, worked for twenty years on a London paper. Each of them, she gathered, had immediately recognized the smell of ink upon the other, and they were now as brothers in the bar parlour of 'The Half-Moon' where they discoursed nightly, with love and longing, of a London they had left for ever. It was this printer chap, Frank said with deep feeling, who was keeping him sane until the great day when she and the children arrived and he was an exile no longer. 'And talking of Fleet Street, Hilda, show me the cutting this fellow Edmonds gave you.'

She produced it. Frank read it, muttered something which she squeamishly translated as 'castrated hogs', and there and then wrote a brief letter to the Editor of a powerful and popular daily, enclosing the advertisement. 'Once a journalist, always a journalist,' he said with a grin. 'It's news, or damned soon will be. I've sent it in your name, by the way, for it's even better news, coming from a woman; it's your "story" anyway, and will buy you a new hat.'

And news, engrossing and national, it became for an entire week. The powerful daily and its evening counterpart appeared with the dramatic headline: *The Forbidden Baby!* The newsboys' posters displayed it, and a prominent Member of Parliament gravely raised the matter in the House. Hilda, forgetting that all this was due to Frank's perspicacity, warmly congratulated herself on having struck a telling blow for social justice and, when she received a telegram from the paper requesting her to telephone them at once, she did so with an air of self-importance that was completely wasted since there was nobody to see it. But all the paper wanted to know was the date of the advertisement. She gave this and was about to ring off when the questioner said pleasantly: 'It's a jolly good story. I hope you'll send us some more. We can take any amount like this one.' At this gratuitous invitation to coin money she felt justified in putting through a call to Frank in Batsford, only to be told that if he could pull off such a scoop every day of his life he would not, at that moment, be drearily contemplating something he called a 'lay-out'. But, as an old lag, he advised her to keep her eyes and ears wide open and thereby be ready, now that she had been initiated, for any further such lucky scoops.

CHAPTER XI

AN INVOLUNTARY REUNION

HILDA's fears that she had been too impulsive in succouring the Edmonds family were not wholly justified. Alan Edmonds was certainly commonplace, but his wife was not, and the two young women struck up a warm friendship, finding in their children a topic of delightful and enduring interest. Each privately deemed her own daughter to be the prettier and more intelligent; each complacently regarded herself as an exemplary wife and mother; each was charming to look upon, and both were supremely confident that for them and theirs the future held nothing but good. They knitted and sewed and gossiped; shared the household tasks equably, took their children for daily airings along the Front and on the Pier, and generally behaved as though the world had been specially created for themselves and their families. Marjorie Edmonds was the first engaging friend of her own age that Hilda had made since she left her native Lancashire. Looking back to the adolescent years with her aunts and uncle in London, she could not recall one of their numerous friends who had not seemed to her to be really old, with the exception of Frank; and Frank of course was a law unto himself, ageless, and, to her way of thinking, totally different from all other men. Unlike Alan Edmonds, Frank was never coarse, and she felt the deepest compassion for Marjorie, so gay, so pretty, doomed to pass her life with a husband whose chief recreation, so Marjorie confided sadly, was making unending love. Captain Edmonds possessed yet another claim to distinction. He had a horrible facility for inventing rhyming doggerel by the yard, even, so Hilda and Marjorie sometimes felt, by the mile, and their bubbling spirits wilted as he read to them one ghastly sheet of rhyme after another. This infliction, however, was not without a corresponding compensation, for it enabled both girls to grow invisible earflaps as a natural defence.

Mary and Stella, like their doting mothers, also became bosom friends, though, unlike their mothers, they quarrelled passionately and often. Stella was a year older than Mary, and it was enchanting to listen secretly as, revelling in her superior accomplishments, she gravely conducted her junior through the perils of the English language, of which she had an astonishing command. Mary, her soft blue eyes fixed in humble admiration on Stella's grey ones, would stumblingly and unwearyingly repeat words and phrases, and, if the lesson was at first beyond all comprehension, she would abase herself eagerly as Stella, with a scornful sigh, repeated it, slowly and impressively. Then, having at last grasped the wondrous thing, she would rush out, Stella smugly following, to seek her mother and pour out her new knowledge in a torrent, so fearful was she of forgetting it before Hilda had heard it and petted her for being such a good pupil. She would then, in a jubilant whisper, repeat it to the slumbering Nicky, with Stella again at hand to correct and admonish should there be the slightest backsliding. One morning, hearing an affronted squeal, Hilda found teacher and pupil, disgusted by Nicky's indifference to their learning, shaking him awake. Mary, having apparently decided that whispering was inadequate, was crying loudly: 'Not *that* way, Mary! *This* way!' But Nicky, a natural philosopher, settled the matter by amiably falling asleep again the instant he felt his mother's touch.

The little girls were happy all day long, even, so it seemed to their mothers, enjoying the fierce quarrels that blew up so quickly and subsided as rapidly. They generously shared all their toys with the exception of Mary's now unrecognizable fairy doll, which was sacrosanct, and which she was prepared to defend with her life; and an empty scent bottle of Stella's, dear to her above all else, which Mary yearned to hold and smell but which Stella guarded just as warily as did Mary the battered doll. Marjorie and Hilda had endless fun observing the children as each cunningly bided her time to seize and hold, for a magic moment, the other's beloved. Stella won this waiting battle and Mary, sobbing violently, was discovered sitting squarely upon her, determined not to budge until she disgorged her booty. Stella, too breathless for speech, was thrashing out with her feet, but despite all Mary's efforts she obstinately clung to the doll. Choking back her laughter, Hilda, spying the now unguarded scent bottle, judicially handed it to her daughter and then, with Marjorie, retreated to watch from the doorway. Mary's face, when she realized that she actually held the coveted bottle, was a miracle of joy, while Stella, shattered through all her being, lay still, her enormous eyes fixed upon Mary's hands. Beaming, Mary clambered into her cot, and there she turned the bottle over, stroked it, murmured to it, and finally, with a look of wicked triumph, took a long, delicious sniff. It was too much and Stella, with an agonized wail, ran to her mother and shrieked: 'Mary's smelling my smell! Look at her, Mummy! She's doing it again! Stop her! It's *my* smell!'

Marjorie, with an amused glance at Hilda, held her while the latter went over to the cot. 'Now darling, you've had it long enough and you must give it back to Stella at once.' Mary, her mouth trembling at this obvious injustice, mulishly held on to the bottle and protested: 'But you gived it me, Mummy, didn't you?'

'Yes, but only for a minute, only while Stella holds your doll. Give the bottle back to Stella, and then you shall have your doll again. That's fair, isn't it?'

Mary, uncertain about the logic of this, but aware that she would have to obey, took another prolonged sniff and yet another before the beseeching gaze of her friend and then, with a last caress, sheepishly held out the bottle and received in exchange the doll. The two children stood glowering at each other until Marjorie asked them to kiss and make up. Stella was the first to respond. She gave Mary a possessive hug and said magnanimously: 'You can have another smell, Mary. A big smell. And I don't really want your doll. She's dirty and she hasn't got no face.'

Mary, too overwhelmed by this offer to resent the slur upon her doll, indulged in another prolonged sniff, and thereafter showed no further interest whatsoever in the scent bottle.

At the end of the second month Frank again came home for the week-end and reported that all was still well in Batsford, particularly, Hilda could not help reflecting, in 'The Half-Moon'; for this time he said noticeably little about the Mossop family, and a very great deal about his brothers-in-exile, the Cockney printer and a peculiar individual they had nicknamed 'Each Pay Our Own' because of his reluctance to buy a drink for anyone but himself. Hilda, vaguely disquieted by the knowledge that Frank was passing all his evenings with these queer persons, and consequently spending far more than he should in the circumstances, ventured to remonstrate, but was assured that it was not only infinitely more rewarding than staying night after night in the hotel, but also far cheaper. She conceded the latter, but was secretly shocked that he should find it essential to pass all his leisure hours with his new acquaintances; surely sometimes he might spend a quiet evening in his hotel yearning for his wife and children, just as she never ceased to yearn for him. He made her laugh so much, however, over 'Each Pay Our Own's' idiosyncrasy, and drew such a bleak picture of his utter misery without her, that she ended by being ashamed of her disloyalty in criticizing him. 'It's damned lonely in the hotel, darling. I sit and think of you until I can't stand it any longer and have to go and see a few friendly faces to save my reason. But only think, Hilda, in a matter of weeks now I shall never have to leave you again.'

'It really is going to be all right, Frank? What about the house Mr. Mossop mentioned? You haven't said anything about that. Have you been out to see it, and when will it be vacant?'

'Leave everything to me, dearest. Be happy and see what Mossop Bros. will send you. Now what about the Edmonds family? Hadn't you better introduce me? He sounds an awful bounder from your letters.'

'Oh, he's not too bad. He's merely deadly dull. He's going to be demobbed in a week or two and then he'll have to find a job. He wants to get into a business of his own, or with a partner, but Marjorie says that he'll only have his gratuity money.'

'Poor blighter, he won't get far on that! He'd much better go back to Canada. Well, ask them in and let's get it over.'

As Hilda had feared, her husband did not take kindly to Captain Edmonds, but he liked Marjorie and for her sake consented to take back with him to Batsford an immense roll of doggerel on which he promised to give his professional opinion, and advise the author where, if good enough, it might best be placed. Again the golden hours flew cruelly past, and again they kissed goodbye as if Batsford was at the ends of the earth. 'Cheer up, sweetheart. It won't be long now. Brother Geoffrey is champing to get you into his fold. He's inquired after you more than once. I shake whenever we meet lest he becomes interested in *my* spiritual welfare. I've seen it in his eye, but so far I've been lucky.'

They were to meet again sooner than they thought, for Frank had only been gone just over a week when Hilda received an oddly brief and disturbing letter from him which read: 'My Beloved, I have been quite mad. I don't know what will be decided. There's to be a Board Meeting. It's that canting old bastard, Geoffrey. I love you. I shall always love you. Kiss Mary and Nicky for me. Don't worry. We shall come through. I still have some friends at court. Ever, dear heart, Frank.'

In her dismay and apprehension she showed it to Marjorie, who suggested that she should telephone to Batsford, but something warned Hilda that this would be unwise. Marjorie then proposed that Alan should be consulted on his return that evening. Hilda, however, could not wait until then. It was obvious that some calamity had befallen her husband and it was her duty to go to him without delay. She asked Marjorie to look after the children for a day or two, and then packed a small suit-case while her friend sent a telegram to Frank announcing her arrival. Hilda purposely gave him no time to reply but caught a London train almost at once, and was fortunate enough to catch another after lunch to Batsford. She found that she had a few minutes to spare, and telephoned Rosa, to whom she read the cryptic missive. Rosa, deducing the worst from its melodramatic wording, concealed her fears and strongly advised her young friend to return home and there await more explicit information. With admirable lucidity she reminded Hilda that if there was one thing in this world that could always wait it was bad news. 'Come along to me, dear, and we can go out for a cup of coffee and talk. Then you must go home, for there's sure to be a further letter from Frank in the morning, and it may be nothing very dreadful after all. I expect he dashed this note off after he'd had a drink or two. Do be sensible, Hilda. I'm positive you ought not to go rushing up there until Frank specifically asks you to.'

But Hilda, as always where her husband was concerned, did not want advice. She wanted assurance that if there was trouble he was the victim and not the aggressor, so, pleading that she was in danger of missing her train, she unceremoniously rang off. All the way to Batsford she tried valiantly to assure herself that nothing had occurred which the Board Meeting could not put right. 'No sense of responsibility.' The disquieting phrase kept breaking in upon her muddled thoughts, as did Frank's racy picture of his cosy evenings in 'The Half-Moon' with the Cockney printer and 'Each Pay Our Own'. 'So drunk he didn't know he was drunk': with frightening clarity she recalled the scene in the taxi on Armistice Day, and the horrible night when she had actually called a doctor to her intoxicated husband. There were various other uncomfortable incidents as well and, as the train sped on, her imagination had installed him in a police cell to await his trial for being found drunk and incapable on the highway. When the train drew up and she saw him searching its length, looking just the same Frank, her relief was so intense that she startled her fellow-passengers by exclaiming: 'Oh look! There he is! My husband!' and leaning out she waved and called excitedly: 'Here I am, Frank. Here. Be quick.' He came running up alongside the still moving train, and seizing her hand kissed it, to the immense astonishment of a placid husband and wife who had been speculating, ever since they left Euston, upon the preoccupied young woman who had sat opposite to them pretending to read a Temple edition of *Antony and Cleopatra.*

Once in their room Frank showered endearments upon her; he was overjoyed to see her although, the instant she was alone with him, she divined that the trouble was grave. As she washed at the immense toilet stand with its twin ewers and soap dishes, she noticed a tumbler half-full of whisky, and, forgetting that Frank was watching her, calmly emptied it into the china slop-pail. Turning round with a smile she perceived his heightened colour, but he smiled back, repeated again that she was as welcome as a spring morning, and said that he would tell her the whole sad story over dinner. Seated at their table, oblivious to all in the room but their own romantic selves, Frank, observing facetiously: 'The prisoner before execution ate a hearty breakfast, or I should say dinner', asked for the wine list, and carefully chose a Burgundy which he said she would appreciate, and be damned to the expense. Sip by sip her courage mounted and when, after she had emptied her glass, Frank told his awful news, she received it without a tremor.

It seemed that Mr. Geoffrey Mossop, poking his nose in and around Batsford's quiet corners, had observed him enter 'The Half-Moon' on Sunday night and, canting old humbug that he was, had watched the place like a famished lynx. Emerging at closing time with his printer friend and 'Each Pay Our Own', Frank had seen him waiting in the shadow. Even so, he said, all might have been well had Geoffrey only been a gentleman, for man of the world he was not and never could be. But when he had so far overstepped the bounds of decency as to address him directly, informing him that Mossop Bros. was no place for a drunkard, he had naturally knocked him down, and the three of them, leaving him to the night, had gone on their way.

Hilda loyally nodded her approval. 'Served him right, darling. Horrid old beast. But go on. There must be lots more.'

'There is, my lamb, so much more that I hardly know how to tell you . . .' He paused, re-filled her glass, and plunged on: 'A hasty Board Meeting was convened next day and . . . well, the upshot is that I've lost the job. I could kick myself for having been such a tactless fool. Whateley was decent enough to tell me on the quiet that though they all deplored my having made such a bloody ass of myself they deplored still more Brother Geoffrey's sneaking ways; and though they obviously could not say so of their own brother and co-director, felt that he had asked for it. As a matter of fact I gathered that Whateley had actually stuck up for me. Like Mrs. Jos he doesn't give a damn for Geoffrey, but he was out-voted. He insisted, however, on them giving me a chequc for three months' salary. No man's down and out while he's got a fiver in his pocket, and we've got quite a few in ours, so you don't need to worry about anything, dearest.'

'Of course not, Frank. And something else is sure to turn up soon now that you've made a start.'

'A what, Hilda! Never mind — wait — I haven't come to the final titbit. It appears that Geoffrey intends to summon me for assault — I wish to God it had been battery too — and they're all at him trying to make him see sense. Vindictive old beast, isn't he? A good Christian gentleman! To think I sweated in the trenches for him and his kind!'

Hilda, fortified by the Burgundy and her loving conviction that Frank had been cruelly wronged, suffered the shipwreck of all her hopes with comparative calm, even with a certain amount of enjoyment as she pictured the hypocritical Geoffrey lying so deservedly in the gutter; but at the mention of a summons for assault she stared at her husband with terrified eyes. After all he had been through in the war, to have a fanatical old pig like Geoffrey Mossop dragging him into a police court! Oh no!

'It mustn't come to that, Frank. I'll go and see the old beast in the morning and make him change his mind.'

'You'll do nothing of the kind! My wife begging a favour from Geoffrey Mossop? Let's hope he can be got to see reason. Whateley and the family will stop him if they can. We'll get out of this god-damned town by the first train to-morrow. My poor Hilda! A fine husband you picked.'

'Now Frank, stop feeling so sorry for yourself! I'm going to telephone Mrs. Jos and ask if I can run up to see her. If anybody can stop that awful Geoffrey she can. Don't interfere. This is one little thing I can do to help. One woman to another, you know.'

She wasted no time and within a few minutes was asking Mrs. Mossop for an interview. There was a constrained silence, and then Mrs. Mossop, very gently, said she did not think there was anything to be gained by meeting. Hilda, however, persisted so urgently that the other woman reluctantly agreed to see her. A taxi was called, and within a quarter of an hour Hilda found herself, for the second time, in the home of the woman whom she had so counted upon as her friend and mentor in Batsford. Mrs. Mossop, though deeply sorry for her, received her with cold formality, but gradually thawed as Hilda begged her to intervene on Frank's behalf. She was in a difficult position, for, though she detested her preaching brother-in-law, her first loyalty was to the firm. Finally, she did promise to move heaven and earth to help. Her best line of attack, she decided privately, would be through his smug vanity as one of the elect; for a change she would preach a little Christian charity to him. Hilda, all gratitude, rose, and the two women shook hands warmly. Mrs. Mossop was congratulating herself on the way the interview had gone when Hilda, regarding her steadily, asked quietly:

'Was my husband very drunk, Mrs. Mossop? If so, I think you ought to tell me. It may help me.'

'Oh my dear, I'm sorry. I'm terribly sorry about it all. Yes. He was very drunk indeed.'

'Was it the first time?'

'I'm afraid it wasn't. You see, it's so difficult — impossible — to conceal anything in a small town like ours.'

'Thank you, Mrs. Mossop. It's entirely owing to the war, you know. My husband never drank too much before he joined up. His nerves have been in shreds ever since he came back from France, but he's a brave man.'

'Yes, we know he is. And you're a brave girl, too. If only you could have been up here with him I feel sure things would have turned out differently. He must have missed you dreadfully. Now you get back to him, and don't worry any further about my brother-in-law. Goodbye, and good luck.'

Hilda, on the very edge of breaking down, got swiftly into the taxi. 'No sense of responsibility.' She had to face up to it now. All her uneasiness, her apprehensions, her fears, coalesced into an ineluctable certainty. Frank was the most enchanting husband in the world, and she loved him. But what was to become of them all? She didn't mind for herself, but what of the children? What kind of future had they with a father who could so recklessly, so stupidly, fling away such a glorious opportunity as Batsford had offered them for a safe and happy childhood, for their rightful place in the sun? Once they were home she vowed that she would talk to Frank as she had never yet talked either to him or with him. She would make him promise, on his honour as a husband and father, never to touch alcohol again. Her tears brimmed over as she thought of all that had been sacrificed for a the sake of a few chatty evenings in a public-house with a Cockney printer and an avowed miser. The house in the country; the good schools for Mary and Nicky; the marvellous holidays in old, enchanted lands; the distinguished friends, artists, writers, poets, dramatists, who would come to rescue them, from time to time, from the outer darkness of Batsford. All these joys surely could not be lost to them for ever. It wasn't fair. It wasn't right. Frank would be given a second chance. Everybody was given a second chance. She had no grounds whatsoever for this comforting assumption, but it enabled her to return to the hotel dry-eyed and apparently cheerful. Frank, when he had heard her story, wanted her to celebrate his escape from the law with a congratulatory drink, but, hoping to set him a good example, she refused. He thereupon ordered one for himself and reproached her for letting him down on his last night in Batsford by making him drink alone. To please him she asked for tea, and as she drank it reflected bitterly that the only delightful thing they had got out of Batsford was the pretty tea-set which Mr. Mossop had so charmingly presented to her when, radiant at their golden prospects, she had been shown over the great Pottery.

CHAPTER XII

'FACILIS EST DESCENSUS...

A YEAR had passed since the melancholy day when Frank Burton, unsung by either the Cockney printer or 'Each Pay Our Own', had hastened out of Batsford. Fortune, seemingly affronted by his ingratitude, had not smiled upon him since, though Hilda's faith in his star still held, albeit a little shakily. Impressed by his frequent confident pronouncements that he had greatness in him, she continued to believe that any morning a light would illumine the path to that merciful second chance; and she believed this despite the struggle for existence going on all around her. Alan Edmonds, having burned up his gratuity in a partnership with an equally optimistic ex-officer, was now working for a miserable salary with a firm in Sunderland, sending to his wife every penny that he could, and existing in cheap lodgings on the little that remained. In almost every letter he wrote to Marjorie he begged her to return to the only land of promise worthy of the name, her native Canada; for there, he was sure, he would at least be able to support her and Stella in decent comfort.

The bell at 20 Princess Square rang a dozen times a day, and Hilda and Marjorie would sigh, wonder what it could be this time, and take turns to answer it. It was always the same thing; the same heart-breaking spectacle of another poor devil of an ex-officer selling coloured writing-paper, or some ingenious domestic labour-saver which nine times out of ten they could not afford to purchase even had they wished to. Usually, when the door reluctantly opened and the salesman saw a young woman before him, automatically shaking her head before he had time to display his merchandise and commence his agonizing patter, he would accept his bad luck with a gallantry that went oddly with the scented stationery and boxes of violently coloured toilet soap. Though Hilda always managed a cheerful smile, there was no gaiety about the business; none of the engaging jauntiness, the merry quips, the colossal cheekiness, that had made so memorable the itinerant pedlars of her childhood. They had been magicians who never failed to wheedle money from the village housewives no matter how strenuously they might shake their heads. Once, confronted with a more than usually persistent or, rather, desperate salesman, who said that he would not go away until he had made just one little sale for luck, Hilda, who had no money at all in her purse that day, said meditatively: 'My husband is an ex-officer, too. He hasn't had any regular work for a year, and we have two children.' The man gave her a startled look, murmured an apology, and hurried away.

But the household survived somehow, Frank on his diminished pension and precarious free-lancing, Marjorie on the pittance which Alan sent her each week. The two girls did not lose their youthful spirits; they still went about with their heads held high, though every dinner they produced was a miracle of conjuring something out of practically nothing. Stella and Mary continued to quarrel and to make it up. Nicky was now a sturdy boy crawling all over the place and Mary adored him so passionately that if he cried, which was not often, she rushed to him in a panic and wept with him. Stella frankly hated him for intruding, by his woes, into her exciting life with Mary, and one never-to-be-forgotten morning Hilda, who had momentarily left the three children alone, returned to find the jealous little girl stuffing a handkerchief into his mouth to ensure quiet while Mary repeated a nursery rhyme after her. Nicky's face was almost black and Hilda, her heart turning over, screamed for Marjorie, who came running. The poor little boy lay passively in his mother's arms and looked up at her with such bewildered eyes that, forgetting the presence of Mary and Stella, she cried over him. Stella was soundly smacked, put to bed and informed that if ever she dared to touch Nicky again she would be sent away from Mary for ever. Mary, stroking her brother's face, whispered: 'Good little Nicky. Dear little Nicky' in a transport of love, and Hilda talked earnestly to her, telling her that she must always look after Nicky because he was so small, and that she must never let Stella frighten him again. One day, Hilda promised, Nicky would be big too, and then he would look after her, his own little sister. Mary, her charming face puckered in an effort to comprehend, nodded vigorously. 'Me look after Nicky. Good little Nicky. Nice Mummy. Nice Daddy. Nice Mary. Naughty Stella. Bad, *bad* Stella!'

'No, darling. Nice Stella too. She won't hurt Nicky again, not with you to watch him. He's *your* Nicky.'

'That's right, Mummy. He's *your* Nicky.' She tore out of the room and came back with her dreadful old doll which, with a sweet gesture of renunciation, she placed by the now sleeping boy.

'You're a very good girl. Nicky will be so pleased when he wakes up, and I shall ask Daddy to buy you a new doll, a great big one.'

'Oh Mummy! Big as this?' Wide-eyed and trembling with joy, Mary stretched her arms to their fullest extent.

'Yes, as big as that. And now I want you to take care of Nicky for a minute while I go to the kitchen. Don't move, will you?'

Mary vigorously shook her head, and assumed such an air of importance as she plumped down beside her brother that Hilda, to hide her laughter, precipitately fled.

When Frank, who had a temporary job in London for a few weeks, came home that night and was duly informed about the potential murderess, he listened so abstractedly that Hilda, whose premonitory senses were becoming more and more acute, fell silent and waited for what she knew would be unwelcome news. Frank, making great play with the re-filling of his pipe, at last said nervously:

'Would you mind very much, darling, if we were to go back to London? If I'm ever going to land a decent job again, I've got to be on the spot, but I know how you love it here and how splendid it is for the children.'

Hilda, dismayed, was about to protest, but he continued quickly:

'I simply must be in London, Hilda, and — oh hell! — it's no use beating about the bush; I had a letter this morning from Cohen, and we've got to leave the maisonette anyway. The time has come for him to collect his pound of flesh.'

'Whatever do you mean, Frank? His pound of flesh?'

'It's that damned bill of sale. He says he can't renew it again. In other words, he wants to see his money back.'

'You're not telling me that he's going to take our furniture? That we shan't have a home any more?'

'Oh, Hilda, I'm sorry! But we'll get a furnished place in London. Don't cry! That's just about the last straw. I can't stand it!'

Shocked into self-control by this heartlessness, she argued: 'But surely Mr. Cohen need not take everything. If he only takes enough to repay what we owe him, then it won't be so very dreadful, will it? We can find unfurnished rooms, can't we? The prospect of having to live in furnished rooms again is awful. I can't bear to think of it after this lovely home.'

'I know, pet. I know how you feel, but the plain truth is that I've had to let the rent slide for months. That is the real trouble with Cohen. We've got to leave here, Hilda, and you're not helping any by looking so martyred. Do you think I'm enjoying myself?'

Hilda, deeply affronted, persisted: 'Do you really mean me to understand that Mr. Cohen is going to claim every single thing we possess? That he is actually going to make us homeless?'

Frank groaned. 'I'll find somewhere for us, dearest. And you must take my word for it that in the long run it will turn out for the best — being in London, that is. But no more suburbs. If we get bogged in one, we may not get out a second time.'

Hilda thought sadly of the pleasant Staffordshire country-side where she had so longed to be bogged for ever; where their life would have been unending summer. Now, con-fronted with the loss of her home, she reproached him savagely, and for the first time, for his brutal selfishness in having flung away the Batsford chance of sweet security for his children and herself.

'You got drunk every night you were in Batsford,' she said witheringly. 'Every single night! It's no use your denying it. Mrs. Mossop told me so herself. And another thing, Frank. I'm tired of hearing you blame the war for all your misfortunes. Other men don't get drunk when they have a family dependent on them. And you lie and lie and lie to me. Look how you lied about my ring! I know I'll never see it again. And see how you've lied to me as to how matters stand with Mr. Cohen. Why can't you ever tell me the *truth*? You're a coward, aren't you? A moral coward, I mean.'

'Am I, Hilda? It's not easy for a man to tell his wife that things are going wrong with him. And whatever you may think, it *is* the blasted war. I needn't have joined up, don't forget. I could have stopped at home and kept both my job and myself intact.'

'I wonder how long, though, you would have kept your job? My Aunt Helen has hinted all sorts of things about you.'

'Damn your Aunt Helen! Oh, I'm sorry! I don't mean that. What are we quarrelling for? What good will it do? As for the Mossop affair, it's rotten of you to drag it up. Even if I hadn't seen red that night and knocked Geoffrey

Mossop where he belonged, he'd always have had his knife into me for daring to have a drink now and then. We shall get by, Hilda. I'm not done for yet, though I should be, without you to cheer me on. You deserve a better man, darling. A better and a younger man — not a war-battered crock like me.'

He smiled at her so confidingly that, despite her irritation at his harping on the war as the cause of all their misfortunes, she glowed with the fire of sacrifice and, as he had intended, was quickly ashamed of her selfish outburst.

Trouble shared was trouble halved, Hilda kept assuring herself, but this fact did not make it any less mortifying to hear their goods and chattels cheerfully depreciated by the rough but agreeable person sent by Mr. Cohen to make the valuation. Frank, his nerves at their jumpiest, had begged her not to be present at this transaction, but she insisted on seeing it through with him. It was her job, and she also nourished a private hope that her charms would so affect the valuer that he would rate their possessions at what she felt them to be worth — even, perhaps, at more than they were worth.

Mr. Tippet, astonishingly attired in an impeccably tailored 'British warm', from which he had prudently removed all badges and buttons, a rough tweed cap, and a loudly checked muffler, proceeded briskly from item to item, rolling his shrewd brown eyes and twitching his enormous nose in a most alarming fashion. Every now and then, actuated by sheer natural mateyness, he thumped a huge fist into the middle of Frank's back, winked at her, and leered at Nicky who, for greater appeal, she carried round with her. Throughout he addressed her as 'Missy', Frank as 'Cap'n', and Nicky as 'young 'un'. Running his thumb along a shining surface he pronounced reflectively: 'Now this piece ain't so dusty. Well made. Good grain. Fetch its price at auction. Um — um — ' and with a dramatic flourish of his pencil jotted down a figure. Then, rolling his eyes and tapping the side of his nose, he would barely glance at some other cherished possession and remark non-committally: 'Um — um — might go — um — um — might not — can't tell.' Another figure was jotted down, this time without a flourish. Thus, from room to room, they proceeded; and when he had appraised and noted down every single thing, even the kitchen pails and the dustbin, he snapped a stout elastic band about his sinister little book, bestowed an extra hearty thump upon poor Frank, a terrific wink upon herself, and concluded genially: 'Well, cap'n, I think that's the lot. Not so bad. Not so bad. And see here, missy, when you and the cap'n sets up house again, don't forget Bob Tippet of The Lanes. Been in the trade all me life. Never touch rubbish, only good, solid stuff like you've mostly got 'ere. Pleased to fix you up with any mortal thing. Aspidistras — flat irons — chamber pots — a rocking 'orse for the young 'un — anything you likes to mention. All cheap but all good. All good but all cheap. That's Bob Tippet. Thank you, missy. Thank you, cap'n. Much obliged I'm sure. Good day to you, and good luck.'

He went, and Frank and Hilda, bereft of their home, stood gazing at each other in tremulous silence. Then Hilda laughed. All these charming things were irretrievably lost to them, but the sword of Damocles had hung over her head for so long that now it had fallen she almost felt a sense of relief. As Frank was always saying, they would soon be on their feet again, and since, unlike the Bourbons, she had forgotten everything, she believed that it would be so. But, to his amazement, she steadfastly refused to return to London until he could provide a proper home there and a reasonable income. They quarrelled, and he accused her of being both selfish and stubborn; then he coaxed and pleaded, but all to no purpose. She argued that there was still plenty of unspoilt country near to London where they could hide their poverty and yet be happy; also it would be better for the children. She suggested that somewhere in Surrey, along the Thames, would be ideal for the time being. She charged him to find a furnished cottage as remote as possible from other human habitations; but after a prolonged search, or so he assured her, he reported that not only were such cottages beyond their present means, but they were also totally inaccessible to any form of transport. What he did not report was that they were also totally inaccessible to any kind of pub, though this disqualification had not occurred to her. After some days he announced the discovery of the very thing — a really rustic cottage on the outskirts of Chertsey. True, it was already occupied by the owner and his wife, but they were willing to share, and since they had a little girl of their own they did not object to other children, an important point which decided Hilda in its favour. Also it contained every civilized amenity and its only drawback was that she would have to share the kitchen. This was indeed grave, but Hilda felt quite equal to coping with it after having shared her own kitchen so successfully with Marjorie.

It would be very sad to lose her friend, who would now join her husband in Sunderland, and she felt sad also when Millie called unexpectedly, a confused, blushing Millie, amusingly unfamiliar in the uniform of the Salvation Army which, she explained gravely, she had joined because it made her feel nearer to her dead mother. She sat nervously on the edge of her chair, fumbling in a capacious string bag from which she produced a giant marrow, grown, she said proudly, on the rubbish-heap in the back garden. Hilda graciously accepted this trophy and Millie, taking a deep breath and fiddling with her bonnet strings, muttered: 'I've come to confess, madam. I was a sinner when I worked for you. I stole these.' Again she delved into the bag and brought forth a lace-edged handkerchief, a pair of white kid gloves, a pair of pretty side-combs, and a snapshot of Mary, sitting in her pram and beaming at the ocean. 'And I stole some of your mince-pies at Christmas to take home to Mum. I told her you'd sent them. I can't give those back to you, but I feel better now I've owned up, and I'm very sorry I ever took anything, madam.'

'Oh, Millie! It doesn't matter. Why . . . I never even missed them. Don't cry. Here, take them back. I'd like you to have them.'

'Thank you, madam, but I couldn't keep them now, except the picture of Mary. I would like to have that, please.'

'Of course, Millie. And what do you think of *my* picture? There — on the mantelpiece.'

Hilda was excessively proud of this studio portrait, which she had had taken as a birthday present for Frank, and for which she had worn her one and only evening dress.

Millie looked at the portrait quickly, and as quickly looked away; then, after a slight hesitation, said primly: 'It's a very good likeness, madam, but it isn't godly to wear a dress as low as that, is it?'

'Millie! What a thing to say to me! But never mind. How long have you been in the Salvation Army?'

'Only a few weeks, madam. Dad's always been in it, you know. He plays in the band, and he's ever so pleased with me for joining. Since Mum died, I've kept house for him.'

'Poor Millie. I wonder if your uniform would suit me. Let me try on the bonnet and tunic, please.'

'Oh, madam! That's only vanity, like your evening dress,' Millie protested.

'Rubbish, Millie! Well, let me just try on the bonnet. It's so pretty, and it looks much more ungodly than my evening frock. Captain Burton says that he's never seen a really plain face under a Salvation Army bonnet.'

'I wish you wouldn't say such things, madam. Now I'm in the Army, I don't think about my appearance at all. I only want to look clean and tidy for Jesus. Well, if you're so set on wearing my bonnet perhaps there's no great harm to it, though the Army wouldn't like it.' She handed the bonnet over, and Hilda ran to find Marjorie that they might both see themselves for a second as Salvation Army lasses.

Dear Marjorie! When the time came for her to join her husband, the two girls wept and vowed everlasting friendship, no matter how widely their lives were separated; but apart from this Hilda bore the departure from Princess Square with fortitude. When the last morning came she went round every dearly-loved room to bid a silent farewell to its furnishings; automatically she plumped up a cushion here, straightened a curtain there, and with needless masochism deliberately recalled the wonderful day when she and Frank and Mary had entered so gaily into possession. Mr. Cohen, in response to an appealing letter which she had sent to him, had allowed her to keep a few intensely personal treasures, such as wedding presents, Mr. Mossop's delightful tea-set, the children's cots, and her household linen.

As they drove out of the beautiful, tree-shadowed square she closed her eyes and kept her mind resolutely fixed upon the fresh fields and pastures new ahead, but the moment she entered the cottage in Chertsey panic seized her, for Mrs. Savage, the landlady, was of strangely forbidding mien. She was very old, Hilda thought, to be the mother of an eight-year old girl; her heavy face was deeply lined and her hair, piled beneath a coarse net, was uniformly grey. She was neatly but dowdily clad in a black blouse and skirt and capacious white apron. She looked exactly like a lavatory attendant, Hilda reflected uncharitably, and when she put out her hand in greeting her new tenant felt like dropping a penny into it. She surveyed Hilda's rosy face and slim figure with obvious disapproval, and stared at her high-heeled shoes as if they were an outrage. Hilda, in no position to do anything but ingratiate herself as best she could, pushed Mary and Nicky forward, but their innocent charms also were not appreciated. Hilda clutched at Frank, who suggested that they should be taken forthwith into their part of the cottage. The rooms, two bedrooms and a sitting-room, were cosy and prettily furnished. Everything was spotlessly clean, and the view stretched illimitably over unspoilt country. But for the presence of Mrs. Savage, it seemed quite perfect, and the instant she left them husband and wife looked at each other in consternation.

'Oh Frank, what a terrible woman! She doesn't like me. I can feel it. Did you notice how she stared at my clothes? I feel sorry for her husband, and for the little girl, too. I wonder why she took such a dislike to me?'

'You're imagining things, darling. She's just a naturally graceless person. Perhaps she's unhappy. I think she doesn't like letting rooms at all, but evidently needs the money. She wouldn't be any pleasanter whoever the tenants were. Keep out of her way as much as you can.'

'Don't be so idiotic! How can I keep out of her way when we've got to use the same kitchen? I feel frightened of her. Oh look! There's her little girl, coming home from school I suppose. She doesn't look very strong — not like Mary. Why, Mrs. Savage is kissing her!'

'And what's so astonishing about that, stupid? But you like the rooms, don't you?'

'Of course. It was clever of you to find them, and it will be lovely here for Mary and Nicky. Every prospect pleases and only Mrs. Savage is vile.'

'Don't worry about her, Hilda. Be diplomatic and keep on the right side of her for all our sakes. You can do it all right if you make up your mind to it.'

But Hilda found that there was no right side at all to Mrs. Savage. With outward meekness she did her utmost to submit to her landlady's rigid routine in all matters pertaining to the kitchen, but there was no pleasing her. She was a woman with a perpetual grievance, and although this grievance was the equally unhappy Mr. Savage, it was upon Hilda's thoughtless head that she vented her spleen. Everything that Hilda did in her wretched, gleaming kitchen seemed to arouse her disapproval. Even so, Hilda, who thoroughly appreciated her own pleasant rooms, was happy. Whenever the sun shone and soft breezes from the surrounding meadows wafted through the cottage, she lifted up her voice and sang as she went about her housework. Her repertoire was catholic in the extreme, ranging wildly through Handel, Moody and Sankey, the Bing Boys, and the current song hits. Once or twice she caught a muttered 'Miss Flibbertigibbet' as Mrs. Savage, scowling, slammed a door upon the gaiety cascading from her tenant's apartments, but Hilda only smiled and sang the louder. All the morning Mary and Nicky played in the garden, and every afternoon she took them into the deep country and there, while they tumbled joyfully about, she read her book, thought tenderly of Frank, and thanked her God for the splendour of the world.

For the first few weeks of this dream-like existence Frank came home on most nights with praiseworthy regularity, and with sufficient money for their unexacting needs. Hilda had never felt happier; never so deeply in love; never so proud of her children, or so satisfied with her own perfections. But there came a morning when Mrs. Savage, irritated beyond endurance as the uplifting strains of 'Jerusalem' went whirling around the cottage, knocked loudly upon Hilda's door and without preamble demanded the month's rent that was owing to her. Hilda, speechless before this further example of Frank's duplicity, trembled. Mrs. Savage, always so stiff and reserved, was weeping, and as she wept she talked bitterly of folk who had no right to be so pleased with themselves singing all over the place as if it belonged to them and being regarded by their husbands as if they were angels from heaven.

'My husband hasn't touched me since Delia was born. Isn't that a nice thing for a woman to put up with? He hates the sight of me. If it wasn't for Delia, he'd have cleared off long ago.'

'But you sleep in the same room,' Hilda stammered.

'Yes. And in the same bed, too. Back to back and never a word, as I stand here a living woman. Well, I want my rent and I want you to go. He likes to hear you sing, if you can call it singing. You fancy yourself, don't you, painting your silly face up like a tart, and you the mother of two children. And can't pay your lodging. The sooner you get out the better I shall like it. Understand?'

'Yes. I quite understand, and I'm not surprised to learn that your husband detests you. All you ever think about is cleaning and scrubbing. Why don't you go out in this lovely weather and enjoy the green world like I do? You never even think of taking Delia for a walk or a picnic. She's always cooped up indoors, poor little girl.'

'You leave my Delia alone. She's as healthy as your two, any day.'

'Is she? Then why are you always giving her Parrish's Food?'

This shaft went home, and Mrs. Savage turned sulkily away. At the door she paused, surveyed Hilda with malicious eyes, and said coldly: 'Take a week's notice from Saturday, and you can tell that precious husband of yours that if he doesn't pay up I'll summons him.'

'Oh, go and drown your miserable self!' Hilda blazed at her.

Mrs. Savage, too angry to reply, slammed the door behind her, and to soothe her own ruffled feelings Hilda lit a cigarette. What an old harridan! And poor Mr. Savage! Until now she had scarcely given him a thought, for he was hardly ever visible, and he was always silent. Like his unhappy wife he, too, was grim and middle-aged and corrugated, and no wonder. Every week-end he went fishing, and the only time she had seen a light in his face was one morning when the postman brought a long, narrow, wooden package for him. Hilda, who happened to be at the gate, took delivery of it, and when she gave it to him his face lit up and he looked for all the world like a stone angel miraculously imbued with life.

'It's my new rod!' he exclaimed softly. 'Now I can give them roach something to think about.'

His wife entered the room, and flushed when she saw him stroking the box, but to Hilda's amazement he did not turn to her and display his treasure as Frank, in like circumstances, would have turned to herself. The light in his face vanished as though a shutter had dropped over it. He was no longer a great stone angel quick with life, but a grey block of a man, awkward and dumb. With the box under his arm, and without a word or glance at the two women, hc walked heavily out of the room.

CHAPTER XIII

. . . *AVERNI'*

THOUGH distressed because they were again in debt, again under the necessity of seeking a roof for their heads, Hilda had sense enough to realize that after Mrs. Savage's embarrassing confession it would be unwise to attempt conciliation, reluctant though she was to leave these pretty rooms with their unbounded view over the de Wint-like landscape. She had hoped to remain in them until Frank was rooted again in Fleet Street. Since, however, they were bound to pitch their tents anew, he begged her once more to live in London, and once more she obstinately refused. Mary and Nicky, brown as ripe hazel huts, glowed with health, and if her days were uneventful at least she never found them dull. But, as she had once yearned in her childhood to achieve honour and glory and power by teaching herself the French tongue, so now she yearned to achieve real distinction by becoming familiar with the classics, and Frank was astonished and delighted when she gravely requested him to teach her Latin. This worthwhile ambition, she pointed out, would lift her for a few hours every day right out of her narrow domestic ritual, to say nothing of the enchanted evenings which they would pass as teacher and pupil.

Somehow Mrs. Savage was paid, and after a brief search Hilda engaged two immense rooms at the top of a tall old house in the High Street. They were a sharp contrast to the rustic cottage, but they were flooded with sunlight; they were also fantastically cheap, and the landlady was as pleasant as Mrs. Savage was dour. Mrs. Springett endeared herself immediately to Hilda by remarking that, after her own children, Mary and Nicky were the bonniest pair she had seen for a long time, and when Hilda naively poured out to her the tale of Frank's undeserved bad luck since the heroic days of his military service, her compassion was warm.

They moved in, and for some weeks, despite the absence of nearly all essential amenities, life continued serenely and, thanks to the ardour with which Hilda pursued her Latin studies, not unprofitably. She now had no kitchen at all, merely a landing on which stood a gas-cooker and a shelf for pots and pans, but except for one room occupied by a young married couple, both out at work all day, she and the children had the whole airy region to themselves.

'Amo, amas, amat, amamus, amatis, amant,' she carolled cheerfully as she went about her morning housework, and Mary and Nicky, sharing her enthusiasm for this fascinating new game, echoed her with glee. Thus marking time, as she fondly believed, she had no reserves with which to meet the dreadful night when Frank neither came home nor sent her a message. She stayed peering down into the darkened High Street for hours after the last London train had gone. It was a severe shock, for whenever he was exceptionally late now she was no longer tormented by visions of him lying dead or injured as the result of an accident. If he had fallen at all, it was among 'friends' all as drunk and unprincipled as himself. Finally she lay on the bed, sleepless, reviling him for a heartless brute, and resolved that when he did return she would be cold, dignified, and contemptuously disbelieving of whatever excuse he dared to offer. Anger, alternating with drenching self-pity, sustained her until night again fell, and still he neither came nor sent her word. She had no money, and no reserves of food. Surely he would never leave them to starve. Pride restrained her from confiding in her good-hearted landlady, and she stubbornly set herself to await deliverance.

Another day and night passed. The children were living on bread and milk, and herself on bread and tea. She felt so hungry and light-headed that in a fit of recklessness she tapped at the door of the young married couple, although she knew that they would not be home until evening. With her heart knocking she listened to the silence within, then stealthily turned the knob and entered. Half-paralysed with fear lest she should be discovered, she stood still and listened again to the silence, which seemed to be alive and watching her. Her cheeks burned as she forced herself to search for food — to steal from a trusting neighbour. In a huge cupboard she found plenty, but there appeared to be nothing she could purloin safely but a quantity of dripping. Of this there was an outsize bowl — rich, yellow, crumbly beef dripping — and on tiptoe she returned to her rooms for a plate and knife. She helped herself to a big wedge, and resisted the fierce temptation to add a couple of eggs for the children. The silence now pressed upon her like the weight of twenty Atlantics and seemed to surge after her in heavy waves as she tiptoed away with her booty. She felt so frightened, and so guilty, that safely back in her own rooms she locked the door and stayed listening by it for several minutes — but all was quiet outside. She made dripping toast for the midday meal, and Mary, as she munched it with relish, gravely remarked how funny it was to be eating breakfast at dinner-time, and in the same breath demanded to know why her daddy did not come home and bring her and Nicky some sweeties.

'He'll be home tonight, darling. Then you shall have a sweetie. Two sweeties if you keep on being a good little girl, for you are a good little girl.'

'That's right, Mummy. I *am* a good little girl, and Nicky's good, too. That's right, isn't it?'

'Yes, both of you are very good; and now I want you to help me by keeping him quiet while I write a letter. Take him into the bedroom for his rest and sing him to sleep; and you try to have a little sleep, too, then when Nicky wakes up we'll go down to the river and watch the lovely boats sail by.'

'Come on, Nicky,' Mary commanded importantly. 'Come on, darling, and go to sleep for a teeny weeny time because you are only little — not big like me. Come on.'

Nicky, meekly acquiescent, trotted away with his sister, and to the strains of 'Ride a cock horse' in Mary's quavering treble Hilda wrote to her Aunt Helen, baldly described her dreadful predicament, even to the theft of the dripping, apologized for having to send the letter unstamped since she had not even a penny in her purse, and asked for help.

Sunday passed in a daze of worry and anger, and on Monday morning there came a wild letter from Frank, enclosing two pounds and stating, somewhat superfluously, that he had been completely mad and had no recollection whatever of what he had been doing. He begged abjectly for her forgiveness, said that he had several irons in the fire, and would be home that evening. In the afternoon, sent down by passenger train, an enormous hamper of food arrived from the Army & Navy Stores, and inside was a letter from her aunt, enclosing a pound note, and informing her that Phillip was responsible for the hamper. Helen, while professing the greatest sympathy for her misfortunes, and profound disgust at Frank's dastardly behaviour, made it abundantly clear that she did not care for her niece's apparent assumption that in time of trouble 'there is always us'. She pointed out, at great length and with many quotations, that a married woman must learn to adapt herself to the changing wheel of fortune. In conclusion she reproved Hilda for having been so stupid as to steal, painted a terrifying picture, quite unnecessarily, of what might have happened had she been caught, and urged her not to frivol away the pound, which, she underlined heavily, must be regarded as a loan and not a gift. She made no mention of coming down to see her.

While the children danced gleefully around, Hilda began to unpack the magic hamper. Her uncle had seemingly forgotten nothing, for not only was there a profusion and variety of essential nourishing foods, but there was a box of cigarettes for herself and a luxury box of chocolate animals, wondrously wrapped in brilliantly-hued tinfoil, for Mary and Nicky. Their eyes grew rounder and rounder as she showed them these delights, and allowed them to choose one each for immediate consumption. Mary, cruelly tempted by them all, considered for a long minute, and then selected a sheep. Nicky, demented by the bewildering choice, at last drew out a scarlet pig. All three were sitting round the hamper, nibbling at chocolate feet and tails, when Frank walked in and stared down at them. Hilda, her cheeks flaming, did not look up at him. He bent to kiss her, but she turned her face from him, and lit a cigarette as steadily as she could. The children, excitedly pointing out their treasures, chattered nineteen to the dozen, and the noise was deafening. Suddenly, her nerves snapping, Hilda seized them roughly, dumped them upon the couch, and in a voice that made them gaze at her, for the first time in absolute terror, bade them sit still and be quiet. Mary, her soft mouth quivering, hugged Nicky, and for a full second they sat there like two apprehensive squirrels. Then, remembering their interrupted feast, they began to nibble joyfully again.

Hilda, completely ignoring the return of her hero, busied herself with the hamper, determined that she would not be the first to speak. The children were withdrawn into their own private world, and the silence was horrible until Frank, in a low voice, broke it.

'I deserve whatever you have to say to me, Hilda. I've been mad. You got my letter this morning? Oh, for Christ's sake stop fiddling with that blasted food! Say something. Abuse me, but don't sit there as if you were playing at bricks.'

'All right, Frank. I will say something. What did you imagine I was going to do, marooned here without money, and without news of you? You knew I hadn't any money.

I couldn't even telephone to anybody for help. How did you think we were going to exist? And what have you been doing all this time? Drinking yourself insensible, I suppose. I've been reduced to stealing food. All we had was bread and tea. I stole dripping from Mrs. Abel's room just to make a change for the children. They haven't been hungry, but I have. Think of that. Your wife was hungry. I wrote to my Aunt Helen for help, and I hadn't even a penny for the stamp. Uncle Phillip has sent me this lovely hamper. Now what have you to say to me? What *did* you imagine I was going to do? I want to hear.'

Frank, unable to meet her scornful gaze, muttered that from day to day he had counted on something turning up — an article being accepted, or a loan contrived — but Hilda did not believe him.

'How have *you* been living this last week while your wife and children were left to starve? On the Embankment?'

'Yes,' was the amazing answer. 'For two bloody nights. The other nights I stayed with old Benfleet in his attic. But for a couple of nights I went all romantic and studied the heavens. I learnt quite a lot about the stars. More even than I learnt in France. But the experience paid for itself, for I got an article out of it. That was the money I sent to you.'

Hilda, shocked to the bone, was silent. What a pass they had come to! Until this past week they had been getting steadily poorer, but they had not been threatened with actual want. As for Frank having to sleep out like a tramp, that was beyond everything; her mind refused to take it in. He must have had some money. One couldn't live for a whole week in London without any money at all. Tenaciously she harked back to her real grievance against him.

'Why didn't you either come home or write? If you'd been on the other side of the world I could understand it, but to be only a few miles away . . . .'

'I've told you, dearest. I must have been crazy. I don't really know what I've been doing. Well, here I am now at any rate, so why not make the best of me, if you can. Our luck is bound to change, but there's one thing you must agree to after this. We must live in London. Then I can at least walk home.'

'All right. I couldn't stand another such week. And you must promise me never to sleep rough again. It's too horrible. My husband sleeping out like a . . . '

'Like a rogue and vagabond,' he interrupted.

'Like a vagabond,' she corrected, all her deep tenderness for him rushing back and blotting out the memory of her recent vigil. 'But just look at this marvellous hamper! We can have a feast. I'm hungry — empty hungry. And so must you be. You can kiss me now, and we'll go back to London as soon as you can find a home for us. I wish I hadn't written to Aunt Helen as I did. Anyway, now you're here, I shall return the pound she sent me by the very next post.'

'Don't be such a simpleton!' Frank protested quickly, in tones of deep horror. 'If you want to be quixotic you can give it to me, and let that stingy aunt of yours whistle for it.'

Hilda, shaken by his lack of all ordinary, decent scruples, gave him a dark look. She was well aware that her aunt could afford to lose any number of pounds, but she had been so mortified by her self-righteous letter that not all Frank's persuasiveness could alter her decision to return the pound forthwith. She therefore enclosed it, with a triumphant little note to the effect that Frank was now back and that all was well. Frank offered to post it for her, but she did not trust him, and went to do this herself. The instant she heard it plop into the letter-box she knew that she had acted like a fool. A whole pound, enough to support them in food for a week, flung away to salve her miserable pride. When she got back Frank was playing at bears with the children, and he gave her a queer, sulky stare. Mary was jigging and whooping on his back, and Nicky was fidgeting to be given a ride, too. Hilda dropped to her knees, Nicky clambered up, and away they went. The two bears met, stared defiantly at each other, then burst into laughter.

'What a little ass you are, Hilda!' Frank said mockingly. 'Do you feel better for being so noble?'

'No, though my Aunt Helen will. That's why I feel such a fool.'

'Never mind, pet. If ever we're up against things as badly again, you've paved the way for a further appeal in that reluctant quarter. Damn it, it should be a pleasure for her to help her one and only niece. That's how you ought to look at it. That's the way I look at it.'

'Then don't,' Hilda advised him tartly. 'She doesn't like lending, and I don't like borrowing — at least not from her. She's never been poor and she hasn't any time for people who are. I hope you won't make it necessary for me to ask her again, and if you knew how hard it was for me to do it you wouldn't joke about it. Give me your word of honour that you won't let it happen again.'

'Word of honour, Hilda. Within a few days we shall be settled in town, and then things will begin to move. You'll see, darling.'

Despite her earnest request, Hilda had singularly few illusions about her husband's sense of honour, for even to her accommodating ears it had a somewhat Falstaffian ring. In spite of this, however, she could not but believe him to be a deeply-wronged man, for was he not perpetually telling her so? However, as he said, things were bound to move forward some time, and therefore hope once more reared its vernal head within her all-too-human breast. Once more she mused romantically upon that place in the sun which awaited the Burton family. And how wonderfully they would adorn it! What fun they would have — what joys were in store for Mary and Nicky — what a deep, full life for Frank and herself! How patiently she would learn to become a personage—to do something — to be somebody — a fit wife for a distinguished man. *Amo*, *amas*, *amat*, *amamus*, *amatis*, *amant*. She and Frank would never snarl at each other as Mr. and Mrs. Savage snarled. Sustained by these reflections she gazed ahead with a dewy optimism that neither a Bourbon nor a Micawber could have rivalled. She now deeply deplored her pig-headed refusal to go direct from the Savage household to London, for though Frank had not actually said that their continued sojourn in the country had been a brake upon his progress he had nevertheless subtly contrived to make her feel in part responsible for his recent alarming defection as a husband and parent.

When, however, they eventually arrived at the squalid street in Chelsea where he had taken a furnished flat, this guilty sense of responsibility vanished, and with it all the bubbling exaltation on which she had been living. Apprehensively she followed him into the deep basement of a tall, narrow, tenement house, and in tearless misery stared about her while Frank hastily went out to buy cakes for tea. So this was the London 'home' that was so essential to their progress. She had trusted him implicitly to find something clean and comfortable, and he had found them this! She knew, of course, that with very young children, or indeed children of any age, it was a problem to find furnished rooms at all in London at a rent they could afford; but surely he need not have brought them to a dungeon, for a dungeon this certainly was. It consisted of two vast bleak rooms and an elongated strip that called itself a kitchenette. There was no bathroom, and the lavatory was outside the kitchen door. Their rooms at 'Catriona' had been luxurious by comparison, while as for her dear home in Princess Square — well, that now appeared to her as a mansion of celestial light and beauty.

She inspected the bedroom, which contained a double bed covered with a greyish Marcella quilt; a marble-topped washstand with a white enamelled jug and basin upon it; a nondescript dressing-table; an immense pitch-pine wardrobe that made her shudder; a dirty white chest of drawers, and two sagging wicker-work chairs. The floor was covered with a worn linoleum that had once boasted gigantic yellow flowers of tropical splendour, and on either side of the bed there was a brown, grease-smooth drugget that stank disgustingly of urine. The bay window with its lace curtains and broken venetian blinds looked upon a cemented area, about two yards wide. The whole room smelt of dirt, sweat, urine and tobacco. Fortunately the children had their own cots, and fortunately, too, she had her own bed linen.

The sitting-room was even more appalling. It boasted a square dining-table covered with a stained green chenille cloth; a horsehair couch; two unspeakable-looking armchairs; a deal sideboard, and various odd wooden chairs and boxes. The floor, as in the bedroom, was covered with threadbare linoleum and more strips of foul drugget. There was a high black mantelpiece with a tin tea-caddy at each end; a cavernous hob-grate, a rusty steel fender, and a quantity of steel pokers of varying sizes and designs. Through a glass-panelled door she espied a steep flight of worn stone steps, leading presumably to a garden, and trusting to discover something clean at last she mounted them hopefully, only to find herself surveying a long, desolate wasteland that had once been a lawn bordered by flower-beds which were now stubby with black and withered foliage. Looking up she saw a tier of 'flats', with here and there a curious face peering down at her. After the trim lawns and bright flower-beds of Princess Square, and the charming country they had just left, this slice of a slum back garden sent a chill through her blood, and she returned almost gladly to the dungeon. She explored the 'kitchenette', which contained a dirty gas-cooker, a yellow sink of vast proportions and depth, a cell-like window high above her head, and two shelves upon which was a heterogeneous collection of coarse and chipped crockery and several large iron saucepans.

Mary, proudly keeping guard over Nicky, gleefully clapped her hands as a cuckoo clock chimed four. In this abominable hole to which their father had brought them the children were a marvel of purity and colour, and in the enveloping greyness glowed like tiny jewelled windows. Oh! How could he have done such a dreadful thing? And what would her aunts think should they ever visit her here? She would certainly never invite them, nor indeed anybody at all save Rosa; but at any rate, she reflected grimly, there would be no more painful refusals to purchase scented stationery and soap at the door, for not the most desperate salesman would dream of wasting his precious time and energy knocking on area doors in such an abomination of desolation. She found the gas-meter, inserted some pennies, and prepared to make tea and heat some milk. She longed to have a thoroughly good cry, but even this balm was denied to her, for there was nowhere to escape Mary's troubled eyes if she gave way. Horrible though the place was, it would not be unendurable for herself and Frank; but for the children it was out of the question. They must not remain here to have the colour sucked from their rosy faces and the sparkle struck from their eyes. Sweet air from heaven they must and should have, poor lambs.

When Frank returned, with a bag of little pastries and a bunch of thirsty marigolds, Hilda gave him a look that sent the blood to his face, and he roamed about wretchedly, silently, while she prepared the tea. She, too, was silent as she sat, with Nicky on her lap, holding a cup of milk for him and keeping an eye on Mary, who was clamouring for a pretty cake before she had eaten her bread and butter. The marigolds lay gasping on the sideboard and Frank, for something to do, placed them in a tumbler of water. When at last Mary had earned her cake and was far too engrossed with it to hear anything that was said, Hilda asked tensely:

'How soon can you take us away from this place, Frank? Why didn't you tell me that it was below ground? Don't you mind about Mary and Nicky? Do you *want* to see them gasping for air? Wilting for air and light! After Princess Square! After the country! You must have been either drunk or mad or both when you took these rooms. Oh! If only I'd had the sense to ask Rosa to find somewhere for us. She wouldn't have done such a silly thing. We can't stay here. It's plain murder for the children.' Her voice was unsteady with anger, and Mary, quick to sense that something was wrong, looked up wonderingly and was immediately given a second cake to keep her profitably occupied.

Frank, crushed by these reproaches, fumbled with his pipe, but Hilda did not offer to strike a match for him. She told the children they could leave the table and play, then, cupping her chin in her hands, elbows on the table, waited relentlessly for him to speak. The silence was acute, but at last he said abjectly: 'I'll have you out of here in a jiffy, Hilda. It was the only place I could afford where children were not objected to, and remember how insistent you were on my finding somewhere self-contained. It is that, at any rate.'

'Oh yes, it's self-contained all right. So is the grave.'

'Please, Hilda, please! Try to put up with it for a week or two. I'll ask Rosa to come along and cheer you up. And any night you want to go and see your aunts or your friends, you can rely on me to look after the children.'

'I shouldn't dream of going to see anybody until we get out of here, least of all my family. I don't want them to know about this cesspool. I wouldn't mind about Aunt Mildred or Uncle Phillip, but as far as Aunt Helen is concerned we're a nuisance and a disgrace to be as poor as this.'

'Don't be so bitter, darling. Let's be pals again. We're bang up against it, but it can't last. In a few weeks this place will have vanished like a bad dream, eh?'

He smiled at her so pitiably that, in spite of a violent desire to hurt him for daring to bring the children here, she could not prevent an answering smile; and as soon as the children were in bed and asleep, she and Frank set to work and scrubbed and scoured and polished. The smelly druggets were rolled up and thrust into the fearsome coal-cellar under the street pavement; her lovely old tea-service made a charming frieze of green and white upon the high mantelpiece, in the centre of which her little silver clock shone like a star in a frosty sky. Mr. Mossop's flowering china was displayed formally upon the ugly sideboard, and the marigolds, stiffly holding up their heads again, glowed upon the table. In the bedroom she stripped the bed of its unsavoury coverings and substituted her own linen, and through all the bustle and activity the children slept serenely. It was long past midnight when they had finished to her satisfaction; looking about him as they drank tea and smoked and chatted, Frank complimented her upon her gift for making the desert blossom so sweetly, and repeated his assertion that their sojourn here was, speaking figuratively, no more than a halt in the wilderness; a dark interlude out of which he would soon lift them into the sunlight.

Hilda, charmed and softened by their deep and lovely comradeship, went to bed, and as she listened to the gentle breathing of the children tried to assure herself that life was still glorious. A few weeks here would make no odds. They would slip away fast enough and if she could not, meanwhile, make the best of things, then she was no fit wife for Frank or any man.

CHAPTER XIV

MÉMOIRES D'OUTRE-TOMBE

WEEK followed week, month followed month, and the Burton family, still entombed, continued to make the best of things. Hilda, her whole energies concentrated on the well-being of her children, was beginning to lose her natural resilience and to despair of ultimate rescue. She was thankful if she could manage to get through a day with sufficient food for them all, and she frequently had to wait for Frank to return with a few shillings, raised from heaven knew where, before she could explore the cheapest shops and purchase their next meal. Once, when they were at their very lowest ebb, she had again stolen food, slipping it beneath Nicky's pram coverlet, and all the way home, shaking with fear, she expected a constable to catch up with her and request her to accompany him. When she placed before Frank that evening a succulent meal of roast chicken he, having left her in the morning with only a few pence, made a facetious remark about manna from heaven. Completely overwrought, she burst into tears, and he sat, white and silent, as she explained about the chicken. He begged her to promise him never to run such a terrible risk again, but she turned on him savagely and said that he was entirely to blame for having once seriously extolled to her an epigram of Oscar Wilde's — something about the best way to combat temptation being to yield to it. 'It's quite a comforting doctrine. Besides, I wanted to give the children a treat. They're sick and tired of bread and milk. I should steal all sorts of things for them if I wasn't so scared of being found out. It's quite easy in a shop where they know you well. I stole this too' — she produced an outsize slab of chocolate — 'it will last them for ages.'

'Hell! God-damn bloody hell!' Frank exclaimed. He pushed away his untouched plate, and saying that he had just remembered he had to make a phone call, rose to go out. Hilda, who did not for a moment believe him, tried to detain him, but he shook her off and said he would not be more than a few minutes. She knew that he would not return for hours, and that then he would be drunk — not gaily drunk as he was after spending an evening with old friends in Fleet Street. When he was in this genial state she did not mind very much, except for the precious money involved, for he made her laugh, and discoursed so fluently about most things under the sun that he practically talked himself sober. But tonight, ashamed and defiant because of what she had done, he would drift from one local pub to another, drinking morosely and alone; and with each successive drink he would feel sorrier and sorrier for himself as a victim of the war — as the only victim of the war. When he came home in this condition she, thinking of Mary and Nicky condemned to this airless basement, and of her ceaseless pinching and scraping and planning to make ends come even within bowing distance, had no need of Rosa's advice to keep silent. She felt too bitter to speak. She would merely look at him, her heart aching because she was capable of so regarding him; and reddening beneath her gaze he would shout aggressively: 'I know you think I'm drunk, Hilda. But you're wrong again, so don't stare at me like that,' and still silent she would leave him slumped in his chair and go sadly to bed.

She now cleared the table, saved the food he had not touched, and washed up, her tears dropping fast into the soapy water. Why were they still so poor? Why was everybody in this dirty neighbourhood so poor? Things had been cut to the bone for months in Princess Square, but in those charming surroundings, and with dear Marjorie to share her plight, life had never been unbearably hard. But here there was no respite from the day-to-day, meal-to-meal, struggle for existence.

Only that morning, just after she had purloined the chicken, a young woman had come into the shop and asked, in an embarrassed whisper, for a pennyworth of cheese. The astonished assistant said that he could not serve her with such a small portion and the girl, flushing to her ears, turned quickly away. Poor thing! All she had was one penny. Well, she and Frank had once been so reduced that they hadn't even got a penny. In despair she had examined her depleted wardrobe and found only one garment which she could dispense with, a summer dress which Marjorie had made for her. It was a charming dress of cream flannel with narrow stripes of indigo blue, an exact replica of an advertisement for a famous pocket camera. Marjorie had made a similar dress for herself, and the two young mothers had worn them proudly as they played with their children on Brighton beach. She held up the dress sadly, reluctant to part with it. All summer was in it. All the happy, dreaming days of her life in Princess Square; but their need was great, and she smoothed it out for folding. As she did so her fingers felt something hard and round. Miracles still happened, it would seem.

'Quick, Frank! The scissors from my workbox!' Laughingly she explained her find — authentic treasure trove. The floating side-panels of the dress were weighted down with pennies. She unpicked eagerly, and from each panel collected four pennies. By judicious marketing she had bought a wonderful meal with those eight pennies, four pennyworth of stewing beef, two pennyworth of vegetables, two pennyworth of damaged fruit, and she had kept the frock into the bargain, for the next post brought Frank a temporary job writing the press propaganda appealing for funds for a great hospital. He went off in tremendous spirits, saying that he would ask for some payment in advance. Hilda, waiting expectantly for him to bring back something for the midday meal, heard a taxi stop, and then his voice excitedly calling her. She rushed up the area steps to find him as hung about with parcels as a Christmas tree, and there were still more in the taxi. He had bought cold meats of every kind; salads; jellies; trifles; pastries; fruit and chocolate and cigarettes. A bottle of sherry, a bottle of Burgundy, toys for the children, and a bunch of heavenly roses for herself. He had certainly been drinking, for he was flushed and triumphant, but she pretended not to notice. It was splendid of him to have raced back to her with all these delicacies, and it was wonderful to watch the children's faces light up over their new toys. Hilda's spirits matched his, and once more the path to security opened wide and clear before them. Frank had work for which he was to be adequately paid. She had money in her purse which was not borrowed, and delectable food on her shelves which had not been stolen. She experienced a mad longing to set forth at once and find a flat into which the sun shone, but prudently decided to wait until Frank was really safe.

What ages ago that had been, and here they still were, avoiding everyone but Rosa and her mother. Her aunts, perturbed by her strange silence, had called unexpectedly one afternoon, and been shocked to find her living so grimly. In her infrequent letters to them she had been reticent, indeed unnaturally so, hence their visit. It now transpired that times without number Frank had borrowed from her Aunt Helen, asking her to send the money to some club in Fleet Street, and he had not repaid a solitary shilling. Questioned directly, Hilda revealed the whole miserable story from Batsford downwards, and Helen, though prodigal with advice upon the getting of wisdom, nevertheless implied that having so obstinately chosen her bed her niece must now lie in it with what fortitude she could muster.

'I simply can't understand Frank,' she exclaimed. 'He's a capable journalist, so it can't be his work that's at fault. Does he drink very hard, Hilda?' Hilda reddened, and Helen continued: 'So that's it! I thought as much. I suppose the fact is that he can't be relied on. But a man with a wife and two children to go losing job after job! I know, dear! You must get him to sign the pledge,' she said brightly, sublimely unconscious of how funny this fatuous suggestion sounded.

'Well, Hilda, we must be getting back. Bring Mary and Nicky to tea one day. Come at a week-end, when Phillip's at home. It's ridiculous to think he's never seen them except in a photograph. He sent his love to you, by the way. Now don't get too despondent, my dear. It's a long lane that has no turning. And don't let Frank ask me for money again. He owes me over fifty pounds and I do really think I've done all that can be expected.' She kissed the children, remarked on Mary's growing likeness to her mother, said that Nicky was a sturdy little fellow, kissed Hilda, urged her to move to a healthier flat at the first opportunity, asked what she had been reading lately, recommended various new novels, and concluded by advising her on no account to miss the new play at the Haymarket. Mildred, who had been almost completely silent, but whose observant, loving eyes had noted various distressing signs of abysmal poverty that had escaped her volatile and voluble sister, warmly seconded the invitation to tea, and the instant Helen went out to the lavatory, gave Hilda two pounds, saying in a frightened whisper: 'Don't let Helen know. I'm sorry, darling, about all this. Poor old Hilda. It's not fair.'

They left, Helen unfeignedly glad to be out of the detestable place, and Mildred wishing in her heart that she could take Hilda and the children back with her until Frank found a decent home for them. As they awaited their bus Helen, irritated by her sister's troubled face, attempted to justify her apparent harshness with Hilda.

'I'm quite as distressed for her as you are, Mildred. But what remedy is there? Have you forgotten how hard we tried to persuade her to wait a year or two before marrying

Frank? That business in Batsford seems to have been shocking. What a magnificent chance thrown, literally, into the gutter. Oh well, I suppose they'll get along somehow. For heaven's sake say something! Don't you agree that I'm right about making her realize that I can't keep on helping Frank?'

'Yes, but you're not being fair to Hilda. She's not learnt yet how to conceal her feelings. It was a nasty surprise to her to discover that Frank has been such a consistent cadger.'

'It's a thousand pities she couldn't have concealed her silly feelings when she first met him. If she had, she might now be married to a responsible young husband eager to make his way in the world. She'd no business to have that second child, either, though I suppose one can hardly blame her for that misfortune. But what's the use of talking? She must do the best she can for those children, and I wish to goodness she wouldn't talk about their father as if he was the eighth wonder of the world. The sooner she comes down to earth about him, the easier she'll find it to cope with things. Ah! Youth! Youth! How sad it is. Thank heaven this is our bus.'

As for Hilda, though she had enjoyed seeing her aunts, she was thankful to see them go. She fought shy of everyone except Rosa, even their old friend Dermot McGilray, who actually lived in Chelsea. She dreaded running into him, but one afternoon, wheeling the pram along the King's Road, she caught sight of him on the opposite side and prayed that he had not also seen her. But he had, for he waved and crossed over as soon as the traffic allowed. In the revealing sunshine she felt disgracefully shabby, worlds away from the gay, would-be-sophisticated young person whom he had always so enjoyed taking about until the momentous night when she had first met Frank at his house. The children, at any rate, were looking sweet, though Mary stared at him in terror when he gravely introduced himself to her as an old, old friend of the family; while the impressionable Nicky, utterly overwhelmed by the sombre black hat and general appearance of gloom which Dermot, a cheerful man at heart, shed around him through his antiquated dark clothing, gave a scream and commanded his mother, in a language which she alone comprehended, to send him away.

Dermot greeted her with sincere affection. 'Well, Hilda, what a charming trio! The last time we met you were an enchanting young bride; now, you're a beautiful young matron! What have you been doing with yourself all this time, apart from having babies? Nobody's set eyes on you for ages. I see Frank in Fleet Street occasionally, and I've asked him over and over again to bring you along any Sunday evening, but he's damned reserved these days. Where are you hiding, and why, if an old friend may be allowed to ask?'

Hilda, warmed by his obvious pleasure in seeing her again, and feeling for him in consequence all her old confiding friendliness, explained frankly how matters stood; how unjustly Frank was being treated by a world which owed him so much. Dermot, she reflected, might be able to help him to a job, for he was not without influence if he cared to exert himself; but though he listened sympathetically enough she realized that, as a carefree bachelor with an assured position, he had not really grasped the magnitude of their plight; indeed, from his next remark, she gathered that he did not even regard it as anything out of the ordinary. 'It's a dog's life, that of the journalist. I think we see more of the seamy side than any other profession. Don't let it get you down, Hilda. Most journalists are perpetually broke. It's a state of mind, though we have our moments. One night we dine at the Savoy, and the next night we dodge the Ritz, if you'll forgive the pun. Old Frank's sure to pull off something decent one day. That's how it goes. If you wanted a predictable future, you should have married a man of business. But you did prefer one of us, you know, and with some good results at any rate.' He gave Mary an approving pat, then fondled Nicky's hands and dropped them as if they held a serpent when the child screamed again and turned his face away.

'Well, being broke is no excuse between old friends for being non-gregarious into the bargain. You and Frank will be welcome at my place any Sunday evening. So long, my dear, and don't forget — any Sunday evening.'

Hilda, heedless of Mary's prattle about 'the funny black man', looked after him wistfully as he walked rapidly away, his silver-knobbed cane lightly tapping the pavement, and the small nosegay of artificial violets in his lapel drawing amused glances from passers-by. With his swarthy complexion and smouldering dark eyes he was the greatest possible contrast to her fair and blue-eyed Frank. Nor did the contrast end there, she admitted reluctantly. For all his Whistlerian affectation in dress, his dislike of green grass and his predilection for artificial buttonholes, he possessed tremendous moral courage. Years ago, so her Aunt Helen had told her, he had looked with such fervour upon the wine when it was red that he, too, had been poor and frequently workless. Then, after a terrible orgy which ended in delirium tremens and Bow Street, he had sworn never to touch alcohol again. He had kept his word and now held down a good job on an influential daily newspaper, the kind of job which Frank ought to have attained by this time. As she continued up Sloane Street on her way to the Park, stopping to gaze at lovely clothes which she ached to buy for herself and the children, she wondered if a good bout of delirium tremens might not be an excellent thing for Frank . . . if it would cure him of his weakness. But she doubted that it would.

Because one or other of them must remain with the children, Hilda did not go to see her old friend, dearly as she wanted to. Frank, who looked uneasy when she told of her encounter, begged her to go, but she said it would be no fun by herself. Instead she urged him to go occasionally, but he made the same flattering excuse, whereupon, to his astonishment, she drily pointed out that he did not seem to mind enjoying himself in pubs without her.

'That's quite different, Hilda. Besides, I never know who I may run into in a pub — in Fleet Street, that is. It's one way of getting to know about any jobs that are going. Now don't be so self-sacrificing. Go and enjoy yourself at Dermot's. You ought to meet people. It's not healthy for you to shut yourself away as you insist on doing.'

'But I thought we were going to know all manner of interesting people ourselves, Frank. It certainly will be fun when we can give parties, too; when we have a home to give them in, that is. Until then I'm not going anywhere except to Rosa's mother, but you needn't think it's dull for me all the time. It isn't, especially when you're at home in the evenings. You said that you were going to take my education in hand and teach me two thousand years of literature.'

'Don't make such wild assertions, Hilda! I said that, poor beggars though we are, we have two thousand years of literature to choose from. But what on earth has literature to do with your going to Dermot's?'

'Quite a lot. I'd far rather listen to you talking about it than go to any old party. If you want me to be happy in this state to which it has pleased you to call me, come home every night and educate me. I like it. It's only when you don't come home that I begin to feel sorry for myself, and very nasty and resentful towards you. Now don't pester me any further about going to see people. Until we get out of this horrible basement I won't go anywhere but to old Mrs. Johnston's.'

The tiny almshouse where Rosa's mother lived was the one spot in London where the Burton family was confident of an affectionate welcome. The almshouses, built in a square around a vast tree-shadowed lawn that reminded Hilda of

Princess Square, were so cosy that she could not comprehend why the old lady was ashamed of living there. After the dungeon, Mrs. Johnston's sunny little home seemed so desirable that one Sunday Hilda made everybody jump by remarking that if only she and Frank might qualify for such a refuge in which to bring up Mary and Nicky, she would expect nothing further of life. Every Sunday throughout the winter they escaped there for dinner and tea, contributing their share to the cost of the plain but wholesome food which the old lady so delighted to cook for them. Frank appreciated these visits quite as much as Hilda, and while she and Rosa washed up he beguiled Mrs. Johnston into reminiscing about old but happy days when, as the esteemed wife of a once-wealthy man, she had wanted for nothing. As his widow, she wanted for nothing now, for in the days of his prosperity he had been a handsome benefactor to the almshouse trust, and when she fell upon evil times there had been no difficulty in securing one of the almshouses for her.

It was the simple comfort of this tiny home that influenced Hilda in her campaign to induce Frank to renounce London for ever and settle permanently in the country, for though she would not face up to it openly she no longer believed that he would ever re-establish himself in Fleet Street. As she washed and ironed and sewed and cooked, she chanted the seasons like a litany and eased the strain of 'making the best of things' by reciting aloud every poem she could remember in praise of things eternal. When Frank saw her seated at the table, staring at a sheet of notepaper on which she had written: *Total weekly income two pounds*, he resigned himself to a disturbing evening as she proceeded to demonstrate that on this modest sum they could all live contentedly in a cottage. She painted a remarkable picture of herself tending fowls and pigs and goats, and flatteringly pointed out that in such a world of light and happiness he would have unending leisure in which to write a masterpiece. Every week she expended tuppence on the journal that had once stipulated 'no children or likelihood', and nearly drove him mad as she read it aloud. There appeared to be no objection to children in the remoter country cottages, and there were plenty advertised at absurdly low rents, some being no more than five shillings a week. All over Britain there were empty cottages waiting for such as themselves. In the Essex marshlands; in green Suffolk; in rich Devonshire; among the Welsh mountains and the Scottish highlands; in the Kentish orchards and in ancient Cornwall. With her head full of Tennyson her immediate preference was for Cornwall; for 'dark Tintagel by the Cornish sea'.

'Oh Frank, just imagine our being able to live facing the Atlantic! No land between us and the other side of the world. Wouldn't it be absolutely glorious?'

Frank shuddered at the frightful prospect of being thus cut off from his fellow-men and felt it expedient to say so forthwith, whereupon she suggested that they ought to be really adventurous and go to live in France. There, at any rate, they would not be cut off from civilization, and while his thoughts turned longingly to the nearest pub she told him about a strange girl she had once known who had gone to Rouen for a week's holiday, fallen head over heels in love with the town, and never returned home. She had taken the only available work — dull, manual labour in a factory — and on a wage of twenty-five shillings a week, with a garret for a home, was completely happy. Why, at the present rate of exchange, they would be almost affluent in the French countryside on two pounds a week! Or they, too, might live in a cathedral-crowned city and augment their two pounds by giving English lessons. And there was the wine! Cunningly, she begged him to consider the wine! So cheap. So good. He could drink his fill with a clear conscience. Corn and oil and wine. What more could they want? Frank shied away from her romantic mood in terror. Except to take her there one fine day for the holiday of their lives, he protested that he had had his fill of France.

'Italy then,' she persisted. 'Why not Italy? Oh Frank, why shouldn't we do something adventurous? Something different? Anything, anywhere, would be better than dragging along here. If you won't take us abroad, then you must take us back to the country, and if you won't live in the country, then we must find a home in the suburbs. I never thought I should hanker after a suburb again, but it would be Paradise after this.'

She returned to the fascinating journal that offered so many different heavens, but at last, unable to stand her fearful concentration on it further, he took it from her and pushed it into the fire.

'Of course we can't live in this hole for ever, but don't keep on so about the country, dearest. We can't live anywhere on two pounds a week. That's why, as I keep telling you, I must stay in London to keep in touch. Cheer up, Hilda. You shall have a country cottage yet — roses round the door, ivy on the walls, no water, no light, no nothing — but you shall have it to play in when you want to, not to live in because you have to. You really must trust me to know what's best for us.'

Hilda, bitterly disappointed that she could not persuade him to share her romantic belief that their salvation lay in a foreign clime, said nastily:

'How can I trust you when all you do is *talk* about what you're going to achieve? I'm only thinking of Mary and Nicky. If it wasn't for them I shouldn't care how or where we lived. You never seem to worry about them at all.'

'Now darling, you don't really mean that. You're nervy. I must go out for a minute for some tobacco.'

'Well, don't forget the whisky to go with it, will you? No matter what happens, you must have your whisky—oh, what's the use?'

He gave her a conciliatory smile and disappeared into the

bedroom. A minute or two later, calling that he wouldn't be long, he went out. Full of grievance against him, Hilda picked up her book and tried to read it, but she felt too restless and angry to concentrate. There was a pile of the children's clothing waiting to be ironed, and she decided to calm herself by doing this mechanical and necessary job. She placed her one heavy flat-iron on the gas-stove, and then fetched her handbag from the bedroom, for she needed pennies for the gas. She extracted her small leather purse that had Brighton Pavilion embossed upon it in faded gold, and tipped its contents on to the table. She picked up the necessary coppers and was about to close the purse when she gave a little cry. There should have been two half-crowns as well as the pennies. She was careless about money even though she had so little, perhaps because she had so little. She searched the handbag; she searched the drawer where she always kept the bag. She combed the whole flat thoroughly, and it was not until she had done this twice over that she knew for a certainty that Frank had taken the money. That was why he had gone into the bedroom just now!

The shock of her discovery brought to mind an incident in Princess Square when a pound note had mysteriously vanished. Frank had helped her to search for it, but it was never found. Her memory, now wide open, went back even further — to an afternoon when they lived in the furnished house in Sydenham. She had wanted to buy some pretty garment for Mary and had asked Frank for the money for this. He had immediately given her two pound notes, which she left on the kitchen table while she went to put on her outdoor things; and when she came downstairs again they had disappeared. She had thought Frank was teasing her, and had demanded their return, whereupon he had looked at her blankly and denied further knowledge of them. It had been a blustery day, and the kitchen door was open. After searching the garden thoroughly she had accepted Frank's suggestion that the notes had literally been blown away through her carelessness. It was, of course, conceivable that such was the case, but even if Frank, having made his effect of being unable to deny her the little pleasure, had re-pocketed the notes, it was not so heinous as the theft of the two half-crowns; for they had not then been as poor as they were now.

She rolled up the pile of small garments, afraid to use her few remaining pence, and sat down to await her husband. But when he came back, some hours later, she saw at a glance that it would be useless to talk to him. She went to bed and lay there speculating about the future of her children. What was to be done about a father who could so shamelessly steal the money for their food and waste it in a public house? How was it all going to end? For end it must, and that quickly.

CHAPTER XV

THE WEAKER VESSEL

Ye husbands, dwell with your wives according to knowledge; giving honour unto the wife, as unto the weaker vessel.

AFTER the estrangement that ensued as a result of the stolen half-crowns a sad peace was entered upon. Hilda's surge of bitterness towards her charming, weak, and treacherous husband gradually receded and gave place to a numbed resolve to make the best of things in the worst of all possible worlds. She still loved him deeply, but they no longer discussed the miracles they would yet accomplish. The only miracle she now attempted was the acquisition of sufficient food and warmth for her family. She had become, or so she believed, the most astute housewife in London. From shop to shop she went, from stall to stall, surveying the damaged 'bargains' with experienced eyes, counting her scanty coins with the absorption of a miser, and hiding her weightless purse so cunningly that Frank was never again able to filch from it. There were times throughout the summer when she had not even a penny for the gas, and to save precious coal would boil the kettle on rolled-up newspapers. Once, in mid-winter, they were actually without a fire, but she was now as resourceful as Robinson Crusoe, and she cheerfully hacked up one of the wretched basket chairs for fuel until Frank came home with the price of a hundred-weight of coal. From time to time he still secured temporary work, and then for a week or two they lived quite splendidly. At such times she prudently laid in a stock of siege provisions, had all their shoes repaired, and bought quantities of wool with which to knit socks and suits for Mary and her brother. The children were sweet and rosy, for in all but the rainiest or foggiest weather she took them out daily to Battersea Park or to Hyde Park. Once there, the dungeon was temporarily forgotten, and she played with them as if she hadn't a care in the world. They adored their father, who made up wonderful stories for them, and though Nicky could not yet understand these properly he would snuggle up against his sister, his brow comically puckered, and laugh when she laughed, clap when she clapped. Mary loved him passionately. She bossed him and fussed over him like a hen with her chick, and every morning her chief delight was to brush his thick, tawny hair, a performance he endured with admirable stoicism, so absolute was his belief in her omnipotence. When Frank undertook to amuse and interest them, Hilda watched and wondered. How could he have such pitiful lapses? How could he ever waste money on drink when he had two such lovely beings dependent upon him? He certainly loved them. Why, then, were they condemned to live like moles? Why wouldn't he listen to her and leave London for good?

One afternoon, during an exceptionally arid financial period, she received a visit from their landlord, Mr. Edwards, a genial-looking person, stout and red of face, with a Cockney accent of quite exceptional pungency. Hilda, though beset by dark premonitions as to the object of this visit, chatted brightly while the children played around. She made some tea and Mr. Edwards, regarding her thoughtfully as he drank, made the curious remark that there was always plenty of money to be made if only people would have the guts to take a risk now and again. Take his own case, for example. By having the nous to buy up vast quantities of ex-army sacks, tarpaulins, etc., for very little, and re-selling them for a great deal, he had been able to purchase whole rows of houses, and by letting them out in furnished flats was now making a regular and substantial income. He advised her to have a heart-to-heart talk with her husband about this simple mode of acquiring money. Nobody with ordinary common sense, he emphasized, need remain poor. Hilda, though by this time fully cognizant of the fact that Mr. Edwards had not called upon her solely for the purpose of demonstrating how she might improve her fortunes, was nevertheless intrigued by the topic and asked for more explicit information.

'Well, Mrs. Burton, it's like this. Say you have five pounds at your disposal. All you have to do is to buy a cheap line of goods, advertise them in the local paper for ten pounds, and there you are! Then you buy another cheap line for ten pounds and sell them for twenty pounds. You've made a start, see? There are so many mugs about that it's as easy as falling off a log. You can't go wrong, see?'

'Yes, it does sound easy,' she agreed politely, wondering meanwhile when Mr. Edwards would get to the real object of his visit. Mr. Edwards, too, was wondering. Like Mr. Cohen of Brighton, he was a humane person despite his ambitious business methods, and he felt genuinely sorry for this attractive young woman and her two charming children.

He drank a second cup of tea, cleared his throat, and said: 'I had hoped to see your husband, Mrs. Burton. I wrote to him and said that I should be calling this afternoon. When's the best time to catch him?'

'Mostly in the evenings, but you can give me a message for him.'

Mr. Edwards did not reply immediately, but lowered his several chins upon his breast, apparently deep in thought. Then he told her the truth, namely that he had not received any rent for weeks; that he had written several letters to her husband, none of which had been answered, and that the final letter, which he must have received that morning, contained notice for them to quit the flat. They must be out by midday the following Saturday.

Genial to the last, he shook hands, gave the children a benevolent pat, and departed. Hilda was neither surprised nor distressed by his ultimatum but merely speculated where, within a few days, they would find themselves, for obviously they must live somewhere. But how cunningly Frank had managed to conceal this calamity, if indeed it was a calamity! At any rate, they would get out of this horrible place. That would be all to the good since they could hardly sink lower; and Frank must have made plans of some kind for them. When he came in, she was singing, a trifle blasphemously: 'There is a happy land, not far away'; and though Frank went rather white when he heard of her visitor, he quickly responded to her mood and cheerfully announced that Mr. Edwards could go to the devil for his rent. Only that morning he had viewed a sunny, delightful flat in Paulton Square, and within twenty-four hours they would be snugly installed in it.

Hilda was overjoyed. Paulton Square was a pleasant spot, and surprisingly quiet considering its near proximity to the busy and noisy King's Road. She had frequently taken the children round it for a quick breath of air after tea, and now they would be free to play on its lawns as they had once played on those dream lawns of Princess Square, Brighton.

'But why on earth didn't you tell me? If we have to be out of here by Saturday there isn't much time, and I shall have *some* packing to do. You might have thought of this, Frank.'

'I wanted to give you a wonderful surprise, darling; also I didn't want you to make a fuss. If I'd told you earlier you'd have found a hundred things to do. Now, you won't even have time to think about them. We just fold our tents and . . .'

'Oh no!' she interrupted. 'We don't steal silently away. Mr. Edwards must be paid.'

'Now, Hilda! Don't look at me in that sideways fashion. I'll settle with Edwards in a day or two. But tell me, whatever did you talk about?'

'Money! How to acquire it easily and quickly. See?'

'No, but I'm more than willing to learn. Carry on, pet.'

Soon they were laughing merrily as, with sly mimicry, Hilda imparted the magic formula and, though he was careful not to say so, Frank decided that in the circumstances Mr. Edwards could afford to wait eternally for his rent. He was always teasing Hilda about what he described as her plebeian attitude towards debt, for which he blamed her strict nonconformist childhood. He had tried to laugh her out of it, but she continued obstinately to regard the owing of money as a major crime, beside which her own occasional lapses into simple theft sank into insignificance.

The next morning Frank went off as usual, gay, tender, and hearteningly confident. Hilda had never really fathomed just what he did with himself all day long when he had no commissioned work on hand, but he had told her that he spent many hours in the British Museum Reading Room on research; also that there was a journalists' club in a court off Fleet Street to which he belonged. He had in fact once pointed it out to her and she had been a little surprised at its outward aspect of decay, though he assured her that it was pleasant enough inside.

The intervening days flew by in a flurry of washing and ironing and packing, and when the morning of deliverance dawned all was in readiness for the new adventure. Twice she had taken the excited children round Paulton Square and shown them their new home, which looked so clean and light and airy. She had been greatly tempted to ring the bell and announce herself as the new tenant of the entrance flat, but remembered in time Frank's charming desire to surprise her. Now, as they sat at their last breakfast in the dungeon, she again plied him with questions about the new home. What was the furniture like? What was the landlady like? How many people were there in the house, and had he glimpsed any of them? To every eager question he gave a perfectly rational answer, and emphasized the welcome information that in the new flat she need not be ashamed to receive old friends. She hadn't felt so light-hearted for months in spite of her fears that at any minute a far less genial Mr. Edwards might appear and demand his dues. She was in a fever to be off; to emerge from darkness for ever. Frank helped all he could to dismantle the cots. She stowed the few remaining oddments in a small hold-all, put on the children's outdoor clothes, likewise her own, and announced that she was quite ready to leave. Frank, too, was ready. He said that he would fetch the taxi. At the door he turned and Hilda, queerly frightened by the strange look he gave her, divined the awful truth. He wasn't coming back with any taxi. He wasn't coming back at all. There was no flat in Paulton Square. He had lied and lied and lied. Instantly perceiving that she knew, and muttering that he would be back in a few minutes, he ran out. Hilda, for once forgetting the children, ran after him, calling him, but he darted through the traffic, disappeared down an alley, and she realized that she could not hope to catch up with him. The coward! The abominable coward! To desert them like this, helpless, penniless, homeless! The children! She raced back, people staring at her in amazement as she flew past them. She hadn't been out more than a few minutes but Nicky was screaming for her, and Mary was half-suffocating him in her desire to comfort him. When they saw her, both children rushed headlong towards her, shrieking 'Mummy! Mummy!' in such terrified voices that she lost her customary self-control before them, gathered them to her, and wept as childishly as they. They clung to her in utter bewilderment, their small world suddenly unsafe. Ashamed of herself, she hugged them and soothed them until their terror passed and they were playing and laughing again.

What was she going to do now? Frank had obviously given up the struggle. He would not return here. And she had to be out by midday. If only he had not lied! If only he had been a man and stayed with her to face the music — then . . . together . . . they would have managed somehow. But to run away — to leave her, handicapped with two small children, to find a way out as best she could! It was horrible. What a coward he was, and what a liar because he was a coward! She would have to go to her people, and the prospect of relating her humiliating story to Aunt Helen was bitter as wormwood. But there was nothing else she could do. Rosa could not help her; she was far too poor herself. She looked in her purse. She had a few pennies, sufficient for the bus fare to Glynne Mansions. Sick at heart, and with a splitting headache, she prepared to set out. For a melodramatic, self-pitying second she thought of suicide. They had lived for so long in this grave, why not remain in it for good — she, and Mary, and Nicky. But the memory of Mrs. Timms and her ghastly revelations steadied her. Mary being 'nicely set' . . . Nicky's face bound up in snowy linen . . . Her own shoulders being properly 'hunched' in. Oh no! No! Besides, she hadn't enough money for the gas, an incontrovertible fact that made her smile.

Carrying Nicky, and with his sister trotting excitedly alongside, she reached her old home in Glynne Mansions, Chiswick. What decades it seemed since, a gawky girl of fourteen straight from a remote Lancashire village, she had mounted these stairs for the first time, the whole lovely world before her. Breathless and trembling she rang the bell. The door was opened by her Aunt Helen, but there was no welcoming smile upon her face. She smelt trouble immediately, for as soon as they were inside she remarked drily: 'Frank, I suppose! Tell me the worst. He wrote to me the other day, saying he was faced with absolute destitution, and asked for yet another loan to tide him over, but I ignored the letter. I felt the time had come to make a stand. Well, child, tell us what has happened.'

Mildred, giving her an affectionate and encouraging smile, took the children into another room and, with burning cheeks, Hilda told her sorry tale to her aunt and uncle. They heard her in silence, and when she had finished neither spoke for a few seconds. Then Helen, gazing severely at her unhappy niece, said briskly: 'All right. But Frank Burton must be made to understand that he, and nobody else, is responsible for his wife and children. The rotter! Why, the humblest working man would not do such a vile thing. Now, Hilda, listen to me, and don't be upset. This is what you must do. You must go at once, with the children, to the nearest Poor Law Institution. You will tell the authorities there what you have just told us. They will look after you, and within a matter of hours they will have found that cowardly husband of yours. He will then be made responsible for you, and will be taught a salutary lesson. You understand, don't you, that I'm not advocating this drastic course with any other thought but what is best for you and the children. Don't cry, you foolish girl! Can't you see that it's plain common sense? Really, what does Frank think? That by running out of his front door he can push his responsibilities wholesale on to someone else – on to us, for instance! Now don't you see that I'm right?'

Hilda stared at her aunt as she would have stared at some primeval monster that threatened to devour her. Mary and Nicky in the workhouse! The only knowledge she had of the workhouse came from the novels of Charles Dickens, and from dark whispers she had overheard as a child in Moss Ferry about old Mester So-and-So, ill, poor, and with neither kith nor kin, having been taken away to the House. It had happened but rarely, for poor though all in Moss Ferry were, no family had ever allowed this final ignominy to befall 'one of their own'. A corner was found somehow; the extra mouth might mean relentless scraping and pinching, but it was always managed, for did not the Lord expect it of them?

When the cruel thing had happened, when there was absolutely no alternative, the sense of shame throughout the village was so oppressive that even the children were aware of it. Hilda remembered quite clearly how, as she sat reading one night, her foster-parents had talked in low, sad tones about old Matthew Cooper, for whom the time had come to go into 't'House' at Warrington, his wife having died, and he having no kin at all to succour him.

'Ah dunna like it, Joe. 'E's bin mazed ever since she went. When Ah wor coming back from our Emma's Ah cotched sight of 'im traipsing up and down in front of t'cemetery talking to hissel.

' "What's do do, Mat?" Ah asked 'im. "Tha's looking poorly. Art worriting about going to t'House? Tha's no need. Tha'll be easier there than doing for thysel in that owd shack on t'Moss. Tha'll 'ave thi meals regular and a good fire to warm thee, a good bed to lie in, and nowt at all to fash thee."

' "Aye, Lizzie. 'Appen Ah will, but Ah wish 'er and me could 'a bin fetched together. It would 'a saved a mort o' trouble."

' "Nay, Mat. Tha munna talk so wild. Get thee home and 'ave a good sleep and tha'll feel different come morning."

' "A good sleep, eh Lizzie? Thank ye, Lizzie. Good Neet." '

And when morning came Moss Ferry knew, as if it had been painted on the heavens for all to learn, that old Matthew Cooper had killed himself rather than go to the House. Fanny Entwistle, the post-woman, tramping to his lonely shack with an official-looking envelope post-marked 'Warrington', had been balked of the little pleasure she so looked forward to — of reading its contents to the old man, who had never had time to learn to read. She found him, head downwards, in the big rain-water butt outside his back door, his stockinged feet wedged on the rim, and his boots, filled with heavy stones, tied firmly about his neck. As Hilda recalled this tragedy, and pictured her children in such an abominable place as 't'House', her sobs became unrestrained, and she clung despairingly to her Uncle Phillip. His face was grim, but there was that in her own face which gave him the courage to ignore his wife. 'Your Aunt Helen is quite right,' he said gently, 'but all the same you shan't go. We'll think of something, my dear.'

'Phillip, I wish to goodness you wouldn't interfere! What else can Hilda do to bring Frank to his senses? It won't be for more than a day or two at the outside. And she's *my* niece, not yours.'

'She's an old pal of mine, Helen, and she and the children are going to remain here, at any rate for the time being.'

'Don't you become hysterical, too! Frank Burton must be taught a sharp lesson, and if Hilda has anything in her at all she'll act like a sensible woman and do the one thing to teach him that lesson.' She paused, then continued less harshly: 'There *is* another way, Hilda. A cruel way for you, but a way out for one of the children at least. You only want what is best for them, don't you? Have you yet faced up squarely to the implications of Frank's atrocious behaviour? What kind of future is there for Mary and her brother with a father who is so weak and so utterly irresponsible? I'm not going to waste any sympathy on you, though naturally I'm sorry you should have to begin paying so quickly for your first happiness with Frank. But you're young and will learn how to cope with life, as we all must learn. For the children, however . . .' She paused again, and Hilda, terrified by her awful gravity, wondered what the 'way out' was going to be. She proceeded: 'As you know, Hilda, I have a very old friend, Josephine Tranter. We spent a day together recently, and in the course of conversation she asked about you, so I told her one or two things — about that lost opportunity in Batsford, for instance, and the struggle you were having in that disgusting basement. She was all sympathy, particularly about the children, and mentioned some close friends of hers who wish to adopt a child. She said they had been thinking about it for a long time as they are unable to have one of their own. She said they were charming, wealthy, cultivated people, so that if they do eventually adopt a child it will be for love and no other reason.' She paused again and, flushing beneath her niece's puzzled gaze, looked at her husband as if for encouragement. He gave her a faint smile, and she continued: 'Now, Hilda, all I ask you to do is to think very seriously about this childless couple. Why not give up Nicky to them? Try to imagine what it would mean for him. I know it would be a fearful sacrifice for you, but think of him – of his future. Knowing him to be safely provided for, you will be able to take a job and keep Mary. Don't rely further on your husband, my poor girl. He's a broken reed if ever there was one. Of course you would have to get his consent to the adoption, which would have to be strictly legalized. But you'll know how to manage this part. And do believe that I'm only concerned about the children's welfare. Remember that for years yet they must be fed and clothed and educated. Single-handed, you'll never be able to do it properly, so let one of them at least have a decent chance.'

Hilda, for some minutes, was too distressed to make any coherent answer. She looked at her uncle's set face, stared incredulously at her aunt; then, having recovered her senses, said resolutely: 'No! You don't understand, Aunt Helen. I can't separate Mary from Nicky for ever. I'd rather go on the streets than do such an unnatural thing.'

'You're not cut out for the streets, my dear. You'd be no good at all in that over-rated profession. You'd be a complete flop,' her aunt said with a smile.

'Well, isn't that all I should need to be? No! Lend me my fare to Moss Ferry. I'll take the children up there – to my foster-parents. *They* won't send us to the workhouse. I'll find work in Manchester and my foster-mother will look after

Mary and Nicky. They can be educated at the village school, like I was. Nobody seems to have worried over-much about *my* future when I lived in Moss Ferry.'

'Now, of course, you're talking like a fool. There's no question of your returning to Moss Ferry. You'd hate it, and since you don't appear to need advice perhaps you'd like to tell me what your immediate plans are.'

'I've told you, Helen,' Phillip intervened sharply. 'Hilda and the children will stay with us for the time being. I'm going out now to call a taxi and she can come with me to collect her things. The children will be all right with Mildred. Come along, Hilda,' and before Helen, furious and speechless, could prevent him, he had seized Hilda's arm and hustled her out of the flat.

Helen, though she yielded neither gracefully nor silently, did her conscientious best to be agreeable for the brief period that they were with her, but the invasion of her home by two small, happy children tried her severely. Hilda, utterly wretched at her humiliating position, was continually on edge, and before they had been there a week Mary and Nicky were as frightened of Helen as she herself had once been. She lectured them and instructed them as if they were mature school-children instead of mere babies, and when she wasn't saying 'Don't' to one or other of them, she was saying it to their harassed mother. If it had not been for Mildred's warm affection and Phillip's constant encouragement, Hilda would have applied to the Relieving Officer, for she was beginning to think that anything was preferable to Helen's sly innuendos that by refusing even to consider the possibility of adoption she was thinking only of herself; of her own selfish pleasure in the children. A true mother, her childless aunt was never tired of pointing out, would, like the Roman matrons of antiquity, suffer all things for her little ones.

It was Rosa who eventually came to her rescue by finding

a temporary refuge for the children with the daughter of an old servant of her mother's young and prosperous days; and it was Phillip who made this possible by promising to pay for them until Hilda found work, traced her husband, and compelled him to resume his natural responsibilities. To please old Mrs. Johnston, this woman agreed to take Mary and Nicky until their mother was in a position to make other arrangements. Helen, bitterly resentful that the expense should be borne by her husband, did her utmost to induce Hilda to sue Frank for maintenance, but she obdurately refused. In her heart she knew that her aunt was right about this but, even after his cowardly desertion, she could not bring herself to do it. There had been so much between them, such a depth of tenderness, that the very thought of dragging in the law was abhorrent to her. She did not attempt to make her aunt understand this; she unburdened herself only to Rosa, who understood, as did her mother, for though the old lady was grieved beyond words at Frank's behaviour, she calmly advised Hilda to seek him out and make it up with him in spite of everything. 'When you've lived only half as long as I have, my dear, you'll realize that it's handy to have a husband around if only to sit in the kitchen and keep the draught out,' a sentiment with which Hilda, the more she was badgered by her Aunt Helen, eagerly concurred.

Through the active benevolence of her old employer at Pierian Hall, Hilda was fortunate enough to obtain a post as secretary to a friend of his, a wealthy timber merchant. Prior to keeping the interview which Mr. Belton had arranged for her with the timber merchant, she called at Pierian Hall to thank him, and was astonished when her old chief, surveying her critically, said warningly: 'You mustn't go to see Sir Edward looking as you do now. He's a nonconformist. After I'd spoken to him about you he asked me if you were straight. "As a die", I told him, but if he sees you with that stuff on your face he'll take fright and you might lose the job. Well, go to it, and good luck. Come and tell me how you get on. They're good people to get in with, so do your best.'

Hilda, fearful of making a bad impression upon the virtuous Sir Edward, went to the interview not only devoid of any make-up whatsoever, but bravely wearing one of her Aunt Helen's plainest and dowdiest hats, which, she was convinced, proved the deciding factor in her favour. Sir Edward was extremely brusque, but he generously made allowance for her obvious nervousness by slowing down his dictation test; before he could finish this, further help came through the arrival of his son, a boy of fourteen. The boy was worried about his birthday present. He couldn't make up his mind what he wanted. His doting father suggested all manner of wonderful things, none of which appealed sufficiently to the lad. At last, joyfully, as if a light had been shed upon him straight from heaven, he said tenderly: 'What about buying your own present, old chap? That ought to do the trick, eh?'

'All right, Dad. That's fine!'

'Good boy. Go and ask Mr. Findlay to write you a cheque for a hundred pounds. That'll let me and Mum out nicely. Then off you go and buy whatever you like.'

The boy, delighted, hurried away and the test was resumed. Hilda acquitted herself well enough to secure the job, but as she waited for her bus back to Glynne Mansions she experienced none of the comparative elation and relief called for by the occasion. One hundred pounds for a mere schoolboy to spend as he pleased! What marvellous things she could accomplish if only she had one hundred pounds or even half that sum! Why, she could build up a home again. Find Frank. Begin anew. The incident of the hundred pounds had depressed her so profoundly that she felt no desire to rush back to Glynne Mansions and tell her good news. Instead, she was assailed by an unbearable longing to see her husband; to tell him that from this day onwards everything was going to be all right; to hear him promise, as he had promised so often, that he would be strong and resolute of purpose. She took a bus to Bloomsbury, went to the British Museum, and sat upon the terrace there. If he was in the Reading Room, he would be sure to emerge some time for a smoke, but though she waited for over two hours he did not come out. Finally, knowing that he was probably a familiar sight there, she asked an attendant to inquire if he was in the Reading Room. She said that it was terribly urgent for her to speak to him. The man was extremely helpful, but he came back with the information that Mr. Burton had not been seen there for some weeks; he also added that if she cared to leave a message he would see that it was delivered when he next came in. She shook her head, thanked him, and set off for the seedy-looking club in the dark court in Fleet Street to which Frank belonged. There was no uniformed attendant here, but, overawed at finding herself on the threshold of what she imagined to be the sacred haunt of Fleet Street's most famous sons, she gave a timid knock on the shabby door. A startled voice called a loud 'Come in'. She entered and looked shyly around for Frank, but he was not there. Four or five men, standing at a dirty bar with drinks before them, gazed at her in astonishment, and with equal astonishment she returned their gaze. Then the barman said civilly:

'I'm afraid ladies are not allowed in here, madam. Is there anything I can do for you?'

'Well — I'm looking for my husband, Frank Burton. I think he's a member of this club. I want to find him. It's very urgent. Has he been here today?'

Expressive glances passed between the drinkers and the barman. Everybody seemed embarrassed and Hilda, the most embarrassed of them all, gained the queer impression that they were in a conspiracy against her and would reveal nothing they might know concerning her husband's whereabouts. The barman, ignoring her question, began to polish a tumbler, which he first breathed into with vigour; the votaries of the Press, moodily regarding their several drinks, which they had politely refrained from consuming, were obviously wishing her elsewhere, and she, feeling as awkward as if she had unwittingly walked into a gentlemen's public lavatory, blushingly retreated. But she was determined to find Frank, and as the evening wore away she became progressively bolder and poked her head into every likely and unlikely bar in Fleet Street. She was on the point of admitting defeat when, in a small pub at the end of an alley, she saw him, morosely drinking alone, and looking ill and unkempt. Her heart shook, but steadying herself she went up to him and said quietly, as if nothing in the world had happened, 'Hello, Frank!' He spun round, his colour mounting. Then he smiled, took her arm, and piloted her to an empty corner. He brought her a drink, and for a few moments they regarded each other in silence.

'Why did you do it, Frank? Why didn't you tell me how bad things were?'

'I couldn't. I just couldn't face up to it. I knew you could go to your people. I'm no good to you, Hilda. No damned good at all.'

'But the children! We've got to think of our children. We don't matter, but Mary and Nicky do.'

She told him of all that had happened; of her successful interview with the timber merchant. She painted an eloquent picture of how, now that she was sure of a weekly income, they could win through if only they stood together. For the time being the children were all right, and if he would make a supreme effort to do his share they would soon all be united again. As she thus talked so earnestly, Frank became more and more dejected. He was ashamed of himself; ashamed of his children being cared for by others;

ashamed even of Hilda's new air of independence. But she was so overjoyed to be with him again that her bitterness towards him dropped from her like a rotted garment. Yet again she made excuses for him. In spite of all the Medical Boards he had attended, he was not yet free of the war. The war it was that had so altered him, strange though it might be for a physically brave man to degenerate into such a moral coward. She must hold fast to this consolatory belief. They left the bar and, arm in arm, walked down to the Embankment, and sat for some time on a bench near a cheerful-looking coffee-stall. Hilda was ravenously hungry, and though she had never before patronized a coffee-stall, she now felt that she could eat everything on this one, even the piles of round, mustard-yellow cakes lavishly decorated with stringy coco-nut. They investigated their combined resources. They were slender, but sufficient for a mug of coffee and a doorstep ham sandwich. The proprietor allowed them to take this delicious meal to their bench, from which they watched the stall with interest; sometimes there was quite a crowd round it, sometimes it was utterly deserted. What fun it was with Frank to share! Suddenly he gave a low whistle. 'Look, Hilda! See that little chap who's just sidled up. Do you recognize him?' Hilda looked, and made out a dim figure standing at the side of the stall, in shadow, fumbling with a paper bag while a mug of coffee was drawn for him. It was J. M. Barrie who, oblivious to the smallest audience he could ever have had, drank his steaming coffee and ate one bun after another from the paper bag. Hilda found it an enchanting experience; an experience to be enjoyed only with Frank, who was already mentally writing a 'par' about it for the evening paper to which he sent his free-lance articles. Frank raised his mug: 'Let's drink his health, pet. He's paid for our supper. Now perhaps you'll understand why I don't want to live out of London. Where else could we have spent such a fascinating ten minutes?'

He took her back to Chiswick, on top of a bus, where they sat close in their old comradeship. She announced her immediate intention of taking a furnished room where they could begin to save for their own home once more. She asked for his address, but this natural request appeared to embarrass him, and he told her to write to him at the little club, where a letter would always find him. She didn't want to leave him, and would unhesitatingly have spent the night with him in the cheapest lodging-house, or even on the bench near the glowing coffee-stall, but he left the bus at Hammersmith Broadway, and stood smiling up at her until it moved off. With loving eyes she watched him enter the Underground. She had forgiven him completely. What a day it had been! She had found a job, and she had found her husband. Everything would now resolve itself, and they would go forward with one purpose only — the well-being of Mary and her brother. In a mood of frantic exaltation she bounded up the stone stairs of Glynne Mansions, and found, as she had hoped, that everyone had gone to bed. Her Aunt Mildred, always so thoughtful, had left a tray in her room bearing a glass of milk and some sandwiches. She wolfed them up, and quickly undressed. On the bedside table there was a photograph of the children and now, from her trunk, she took out a photograph of Frank and placed it by the other. Oh, it was a grand old world, a wonderful world! And wasn't she thankful that she was still here to wake up in it?

CHAPTER XVI

CAN MOSS FERRY SAVE THEM?

HILDA, taking the initiative, rented a large bed-sitting-room for them both in a quiet Bloomsbury street, settled down to her work for the timber merchant, and planned unceasingly for the happy day when the Burton family would be under their own roof again. She shut her mind resolutely upon the past, for Frank, straining every nerve, was now behaving in the most exemplary fashion as a husband and father. She missed the children keenly, but her work was arduous and throughout the day she could only think of them in dreaming snatches. She did not particularly like her job, but she performed it conscientiously; and what a joy that weekly pay envelope was, and how differently she spent its contents from the carefree manner in which she had frivolled it away before her marriage.

Every week, revelling in the sacrifices it entailed, she contrived to save a few shillings, placing the money in a trinket-box concealed among her underclothes in the chest of drawers. Frank, she now dared to hope, was a genuinely reformed character, but even so she was nervous about leaving temptation in his way. He was still without regular work, but now that she was a bread-winner they were able to manage. Frank paid the expenses of Mary and Nicky, and she did the rest. They were never hungry. They could even afford little pleasures such as an occasional theatre or concert, but the greatest pleasure of all, the one to which Hilda looked forward single-mindedly from one week to the next, was the visit to the house in Woodford where the children were. They seemed happy, for Mrs. Smith was a kind and affectionate woman, but although the air of Woodford blew clear and sweet, they did not look nearly so rosy and sparkling as they had done in the dreary slum in Chelsea. Nicky seemed listless, Mary less vivacious, and it was when having tea with them that she discovered the reason. Instead of giving them milk to drink Mrs. Smith gave them tea, and very strong tea at that. Her eyes sought Frank's unhappily when Mary asked for more, and when he mildly protested Mrs. Smith took offence. 'Oh! don't grudge the child a cup of tea. She loves it. So does Nicky. They're not a bit faddy. They eat everything that's going. What I have, they have. They never say no to a thing.'

Hilda was dismayed. She had always been so careful; such a tremendous stickler, where they were concerned, for plain, wholesome food. She believed in following absolutely the rules laid down in her book for the healthy rearing of children, but of course it was stupid of her to expect Mrs. Smith to take quite the same trouble with them as she did herself. She suspected all manner of horrors; too much food out of tins; too many sweets; too many cakes; insufficient green vegetables and fresh fruit; and above all else insufficient sleep. Rosa, going down unexpectedly one night just to inquire after them, had found them still up and playing at nine o'clock. Poor darling Nicky. He was only a baby and needed long hours of sleep, while both children were accustomed to their afternoon rest, which Hilda was unhappily certain they did not have now. And though they were happy, they were obviously missing her. When she and Frank went to see them, the instant Mary heard her voice she came racing along the narrow lobby, her arms thrust forward, her face aglow, shrieking: 'Mummy! *My* Mummy!' with Nicky racing after her like a small galleon. That possessive cry held so much longing that Hilda actually came to dread it, despite the joy it heralded. Once, prattling innocently, her face extremely serious, Mary had confided that Nicky had been smacked for being a naughty boy. 'He cried, Mummy. He cried a big, big cry — big like this,' and she stretched her arms to their widest extent. 'But he was a very naughty boy. He cried hisself to sleep and I cried too but not a big cry like Nicky and Auntie gived us a sweetie.'

'It was only a baby smack,' Mrs. Smith explained quickly as she perceived Hilda's agitation. 'I didn't really hurt him. He was more surprised than anything.'

'Yes, I'm sure, but he's so little, Mrs. Smith. He doesn't understand yet.'

'Never too young to learn, Mrs. Burton. I don't believe in spoiling them. But you don't need to go worrying about them. You can see they're quite happy.'

'Of course they are, and we're very grateful to you,' Hilda answered as warmly as she could manage, seeing before her not the kind, decent woman Mrs. Smith undoubtedly was, but a veritable monster of cruelty. All the way back she was haunted by that: 'He cried hisself to sleep.' Poor little boy, crying himself to sleep. That was something which had never happened to him before. Frank, watching her miserably, was afraid to speak, and she, too, was silent for a long time, asking herself what she had ever done to be punished like this.

'We'll have one of them with us every week-end,' she said at last, 'in turn, until we have a home again. Don't you think that's a good idea, Frank?'

'It's a splendid idea. I can't imagine why we haven't thought of it before. Don't fret any more over that little smack, dearest. You know that Nicky's forgotten all about it.'

'It's not the smack that's making me feel sick. It's Nicky being left to cry himself to sleep. That was wicked. And you don't do anything about it, do you?'

He did not answer, and they finished the journey in silence, but at Liverpool Street he insisted upon her having a glass of sherry. She felt better for it; it helped to quieten Nicky's sobs, and it made her feel ashamed of her taunt to Frank. 'One whole night and day, every week, Frank. Proper food, proper sleep, and oceans of love. I feel like going straight back for Nicky. Shall we?'

'No, Hilda. It's much too late, but today week will soon come round.'

Though she did not enjoy her new career, when all she yearned for was the care of her own children, she nevertheless learned many wonderful things about woods: mahogany from Honduras; teak from Burma; English oak; English walnut; and strange beautiful woods from Australia. Sometimes people came to this mandarin among timber merchants to beg him, as a great personal favour, to transmute a condemned but dearly-loved tree into some article of furniture, thereby giving it life everlasting. She would listen in amazement as he named a figure for this work that seemed to her out of all proportion to its cost; she always expected the supplicant to withdraw his plea, but this never once happened, no matter how outrageous the sum named. Whenever she got a chance she would talk to the craftsmen and coax them to show her their secrets; they would then discourse to her about wood in reverent tones, caress dead-looking planks with loving hands, planing away the dusty surface that she might marvel at the beautiful grain and see how strongly the wood still burned with life. Such stimulating interludes helped her tremendously to get through the working week, to the day that gave her, for a few sweet hours, Mary or Nicky. Her savings were mounting steadily, and when Frank was safely out of the way she would lift out the trinket box and gloat over them. Her plan for the future was simple. When she had acquired sufficient for the nucleus of a small home she would find some pleasant working woman to run it for her and look after the children during the day, for she had no intention of ever giving up her job. If Frank continued as at present, then all should be well. The children would have their rightful home life. There would be few luxuries, but they would be a family again, beholden to nobody.

But modest though her ambition was, it seemed that the Fates themselves were leagued against her, for there came a night when she waited for Frank in vain; and as the hours passed she realized what must have happened. Old friends. Old pals. How she loathed the very sound of old friends and old pals. Drunkards, all of them. Drunkards and wastrels like Frank, with not a thought in the world but where the next drink was coming from. And where, in Frank's case, had it come from? Palsied with fear, she took out the trinket box. It was still wrapped in a crêpe-de-chine camisole, but even as she unwrapped it she knew that it was empty. She placed it, opened, on the mantelpiece, between the photographs of Mary and Nicky, and waited, with black murder in her heart, for her husband to return. He came in about one o'clock, dead-drunk, and collapsed, unseeing, into an armchair. She stood looking down at him. It was useless to speak to him. She would have liked to photograph him as he lolled there, stupid, hateful, a drunken sot, and compelled him to carry the photograph about him for ever. The camisole that had concealed the trinket box was threaded with narrow blue ribbon. She pulled this out and, with more blue ribbon from other garments, cut it into matching lengths, and these, in miniature bows, she pinned all over him. The blue riband of temperance! She rummaged in her work-basket and found more ribbon — white and red. She added blue and sewed the sections together. Red, white and blue. The Mons ribbon! With atavistic fury she sewed this firmly on the breast of his coat. She degraded and insulted him as he had degraded and insulted Mary and Nicky and herself. She then searched his pockets for whatever might be salvaged, but found only a pound note and some silver. The trinket box had contained twenty pounds, and to acquire that meagre sum she had pinched and scraped for months. She cursed her folly in not having put the money into a post office account, a precaution she had not taken because it had been so rewarding actually to feel and watch her savings grow. While she was about it, she spilled out the contents of every pocket. There was a squalid wedge of pawn tickets, and there were letters from every one they knew, or so it seemed. From her Aunt Helen; from Dermot McGilray; from poor Alan Edmonds in miserable Sunderland; from Rosa; from Julian Stockell in Brighton; and all were delicately couched reminders that he owed them money. There was one from his sister in Gloucestershire, an affectionate letter of sympathy for his misfortunes, which concluded with the words: 'I enclose a pound, Frank dear, but it must absolutely be the last. It isn't fair to Mother; you surely must realize how difficult it is for us to manage on our small income. Good luck, old boy, and our love to you all.'

These letters were old, but presently she came to one of very recent date and bearing the Woodford postmark. Why should Mrs. Smith have written to him? Why not to herself? Fearfully she drew it out and read:

Dear Captain Burton,

It is weeks now since you paid me for Mary and Nicky. I got your letter promising to pay and asking me not to let Mrs. Burton know you owed me anything but I am not able to go on keeping your children for nothing. I have only got my pension and a bit put by so will you please send me the money and then take the children away because I feel I can't trust you to keep sending the money.

And that time you came to see them by yourself when Mrs. Burton was not well you acted so strange it gave me the creeps. Perhaps it was because you have bad nerves but anyway will you please send me the money. I have only let it go on till now without telling Mrs. Burton because I thought you were a gentleman and would be sure to keep your promise. I think Mrs. Burton would be very upset to know you have not behaved right to me over the children and if you don't send me the money I shall have to ask her for it which I don't want to do as you can guess.

Yours truly
Mrs. Smith

Hilda propped the letter against the trinket box. Could this be the reason he had stolen her savings? Somehow she did not think so. He was hopeless, entirely without scruples of any kind. It was infamous of him to owe money to Mrs. Smith. 'Well – it's her worry, not ours', she could hear him saying. And in what way had he 'acted very strange?' He must have gone there when he was drunk. Oh! Poor Mrs. Smith! And poor little Mary and Nicky! She went to bed and, while her husband slept his drunken sleep, she lay awake, pondering the insoluble problem of how she was going to support herself and two children on her present salary. Her Aunt Helen's cruel suggestion about Nicky came into her mind, but she pushed it from her. Not that way. She decided to see Rosa that evening and ask her advice. Also she must go down to placate Mrs. Smith. Before trying to sleep, she sat up and surveyed her be-ribboned hero. If anything could shame him into sanity, surely her charming taste in adornment would. At half-past seven, heavy with sleep, the alarm clock wakened her. Frank was not there, but the hearth-rug resembled a temperance banner, for it was covered with blue ribbons.

As she made tea and tidied the room she had one thought only. What in God's name was she going to do about the children? All the morning, busy though she was, she sought for some way out. She had a raging headache and would have given much to have said so and been told to go home, but as a comparatively new employee she felt that this would be unwise. On the whole, employers were averse to engaging married women, especially married women with children. On the other hand, the timber merchant had no fault to find with her work, and reasoning thus she conceived the bold idea of enlisting his sympathies on behalf of Mary and her brother. He was a good man, and she was made aware almost daily of his goodness. He received shoals of begging letters from all sorts and conditions of men, and these, after a cursory glance, were dropped into a waste-paper basket. But if, through a friend, a case of hardship was brought to his notice, he would always give the matter his gravest consideration. He would instruct his chief clerk to make discreet inquiries and, if that astute person reported that the case was genuine, Sir Edward would either send the sufferer an adequate gift of money, or take infinite pains to find him a job. Nine times out of ten he would do both. His wealth was colossal, and his influence as far-flung as the Antipodes. At a nod from him, tired mothers were admitted to seaside rest homes; orphans were educated; ex-service men yearning to set up in business for themselves as purveyors of cats' meat were enabled, through his goodness, to attain this peculiar ambition. Hilda perceived that he was especially good to ex-service men, for the war, as she also perceived, had been kinder to him than it had been to them. There was no limit to his goodness, and she knew beyond a peradventure that if she could only face the cheerless prospect of having her lovely boy and girl brought up in a Children's Home he would indubitably help her to do this.

But for a long time she could not bring herself to make this appeal. She discussed it with Rosa and her mother until their ears ached. They would not advise her. All that Rosa permitted herself to say was that the years would quickly pass; that Mary and Nicky would be well cared for and educated, and that anything, even a miracle, might yet happen to save Frank from himself, though in her heart she did not believe in such a miracle. In her doubt and torment, and in the faint hope that her Aunt Helen would be too proud to countenance such a solution, despite her own even more cheerless suggestion, Hilda at last consulted her. She was plainly delighted, and smiling her warmest smile said brightly: 'But how splendid, my dear! Why, it's the very thing for them and you. It's a wonderful idea. Speak to Sir Edward without delay. Don't be foolish and sentimental. If you can place Mary and Nicky into a Home, your troubles will be at an end. You'll quickly get on your feet again. Now do be sensible and go through with it.'

'But what about them, Aunt Helen? They'll be unhappy. I can't bear that they should be unhappy.'

Helen, with no smile now upon her handsome face, said sharply: 'Don't be such an idiot, Hilda! Oh, I could shake you! Listen to me. If you don't try to get them into a Home, what do you propose doing? How are you going to keep them, and where? Pull yourself together and do a little hard thinking for once. You'll be able to visit them in a Home; perhaps even have them to stay with you during your holidays. If it is allowed, I might even have them to stay with us when they're a little older. And at fifteen or sixteen, when they're ready to begin making their way in the world, they will be all yours again. Nobody but a certified lunatic would hesitate for a moment. *Think*, Hilda! I beg of you to *think*. Ten years at the most. They'll flash away. You won't let Miss Tranter's wealthy friends adopt them . . .'

'Them! Aunt Helen?'

'Yes, both of them. I saw her again the other day and she told me her friends are eager to have Mary as well as Nicky. I'm not made of stone and I understand how you must feel at the thought of anything so final, but I still think it's the best thing you could do for them. This alternative, however, is not final. They'll be perfectly happy among a host of other little girls and boys, so what, in heaven's name, are you hesitating for?'

Her gaze was riveted upon her niece as if by sheer will-power she could force her to submit, but Hilda stood her ground and said sadly: 'If they go to a Home, they won't be my Mary and Nicky any more. They'll be a lost little girl and boy among hundreds of other lost children. I think I'd almost rather give them up to Miss Tranter's friends, then I should at least know that they had a real home — their home. How can they be loved and petted in that other Home? And perhaps they would be separated. Until they're older, that would be dreadful. You don't know how dreadful. If that were to happen, they could not help being unhappy. Oh! if only I dare trust their father again.'

'If you ever do,' Helen said grimly, 'you'll deserve to suffer, and if it stopped at you, well and good. But what right have you to condemn two innocent children to the care of such a father? You have no right, my poor girl. I'm sorry to have to speak to you like this, but there's a limit to my patience. We should all like to see you divorce Frank and make a new life for yourself. You must get the children settled and then ask him to give you your freedom. It could all be done very quietly, for you can hardly go on deluding yourself further about him, can you?'

'No. But I can't help what I feel about him. That's something else you don't seem able to understand; for that matter I don't understand it either. I know that I'm a fool, and I despise myself for it, but there's something between me and Frank that I can't explain to anybody, not even to Rosa. I've tried to hate him, but I can't keep it up. And he's only got me.'

'And you, unfortunately, have only got him. Naturally I think it's a bad exchange so far as you are concerned, but I'm not quite such a gorgon as you seem to think, Hilda. I do understand about your feeling for him. But talk to Sir

Edward. Be a true mother and think only of what is best for those children; and try to believe that I can see a long, long way further than you can. If only you will be guided by me in this matter, you'll live to thank me. I'm sure of it.'

Hilda, wishing that she could feel equally confident about this complacent prediction, nevertheless felt so bewildered by the reasoning of her overpowering aunt that she meekly promised to approach her employer. She did not, however, think it necessary to inform her guide and counsellor that before taking such an irrevocable step she was determined to make one final effort to keep Mary and Nicky together in a warm, living home for the few precious years of their childhood. It was an idea that had been revolving in her distracted mind ever since Mrs. Smith had asked for them to be taken away; and the more she pictured them, so small, so puzzled, in a vast, impersonal Institution, the more resolved she became to make this last appeal for them. She would go to Moss Ferry, where she had spent her own lowly but wonderfully happy childhood, and she would beg her foster-parents, Joe and Lizzie Winstanley, to care for Mary and Nicky as they had cared for her. If they consented, it would not be for gain, but for love of herself; and, knowing her circumstances, they would accept nothing from her but the bare cost of the children's food and clothing. Frank, surely, would be able to help out from time to time; but even if this hope should prove a will-o'-the-wisp, she could still manage to keep them in Moss Ferry out of her own earnings. The shadow of the great Orphanage which was supported so handsomely by her employer fell chill and dark around her, and she would do anything to keep her children out of it. In Moss Ferry, Mary, followed in a year or two by Nicky, would attend the village school where she had spent such fascinating years in the pursuit of knowledge. In her day no scholarships had beckoned from fair horizons, but now that opportunity for all was the watchword it would be far otherwise for them.

Even in unknown Moss Ferry they would be offered their rightful chance, and she had no manner of doubt that they would grasp it.

Happy in her decision, she announced it quite calmly to Frank, but she did not seek his opinion, and he was too ashamed to mutter more than: 'If you think it will work, Hilda. After all, we shall soon be able to have them back with us again.' She did not reply to this, for there was no point in doing so. Whatever was arranged for Mary and Nicky was her responsibility alone. Without further preamble she decided to go to Lancashire the following Saturday. She would not be able to spend more than a few hours there, for she must be back at work on Monday morning, but a few hours would suffice for her purpose.

It was eight years since, a boastful girl of sixteen, she had visited her foster-parents and dazzled them with a pulsating account of her marvellously exciting life in London. To her shame she had not communicated with them since, for she had wanted to forget them until she could return in even greater triumph with a distinguished husband. She had not written to announce her flying visit, but she suffered no uneasiness on this score. People in Moss Ferry were always at home. The train chugged through the ugly, familiar landscape that stretched like torn and dirty streamers for miles beyond Manchester, and she was nearly at Kilnbrook, the station for Moss Ferry, before the depressing scene gave place to level fields and virgin meadows intersected by sparkling brooks that were still the haunt of coot and hern.

Once again she was the sole passenger to alight and, working in his garden, as he had been working eight years before, was George Partington, station-master, porter, ticket-collector and general factotum. As he jabbed his fork into the earth, Hilda, for a crazy second, felt that she must have dreamed those intervening years. Mr. Partington was bareheaded and in shirt-sleeves, but on seeing a lady standing there, dressed in what appeared to him the very height of fashion, he ceremoniously put on his insignia of office, a peaked and braided cap, and an ample-skirted, brass-buttoned frock-coat of dark, heavy cloth. Then, as befitted one in whom was invested the power and majesty of the great Cheshire Lines, he advanced with measured steps to take her ticket. Hilda gave a friendly little laugh and held out the ticket. 'There you are, Mr. Partington. How are you? You haven't changed one little bit.'

'Eh! Danged if it isna young Hilda Winstanley again! Ah'm glad to see you, lass. You hanna changed ower much either. Filled out a bit, mebbe. It mun be all of ten year since you stood on this very station at this very hour.'

'Eight,' Hilda corrected. 'And I'm not Hilda Winstanley any longer nor all that young either. I'm Hilda Burton now and the mother of two children, a girl and a boy.'

'Danged and you is! No wonder you've filled out a bit. Step ower to t'ouse and show yoursen to Mary Jane. She'll be rare pleased to have a crack wi' you and mak a cup o' tea.'

'No, thank you all the same, Mr. Partington. I have to get back to London tomorrow, so I must push on to Moss Ferry. How are all the Winstanleys?'

'Same as usual — least, same all 'cept Joe. When t'war was on Lizzie badgered and moithered him to chuck up t'road work and go into t'foundry alongside that lad o' theirs, Jack. Wages was big and Joe towd me hissel 'e could earn as much i' two shifts as 'e got in a full week on t'road work. But when t'war finished so did t'money, and by the look of 'im so will Joe if 'e doesna eat 'is pride and get back to proper work on t'road or farm again. Till 'e went into that danged foundry 'e'd never 'ad a day's illness. Now 'e's allus 'aving to lay off work, and when all's said and done they've got nowt to show for them big wages but some new furniture. Reckon you've 'eard as Lily's married too and got a little lad. They live wi' Joe and Lizzie and the new furniture.'

Hilda's spirits sank beneath this shattering news. There would be no room now for Mary and Nicky in the little house in School Lane, no matter how willing her foster-parents might be to have them. Bidding Mr. Partington good night she took the short cut to Moss Ferry along Lovers' Lane and across the silent fields, far too worried and shaken even to think of the boggarts that were known to lie in wait for solitary travellers once the sun had dipped. All the way she tried to assure herself that her journey was not in vain. Well, she would soon know.

CHAPTER XVII

THE END OF AN EDUCATION

But for the absence of Lily, her foster-sister, the scene was almost exactly as she had last seen it, eight years before; and for several choking minutes Hilda, unseen, stood peering into the kitchen where she had spent her childhood. On the wall facing her was the immense oil painting of the grim old woman whose grey corkscrew curls were arranged with such meticulous neatness beneath her snowy goffered cap. On the high mantelpiece the Mazawattee tea-caddy still held pride of place in the centre, and the pair of martial cast-iron horses flanking it still gleamed like black ice as the result of Mrs. Winstanley's weekly assaults on them with black-lead. The whole room was contained in the golden shadow cast from the swinging oil-lamp over the table, and clear in this subdued light was her foster-mother, knitting in her rocking-chair by the fire. She appeared to be knitting a child's sock, and in the silence Hilda could plainly hear the clicking of her steel needles. Her foster-father was asleep in his rocking-chair by the window, and recalling Mr. Partington's grave words she studied him intently. Certainly he looked thinner, and older than he actually was, but there was the same gentleness about his unguarded face that she remembered so well. Drawn up to the table was a child's high chair, and a number of small garments were airing on the wooden 'cradle' that stretched across the ceiling. Over the mantelpiece there was a crudely coloured photograph — obviously an enlargement — of a baby boy, his long curls tied with blue ribbon. Seen thus from the outer darkness the little room had a confident air of complete indestructibility. It was like a van Ostade etching and Hilda, wondering how she could ever have thought it ugly and common, gazed upon it with all her soul. It was a home. Oh, if only she could bring Mary and Nicky here for a few years! For the first time in her life she envied her foster-sister, whose child had the right to be here, the very heart and pivot of the house, while for her children, her sweet boy and girl, that other Home waited. From sheer heartache she cried a little, then crept round to the back door, quietly lifted the latch, and entered. Her foster-mother, without turning her head or pausing in her work, asked equably: 'Is that you, Mrs. Clarke?' evidently supposing her visitor to be a neighbour.

'No, Mother. It's me.'

Mrs. Winstanley dropped her knitting, and without a word held up her arms. Hilda bent down and for a long moment they clung to each other. She looked across at her foster-father, whose gentle blue eyes were regarding her with such trance-like fixity that for a second she wondered if he was really awake.

'Yes. It really is me, Father! I thought it was high time I came and had a look at you all again. I'm married now, and have a son and a daughter. Didn't you know?'

'Us is never towd owt about you, 'Ilda, and 'as got oursen used to it, but us allus knowd as you'd come back again one day — like you 'ave,' Mrs. Winstanley said proudly, and Hilda, as she kissed her foster-father, had the grace to blush.

'But your 'usband and childer? Where han you left them? Outside?' Mrs. Winstanley exclaimed, it being inconceivable to her that a married woman should go journeying without her family.

'Of course not. They're at home. In London. I just never thought of them coming too. I'm only here for this one night, to see you and hear all the news, and tell you about Frank and the children. Mary's the eldest. She's four and a half and Nicky is two and a half. We called him Nicholas John — after your John.'

'You did that, 'Ilda!' Mrs. Winstanley beamed with pleasure. 'Fancy you remembering our John like that! That's summat for me to go ower and tell 'im. Our Lily's married too — three year back. Ted's a steady young chap and works at Morgan's farm. They've only got the one little lad, but Lily's expecting again, and when she 'ears tell as you've got a little wench reckon she'll feel put out if she doesn't 'ave one too. That's 'er first over t'mantelpiece. 'Is name's Ronald. I thowt she might ha called 'im Joe, after 'is granddad, but she would 'ave a new-fangled name. They calls 'im Ron for short, though. They'll be back any minute and then us'll 'ave a bite. You mun be clemmed after coming 'underds o' miles like you 'ave. And just to see us.'

Smiling happily she moved the great iron kettle from the hob to the fire, set the enamel teapot to warm, then bustled about with knives and forks. 'Fish and chips, 'Ilda. Saturday neets they allus steps in to Annie Cooney's and treats us to fish and chips. Reach down them plates, love, and put them in t'oven. Eh! Our Lily will be that taken aback when hoo sees you.'

Lily, however, was nothing of the kind, for although Hilda had not encountered one single human being after leaving George Partington, Mrs. Cooney's fish and chip emporium was buzzing with the news of her arrival. The huge cauldrons of hissing fat, so pleasing to the eyes of hungry patrons, were neglected while everybody informed Lily and her husband that Hilda was actually at home. It was therefore calmly, but quite affectionately, that Lily greeted her. 'And this is my 'usband, 'Ilda. Ted, this is 'er. 'Ave you bin up to see our Ronald?' Lily asked eagerly.

'Not yet, Lily. I'll take a peep at him when we go to bed. I'm dying to see him. I have a little boy too, and a girl. See, I've brought a snap of them — taken with their father — but it doesn't do any of them justice.'

Mrs. Winstanley, her face alight with interest, almost

snatched the snapshot when Hilda produced it from her bag. She took it to the table and there, directly under the lamp, gazed upon it long and thoughtfully. Then, with a wondering look at Hilda, she remarked quietly: 'You didna tak a young chap, 'Ilda. Belike there's a tidy stretch atween you, and it seems like 'e's 'urt 'is arm or summat.'

'A German shot it away in the war,' Hilda explained. 'Frank was an officer. A very good officer.'

'Ay! Us can see 'e's a gentleman. But 'ow fearsome for 'im to be mauled that road. 'Ow does 'e manage?' Mrs. Winstanley inquired, her brown eyes warm with sympathy. 'Does 'e work for a living?'

'Of course he does,' Hilda said laughingly. 'He writes for the newspapers and magazines and different journals, and some day perhaps he'll be famous.'

'Think o' that!' Mrs. Winstanley ejaculated. 'You have done well for yoursen, 'Ilda. Ah'm that pleased to know it, but fancy onyone earning a living out of t'newspapers!'

Being unable to read or to write, her own acquaintance with newsprint was confined to lighting fires with it, lining her cupboard shelves, and using it in the privy. That a man should earn his bread by it was so incomprehensible to her that she darkly suspected Hilda of deliberately concealing her means of support, and sincerely hoped that they were honest.

As, after another prolonged inspection, she handed the snapshot to her husband, she remarked fondly: 'Tak a good look at t'little wench, Joe, for Ah do believe hoo favours us.'

'Dunna talk so daft, Mother,' Lily interjected sharply. 'She's the very spit of 'Ilda.'

'Ah can see that for mysen, but then 'Ilda favours us,' Mrs. Winstanley persisted defiantly.

'Now Mother! 'Ow can that be when 'Ilda's got nowt to do wi' us?'

' 'Ave it your own road,' her mother conceded cheerfully,

'but Ah still say as 'Ilda favours us, and t'little wench does too.'

'I wish I did belong to you,' Hilda said wistfully, and was rewarded with another beaming smile from her foster-mother, and a tender look of unshakeable love from her foster-father. Indeed, he had scarcely taken his eyes off her since that first trance-like stare. What would he say, she wondered, if she told the truth about her visit? He would long to help her, and so would his wife. But Lily was the stumbling-block, Lily and Ted and Ron, and then the new baby that was coming. They couldn't help her in the only way that mattered. Well, there was no point now in laying bare her troubles. Her foster-mother, automatically assuming that by marrying a gentleman she had achieved wealth and splendour, was eager to hear all about this happy state of affairs and plied her with innumerable questions, which Hilda answered with thumping lies; she even went so far as to invite the entire family to visit London one day and spend a holiday beneath her palatial roof.

'Us did go to London once,' Mrs. Winstanley informed her. 'Us stopped wi' our Susannah in Balls Pond Road. Reckon you knows Balls Pond Road, 'Ilda. Us didna know where you was living, but our Susannah took us one time to Hyde Park. Hoo said Hyde Park was the most fashionable place i' London, and the likeliest for us to 'appen on you. But what a big place it is. No wonder us never spotted you, though there was mony a young woman as might ha bin you at first look. Well, reckon it's time to go up to bed. Mun you really be away again tomorrow?' she asked sadly.

'Yes, Mother. I really must. I'm just going to have a look at Lily's boy. He's like you, Ted, judging from that lovely photograph up there.'

Ted, who had scarcely uttered a word, gave her a sheepish smile and exchanged a gratified look with Lily. Hilda followed them up the steep, narrow, but now linoleum-covered stairs, and by the light of a candle was introduced to the sleeping Ron. He was a handsome little fellow, but of course not to be compared with her own beautiful Nicky. She kissed him, and was then shown into the little back bedroom which she had once shared so belligerently with Lily, and which smelt overpoweringly of apples, these being stored under the bed. They kissed good night and Hilda, utterly wretched, wondered what Frank was doing. Was he gaily drinking with his public-house cronies or was he morosely drinking alone? Or was he sitting virtuously in their room and thinking of her? Her thoughts turned to Mary and Nicky. They would be lying sprawled out, their soft faces looking like closed flowers. She ached with misery as she thus pictured them, but she had now made up her mind about them. They should not go to the Home. Like the little fellow next door, they too must have a home of which they were the heart; a home which would grow naturally around them and hold them safe. She would give them up to the new 'mother' and 'father' who awaited them so hungrily. Frank, for very shame, would put up a fine, melodramatic show of rage at this decision, and make the same old promise to do splendid things for them yet. But any home that he built for them would be upon sand. A house of sand fashioned by a man of straw. Hilda, foolish though she might be, none the less knew that she dared not hold her children's future so lightly.

At last she fell asleep, and immediately after breakfast next day bade a long farewell to her foster-parents, the simple man and woman who had never once failed her in affection. They were ardent in their desire to see her husband and children and, fencing to the end, she promised to bring them to Moss Ferry for Wakes Week, at which time Ted and Lily and Ron would be on holiday at Blackpool. She left the snapshot with them, for Mrs. Winstanley wished to show it boastfully to all Moss Ferry as proof that their Hilda had done well by herself and married a gentleman. Hilda, blushing for the said gentleman, laughed a little, cried a little, and kissed them all round. She had asked that nobody should see her to the station, but her foster-father would have none of this and insisted on accompanying her. He was all dressed up in his black Sunday clothes, and she had not the heart to disappoint him. Mrs. Winstanley, who had been up betimes despite the fact that on Sunday mornings she always had a good 'lie-in', placed a brown paper parcel, warm and round, into her hands. 'For your childer,' she explained. 'A sponge a-piece. Ah minds as 'ow you and Lily allus liked me to mak a sponge for owt special. You mun put t'jam in them yoursen. And dunna forget about bringing your 'usband and childer to see us. Us is allus 'ere.'

Few words were spoken during the walk to the station, for Joe Winstanley was not given to speech at the best of times, but simple and unlettered though he was, Hilda realized that in some mysterious fashion he had sensed she was unhappy. Mr. Partington, properly arrayed, opened a carriage door for her, shook hands, and stepped back so that Joe might have the last word. Hilda kissed him, and as the train began to move he said quietly: 'You'll mind what hoo said, 'Ilda. Us is allus 'ere.'

When she reached home that night Frank was awaiting her, and she glanced at him nervously as he jumped up to welcome her. His eyes were very bright and his voice sneeringly defiant as he asked, astonishingly: 'Well! And have you done the deed, my darling? Are you going to park out our children in the industrial north as your sweet family parked you?'

Hilda stared at him. Had he absolutely no sense of shame? No comprehension at all of her misery? She realized that the defiance was due to the fact that he had been drinking, but she was in no mood to make any allowance for this. For some minutes, through sheer anger, she made no answer. He had set out a cold meal, and it was not until they sat down to this that she felt sufficiently controlled to speak.

'No. I have not arranged to park them anywhere. I am merely going to give them away to people who want them. To a man and a woman who need them. In plain language I am going to take Aunt Helen's advice and let them be adopted. And I am going to do this because you, their natural guardian, have betrayed them.'

'The hell you are!' he blustered. 'And do you suppose that I am going to let my children be sold?'

'Who has said anything about selling them?' Hilda retorted sharply. 'Though I do believe that if you were offered blood money for them you would take it; *and* get drunk on it. No, Frank. It's a little late in the day for you to indulge in fatherly heroics. You didn't appear to mind what happened to your children when you left us stranded in that horrible basement. Nor when you left us stranded in Chertsey. Of course, if you can now assure me that you can provide a home for them, then I shall have to think again, shan't I? And what about me? Do you imagine that I want to lose them?'

'You talk as if they were not my children at all. I shall not let you do this thing,' he blustered again.

'Once and for all, Frank, will you please stop being melodramatic. How else should I talk? You've stolen the money that was to build up a new home. You and your dear old pals have had a lovely time on it. On money that *I* have worked for, not you. You lie and lie and lie. You've shown yourself to be quite incapable of providing for any of us. I couldn't arrange for them to go to Moss Ferry, and I will *not* have them carted from pillar to post. It's criminal to bewilder little children in this way. Can't you understand that I want to know they are safe? And safe not only in an affectionate home, but safe from *you*!'

His face flamed, and he strode about the room, dramatically clenching his fist, and muttering strange imprecations, but Hilda continued: 'Yes. Safe from their own father. Would you like them ever to see you as I have seen you? As you let Mrs. Smith once see you?'

'But you can't do a thing without my consent,' he exclaimed triumphantly.

'Can't I? I can take you to court and make you entirely responsible for them. So now what have you to say?'

He stared at her stupidly, and she stared resolutely back.

'I must think,' he muttered. 'I must think.'

'That isn't necessary, Frank. I've done all the thinking, and I've made up my mind. Mary and Nicky are going to have their place in the sun, so you may as well get accustomed to the idea.'

'I should have thought those damned relations of yours might help until I can get square with things,' he said lamely.

'I should have thought so, too. They're not poor. But then, why should they take over your responsibilities? That is Aunt Helen's answer, and I can't help seeing her point of view, particularly after all that has happened.'

Again he strode ridiculously about the room, clenching and unclenching his hand. Hilda, unimpressed, continued remorselessly: 'Aunt Helen thinks I ought to see the Pensions people, and ask them to pay your pension directly to myself.'

'It can't be paid to anyone but me. That's Army Regulations. But I swear I'll hand it over to you every month, Hilda. Then we can keep the children, and start again, can't we?'

Hilda, remembering all his treachery and cowardice and weakness, mournfully shook her head.

'I can't trust you, Frank. Because of them, I dare not. But if only you knew how I want to trust you.'

There was a silence, broken by Frank saying abjectly: 'If I agree, Hilda . . . if they go . . . you won't leave me, too?'

'No, Frank. Leaving seems to be your prerogative. I don't want to leave you. I ought to, but I don't. Never mind about us. Tomorrow night I shall go and see Aunt Helen and tell her what I've decided. Everything will have to be transacted properly through a lawyer. But don't let us talk of it any more until it happens. I'll tell you all the details after I've seen Aunt Helen. It's only nine o'clock. Let's go out somewhere. I should like to hear some lovely music and have a good cry, but that's silly. Let's go and see Rosa. There's one thing, Frank. Please don't go to see them again. Once they are settled in their new home, they will quickly forget you and me, but until they do it is me I want them to remember.'

A month later Hilda saw her children for the last time. Rosa accompanied her, and they went laden with toys, for in a vain effort to ease her misery Hilda had spent a week's salary on these. They took them out to tea, let them eat everything they wanted, played with them on Woodford Green, and returned them to Mrs. Smith tired out but prattling merrily of the lovely holiday they were going to have in the beautiful country, for their new home lay in the very heart of England. Hilda, taking sole command, bathed them and put them to bed, Nicky with his new Teddy Bear that was nearly as big as himself, Mary with her splendid talking doll. They demanded to be told a story, and she made one up for them until their eyes closed and they slept. For a long time she sat on, caressing first one little face and then the other. Her heart almost failed her as, with Rosa, she kissed them farewell. They were still hers. But a picture rose before her swimming eyes. The picture of their father, slumped, degraded, senseless, covered from head to foot with blue ribbons, and among them, showing itself timidly, almost apologetically, the brave ribbon of Mons. She kissed them again, and yet again, so fiercely that Mary opened her eyes and said: 'I s'all send you a postcard, Mummy.' At that she ran from the room, leaving Rosa with them to the end.

The next day they were to be taken by her Aunt Helen to Miss Tranter, and she was to take them to their new 'mother' and 'father', who were already in London eagerly awaiting them. And all that fateful day, as she contrived somehow to get through her duties, she felt as a condemned murderess must feel awaiting the moment of extinction, but all the time hoping, praying, that at the eleventh hour a reprieve will be granted. In spite of all that Frank had done, or rather had not done, in spite of her fierce request to him never to speak of Mary and her brother before her, she yearned for him to ring up and say that he had stopped the cruel business. She longed to hear her Aunt Helen's dominating voice telling her the same thing. She prayed for a miracle to happen, but the day wore on as usual, a day that would be etched in her memory for ever; and in the evening, with her faithful Rosa, she went to Glynne Mansions, aching for the last news. Her aunts and uncle were waiting for her, sadly, nervously. She looked at Helen, and asked stupidly: 'Have they gone?'

'Yes, dear. And they were so happy, and so excited about their holiday. Miss Tranter was enchanted with them, and when I left Mary was chattering away to her like a little steam engine. I'm sure you've done the right thing for them, Hilda. There was no sort of future for them with Frank, damn him! Just think how they're going to be loved and petted and cared for now.'

'They've always been loved and petted,' Hilda said bitterly.

'I know, dear. Of course they have. I didn't really mean that. What I meant to convey was — think of the chances they'll have, their education, their opportunities, and when they're grown up there'll be no strap-hanging in crowded tubes for them. Think of that, Hilda.'

Hilda did think of it. Strap-hanging in crowded tubes had never done her any harm. What an extraordinary, what a fantastic thing for her aunt to say! Hilda stared at her aghast, but she seemed unaware of having said anything extraordinary or fantastic for she continued: 'There's something we want you to know, Hilda. We're not rich — no need to tell you this, of course — but . . . well . . . we haven't anyone but you. You won't need to worry about your own future too much, materially that is. We've left everything to you, my dear. One day you'll have a reasonable competence of your own with which to enjoy a serene old age. That's something, isn't it?'

Hilda felt no gratitude, and for some moments showed none. A serene old age! Mary and Nicky! Her Aunt Helen could have saved them. Phillip and Mildred, as she well knew, had fought hard with her about this, but she had been too strong for them. She didn't like children. She didn't want her agreeable life to be disturbed. She waited now, complacently, for her niece's reaction to the comforting news that her old age was provided for. Collecting her wits Hilda said quietly: 'Thank you, Aunt Helen. You are very thoughtful.' They were all looking at her, apprehensively, but she did not cry. There were no tears left in her. She took Rosa's hand and said they ought to go. They were urged to stay to supper, but Hilda wanted Rosa to go back with her to Frank, for she dreaded being alone with him on this most desolate night.

'I had done a deed, they said, which the ibis and the crocodile trembled at.' Hilda was haunted by the savage, accusatory phrase. It took her by the throat a score of times a day. She was sitting now, waiting for Frank, in the living-room of a tiny flat in Hampstead. Six months had passed since the children had gone, and there was no visible remembrance of them about. Their photographs, snapshots, a green and white painted duck — Francis Drake — which Mary had loved to distraction, a gay little smock of Nicky's which she had made so proudly — all were safely buried at the bottom of a trunk. She and Frank never spoke of them to each other. Whether he ever did so to anyone else she did not know, though she imagined not. For her part she only spoke of them to Rosa and, when she saw her alone, to her Aunt Mildred. Sometimes she woke up in the night crying for them, and Frank lay miserably beside her, not daring to attempt to comfort her. Incredibly, she still loved him, and since the night when she had adorned him so barbarously with her blue ribbons she had never once seen him helplessly drunk, though she always knew when he had been drinking heavily, for at such times he would stay out for hours and not return until he was himself again.

'I had done a deed, they said, which the ibis and the crocodile trembled at.' Had she? Ought she to have done anything, no matter what, to have kept her children? They were happy. Through her friend Miss Tranter, her Aunt Helen was informed that they had thoroughly settled down and were adored by their new 'parents' and a host of 'aunts' and 'uncles' and 'cousins'. Nicky had already been entered for Eton, and Mary had been given a pony. All the nervous little puckerings due to Mrs. Smith's ignorant regime had smoothed out; they were, too, thoroughly and properly naughty, and loved for their naughtiness. Nicky would never again be left to sob himself to sleep. As she sat thinking of them, De Quincey's beautiful phrase weaving among her thoughts like a bright poisonous snake, bitterness flooded through her. Frank was her husband. He had taught her everything she knew. From a vain, ignorant, trusting girl she had grown into a strong, self-reliant woman who no longer believed that the world had been specially created for her. But, even though she loved him, could she stay with him? That terrible phrase leaped out at her again. The children were between them. Not rosy children of flesh and blood, but ghosts, dead children. 'The ibis and the crocodile. . . .'

She heard his key, and watched for him eagerly. Yes. She would stay, for as long as she could. She knew the worst of him, and there was that between them, despite all that had happened, despite the bitterness she could not subdue when she gave way to her memories, that held her to him. Through him she had heard the chimes at midnight: gleeful childish laughter which echoed now as if from under the sea, faint but very sweet. Because of this laughter, which she could summon up at will, the bond between them might wear to an infinite tenuity, but she did not think it would break. Its ends lay in the hands of two small ghosts who, for all their frailness, would hold it fast through bitterness and heartache until time assuaged the memory of that which once had been.